CIPS Study Matters

Level 6

Graduate Diploma in Purchasing and Supply

Leading and Influencing in Purchasing

Gino Franco
University of Derby

THE
CHARTERED INSTITUTE OF
PURCHASING & SUPPLY

Published by

The Chartered Institute of Purchasing and Supply
Easton House, Easton on the Hill, Stamford, Lincolnshire PE9 3NZ
Tel: +44 (0) 1780 756 777
Fax: +44 (0) 1780 751 610
Email: info@cips.org
Website: http://www.cips.org

First published July 2006

Technical reviewer: Tony Davies, Newpoint Consulting

Instructional design and publishing project management by Wordhouse Ltd, Reading, UK

Content management system, instructional editing and pre-press by Echelon Learning Ltd, London, UK

Index prepared by Indexing Specialists (UK) Ltd, Hove, UK

ISBN 1-86124-160-7
ISBN 978-186124-160-3

Contents

Introduction

This course book has been designed to assist you in studying for the CIPS Leading and Influencing in Purchasing unit in the Level 6 Graduate Diploma in Purchasing and Supply. The book covers all topics in the official CIPS unit content document, as illustrated in the table beginning on page xi.

This course book is designed to develop students' leadership skills to enable them to lead, influence and provide direction to stakeholders within the supply chain. Purchasing managers need to be able to operate at a strategic level. They should be able to lead in their defined area or part of the organisation and will be expected to motivate and support supply chain members and stakeholders in achieving objectives and success.

Purchasing managers are expected to lead in a variety of situations and to ensure that they maintain the balance of power required to achieve success. They should be able to demonstrate effective leadership in a variety of contexts, including through change, adversity, conflict and success, in order to maximise the potential of the organisation.

The book is divided into four main parts, which together provide a comprehensive treatment of the subject area:

- leading and managing in purchasing (sessions 1–3)
- leading and influencing in the supply chain (sessions 4–7)
- develop a culture of productivity through people (sessions 8–13)
- lead change in the supply chain (sessions 14–20).

How to use this book

The course book will take you step by step through the unit content in a series of carefully planned 'study sessions' and provides you with learning activities, self-assessment questions and revision questions to help you master the subject matter. The guide should help you organise and carry out your studies in a methodical, logical and effective way, but if you have your own study preferences you will find it a flexible resource too.

Before you begin using course this book, make sure you are familiar with any advice provided by CIPS on such things as study skills, revision techniques or support and how to handle formal assessments.

If you are on a taught course, it will be up to your tutor to explain how to use the book – when to read the study sessions, when to tackle the activities and questions, and so on.

If you are on a self-study course, or studying independently, you can use the course book in the following way:

- Scan the whole book to get a feel for the nature and content of the subject matter.
- Plan your overall study schedule so that you allow enough time to complete all 20 study sessions well before your examinations – in other words, leaving plenty of time for revision.
- For each session, set aside enough time for reading the text, tackling all the learning activities and self-assessment questions, and the revision question at the end of the session, and for the suggested further reading. Guidance on roughly how long you should set aside for studying each session is given at the beginning of the session.

Now let's take a look at the structure and content of the individual study sessions.

Overview of the study sessions

The course book breaks the content down into 20 sessions, which vary from three to six or seven hours' duration each. However, we are not advising you to study for this sort of time without a break! The sessions are simply a convenient way of breaking the syllabus into manageable chunks. Most people would try to study one or two sessions a week, taking one or two breaks within each session. You will quickly find out what suits you best.

Each session begins with a brief **introduction** which sets out the areas of the syllabus being covered and explains, if necessary, how the session fits in with the topics that come before and after.

After the introduction there is a statement of the **session learning objectives**. The objectives are designed to help you understand exactly what you should be able to do after you've studied the session. You might find it helpful to tick them off as you progress through the session. You will also find them useful during revision. There is one session learning objective for each numbered subsection of the session.

After this, there is a brief section reproducing the learning objectives and indicative content from the official **unit content document**. This will help you to understand exactly which part of the syllabus you are studying in the current session.

Following this, there are **prior knowledge** and **resources** sections if necessary. These will let you know if there are any topics you need to be familiar with before tackling each particular session, or any special resources you might need, such as a calculator or graph paper.

Then the main part of the study session begins, with the first of the numbered main subsections. At regular intervals in each study session, we have provided you with **learning activities**, which are designed to get you actively involved in the learning process. You should always try to complete the activities – usually on a separate sheet of your own paper – before reading on. You will learn much more effectively if you are actively involved in doing something as you study, rather than just passively reading the text in front of you. The feedback or answers to the activities are provided at the end of the session. Do not be tempted to skip the activity.

We also provide a number of **self-assessment questions** in each study session. These are to help you to decide for yourself whether or not you have achieved the learning objectives set out at the beginning of the session. As with the activities, you should always tackle them – usually on a separate sheet of paper. Don't be tempted to skip them. The feedback or answers are again at the end of the session. If you still do not understand a topic having attempted the self-assessment question, always try to re-read the relevant passages in the textbook readings or session, or follow the advice on further reading at the end of the session. If this still doesn't work, you should contact the CIPS Membership and Qualification Advice team.

For most of the learning activities and self assessment questions you will need to use separate sheets of paper for your answers or responses. Some of the activities or questions require you to complete a table or form, in which case you could write your response in the study guide itself, or photocopy the page.

At the end of the session are three final sections.

The first is the **summary**. Use it to remind yourself or check off what you have just studied, or later on during revision.

Then follows the **suggested further reading** section. This section, if it appears, contains recommendations for further reading which you can follow up if you would like to read alternative treatments of the topics. If for any reason you are having difficulty understanding the course book on a particular topic, try one of the alternative treatments recommended. If you are keen to read around and beyond the syllabus, to help you pick up extra points in the examination for example, you may like to try some of the additional readings recommended. If this section does not appear at the end of a session, it usually means that further reading for the session topics is not necessary.

At the end of the session we direct you to a **revision question**, which you will find in a separate section at the end of the course book. Feedback on the questions is also given.

Reading lists

CIPS produces an official reading list, which recommends essential and desirable texts for augmenting your studies. This reading list is available on the CIPS website or from the CIPS Bookshop. This course book is one of the essential texts for this unit. In this section we describe the main characteristics of the other essential texts for this unit, which you are strongly urged to buy and use throughout your course.

The other essential texts are:

Management and Organisational Behaviour, 7th edition by LJ Mullins, published by FT Prentice-Hall, London in 2005.

This essential text provides excellent coverage of most generic aspects of management and organisational behaviour.

It covers far more generic material than is required for the Leading and Influencing in Purchasing syllabus, so you should focus on the relevant models and concepts, and not attempt to digest the whole of the contexts of this text. At the same time the text is not written for the purchasing and supply chain perspective, but is a generic treatment. You will need to consider for yourself, how these generic concepts are relevant and can be applied to the supply context. The text also has a good range of practical examples, case studies and practical activities which you should refer to, in order to gain a good appreciation of management and organisational behaviour in the real world. For a more detailed treatment of the supply context, you are also encouraged to refer to the specialist references provided within the various sessions of the unit.

A Manager's Guide to Leadership by M Pedler, J Burgoyne and T Boydell published by Mcgraw-Hill, London in 2003.

In this text the authors argue two key points:

- Good leadership is not just a question of possessing and developing the right skill set or aligning yourself with a guru's particular model. It is about how you respond to tough dilemmas and difficult challenges.
- Leadership does not belong to the business top hierarchy. Everybody faces leadership challenges at whatever level they operate within their organisation.

This book provides students with a range of tools and techniques to help them assess and respond to a variety of difficult challenges.

This text is not as comprehensive as the Mullins text, since its focus is on leadership, rather than the whole area of organisational behaviour. But the treatment of leadership is a good blend of academic theory with practical examples and application into real life situations. The coverage is generic, without a special emphasis on the supply context, so again supplementary special reading is required.

Unit content coverage

In this section we reproduce the whole of the official CIPS unit content document for this unit. The overall unit characteristics and learning outcomes for the unit are given first. Then, in the table that follows, the learning objectives and indicative content are given in the left hand column. In the right hand column are the study sessions, or subsections, in which you will find coverage of the various topics.

Unit Characteristics

This unit is designed to develop students' leadership skills to enable them to lead, influence and provide direction to stakeholders within the supply chain.

Students should be able to operate at a strategic level. They should be able to lead in their defined area or part of the organisation and will be expected to motivate and support supply chain members and stakeholders in achieving objectives and success.

Students will be expected to lead in a variety of situations and to ensure that they maintain the balance of power required to achieve success. They should be able to demonstrate effective leadership in a variety of contexts, including through change, adversity, conflict and success, in order to maximise the potential of the organisation.

Learning Outcomes

On completion of this unit students will be able to:

- Critically valuate the fundamental differences between management and leadership
- Assess a range of leadership styles and apply them effectively within the supply chain
- Develop an innovative and compelling vision for the purchasing function
- Solve difficulties and challenges that arise within the supply chain and threaten key relationships
- Create and maintain a culture that encourages and recognises creativity and innovation
- Lead and influence individuals and teams effectively: encouraging, motivating, supporting and recognising achievement
- Develop a culture of productivity through people
- Successfully employ a range of effective communication methods and messages for the supply chain to support change
-

Learning objectives and indicative content

1.0 Leading and managing in purchasing (Weighting 15%)

1.1 Critically evaluate the fundamental differences between leadership and managing. — Study session 1

- The role of a leader and the activity of leadership
- The leader as a visionary, direction-setter and manager, the person who gets things done
- The key traits of a leader that differentiates from a manager
- What leaders actually do, using Adair's model of action-centred leadership
- The close relationship between leadership and management
- The need for a leader to be a good manager too
- The roles of leadership in a purchasing function including the chief purchasing officer/head of purchasing, the purchasing council and a PLT

1.2 Critically assess the behavioural traits of successful leaders. — Study session 2

- The role of the visionary in leadership
- The terms directive and facilitative and their styles of leadership
- The key components of emotional intelligence (Goleman) and the strong link with leadership skills
- The role of integrity and values within leadership
- Key communication skills for leadership: including promotional, influencing and persuasion and inspirational

1.3 Develop a range of leadership styles and judge when best to use them. — Study session 3

- The three main classifications of leadership styles: authoritarian, democratic and laissez-faire
- McGregor's Theory X and Theory Y
- A continuum of different leadership styles from facilitative through to directive
- The contrasting methods of tell and sell and the other two broad categories of leadership style: consult and join
- The merits of a situational approach to leadership
- The four main stages in Hersey's model of situational leadership and when each stage is appropriate to use in a purchasing context
- Transactional leadership and transformational leadership

1.4 Critically evaluate strategic leadership approaches: — Study session 3

- Strategy
- Human Assets
- Expertise
- Control
- Change

2.0	**Leading and influencing in the supply chain (Weighting 20%)**	
2.1	Continually influence stakeholders within the supply chain through using models of influence. • Collaboration and how this may differ from competition, adversarialism and/or accommodation • What is meant by influencing • The difference between influencing and negotiation • The importance of rapport when influencing and the key components in creating rapport • Interpersonal sensitivity and its importance in managing key stakeholders • Appropriate stakeholder map for a given purchasing activity and how power and dependency issues are identified • Key methods of influencing	Study session 4
2.2	Critically assess how the different sources of power are legitimate and acceptable when leading and influencing areas of the supply chain. • Five sources of power and applying them to the purchasing context • Coercive power • Referent power • Expertise power	Study session 4
2.3	Lead and influence effectively in four different directions. • Manage your manager and identify key methods for managing upwards • A range of influencing styles for leading direct reports and teams, and understanding what is meant by the term readiness in relation to individuals being led (Hersey & Blanchard) • A range of influencing styles for cross-functional leadership, both within and outside the bounds of formal teams • The range of external stakeholders (including suppliers, customers, collaborators and other third parties) and effective influencing styles • The relative merits of escalation as a means of influencing	Study session 5 Study session 6
2.4	Develop a range of tactics and definitions to effectively influence the supply chain. • Rational persuasion • Inspirational appeal • Consultation • Ingratiation • Exchange • Personal appeal • Coalition • Legitimating • Pressure	Study session 6

2.5 Critically assess the outcomes of attempts to influence the supply chain. — Study session 7
- Internalisation
- Compliance
- Resistance

3.0 Develop a culture of productivity through people (Weighting 30%)

3.1 Determine the need for people to work effectively, individually and in work-based teams, and justify their development. — Study session 8, Study session 9
- The range of personal preferred styles for working effectively (including introversion and extraversion) and their relative merits in the workplace
- Team models of the solo leader and the team leader
- Mintzberg's motivational and hygiene factors for leadership
- The need to change roles and refresh the status quo on a regular basis
- Critical individual and team roles, characteristics, competencies plus individual roles and expected behaviour patterns
- The merits of cross-functional teams and the role of sponsorship
- The key stages of team development
- The typical roles/responsibilities of a work-based team in a purchasing project
- The classification of team roles
- The merits of diversity within teams
- The merits of leaderless teams (e.g. T-groups)

3.2 Develop a consensus on how to work together, identifying potentials for pitfalls and conflicts within the team. — Study session 10
- Power
- Politics
- Position
- Lack of resource
- Poor communications
- Poor leadership

3.3 Critically assess diversity issues relating to the success of people and propose approaches to managing them. — Study session 11
- What is meant by the term equality and diversity
- The benefits of diversity to a high-performance culture looking at the advantages and disadvantages
- What is meant by the term equal opportunities, and the issues associated with discrimination
- Potential areas of discrimination in the workplace and the regulatory framework to protect against it (including gender, race, religion, disability and age)
- Proactive measures required to promote equality and diversity in the workplace
- Potential consequences of failing to pursue a proactive approach to equality and diversity (e.g. cultural impact, disaffected staff, reputational damage, potential lawsuits, and ethical issues)

3.4 Determine and justify ways of developing people and increasing their productivity and effectiveness. • Why it is important to develop people in the workplace • The purpose of training needs analysis • The basic process of TNA and the need for independent assessment • A range of skills and competencies for purchasing and supply that can be reliably assessed and measured • Contrast between training and development • A range of training and development initiatives • What is meant by blended-learning and action-learning	Study session 12
3.5 Effectively plan team time, including scheduling, justifying resource, deadlines and delivery dates. • What is meant by project planning and resource scheduling • The key components of a project plan and a resource plan • How a resource plan is developed and monitored for a given purchasing project • The different capabilities required that comprise a purchasing project (e.g. leadership, planning, research, analysis, strategy, negotiation, implementation, management, communication) • Development of a case to justify additional resource for a purchasing project	Study session 13
4.0 Lead change in the supply chain (Weighting 35%)	
4.1 Develop a compelling and innovative vision, values and culture for the future, justifying reasons and benefits associated with change, taking into account the relationship between transformational and transactional change. • The meaning of the term vision • The need for strategic alignment between mission, objectives, strategy and tactics • How a vision can be created and the actions required to gain buy-in: education and communication, participation and involvement, facilitation and support, negotiation and agreement, manipulation and cooperation plus explicit/implicit coercion • The need for vision to be compelling • How a vision should be communicated and reinforced • The meaning of the term culture in the context of the purchasing function • An appropriate range of values for the purchasing function and the benefits of having explicit value statements • The importance of CSR and ethics in building sustainable values within the purchasing function	Study session 14

4.2 Critically evaluate a range of different models of change management and consider the implications of implementation of each one for the purchasing function and the wider organisation as a whole. — Study session 15
- Factors driving change and their effect using appropriate tools (e.g. Lewin's force field analysis)
- The meaning of the organisational development movement
- Lewin's model for planned change and the three key stages of unfreezing, movement and refreezing
- The action research model and what is meant by cyclical change
- The merits of employing external resources to lead organisational change

4.3 Develop an appropriate style for leading and managing the strategic change process that will encourage stakeholders to welcome and embrace change within the purchasing function. — Study session 16
- Crainer's seven skills required for managing change: managing conflict, interpersonal skills, project management skills, leadership and flexibility, managing processes, managing strategy and managing personal development
- The importance of stakeholder consultation and the identity of key stakeholders who should be consulted when leading change in the purchasing function
- Principal methods of consultation and engagement of stakeholders, and the need for communication as a vehicle to assist the change process
- Ways and means of resolving conflict with stakeholders using the Thomas-Klinman conflict model as a framework. And how this applies to the workplace.

4.4 Set and prioritise justifiable objectives for change and identify strategies for achieving them. — Study session 17
- The need for objectives and targets for change programmes
- How objectives are set for a change programme and how objectives should be defined (SMART) and aligned with a broader strategic intent
- The relative merits of incremental versus step [fundamental] change and the respective implementation strategies these require
- How objectives can be broken down to individual tasks and components
- Contrasts between project and programme management
- Ways in which a change programme can be structured using a steering group, work-streams, focus groups, cross-functional teamwork and change agents
- The prioritisation process and allocation of resources to achieve targets

4.5 Determine the resource requirements for the implementation of change within the purchasing function including: — Study session 17
- Human
- Physical
- Financial

4.6 Delegate responsibility for the effective implementation of change including planning and implementation and delegating both responsibility and power to managers. • What is meant by delegation and what are the requisite leadership behaviours that enable effective delegation • Link to Hersey's model of situational leadership • Support needed to be given in order to allow a delegated responsibility to work successfully: clear direction/sponsorship, recognised authority/mandate, appropriate resources, appropriate training and capabilities, reasonable timescales and communication support • How to monitor and review delegated responsibilities and tasks • Developing appropriate rewards and recognition associated with the successful delivery of delegated activities • How a leader might take corrective action and re-direct activities that have been delegated	Study session 18
4.7 Use forcefield analysis to identify forces and barriers to change and determine what needs to be done to develop and assist change. • Bureaucracy: i.e. departmentalism, formality of management • Resources • Politics • Insecurity • Risk • Blame culture • Deference • How individuals respond to change • Link to Lewin's forcefield analysis • Why some change programmes fail • The principal barriers to effective change and the mitigating actions required to overcome resistance	Study session 18

4.8	Negotiate effectively in difficult leadership and management situations, including involvement in negotiating within industrial relations situations. • The negotiation process and the need for planning a negotiation campaign (link to other units) • How a complex negotiation needs careful stakeholder mapping and the importance of power/dependency mapping • The concept of structural power (Cox) in a negotiation context and how this will impact the approach to negotiation • The areas for non-negotiation and potential concession • The need for alignment within the negotiating team and the way in which escalation can be used appropriately for strategic issues • The term industrial relations and the contexts in which such relations are appropriate • When and how the purchasing function may become involved in IR situations • How to approach an IR negotiation and the key differences from a commercial negotiation	Study session 19
4.9	Monitor and control the impact of the change process on the supply chain performance including: • Budgets • Projects measurement • Benchmarking • Auditing • Employee and stakeholder reactions • Appropriate communication programmes involving third parties regarding internal changes	Study session 20
4.10	Manage continuity of performance while implementing change. • The importance of maintaining a business as usual approach for managing supply • The process of internal handover from one individual/team to another • How a supplier implementation programme is organised, including the potential benefits of a trial/pilot period and the ramp-up/ramp-down phases • How existing suppliers can be managed and incentivised to see out the full terms of their contracts without disruption to supply or service-levels	Study session 20

Study session 1

Leadership and management: is there a difference?

Mahatma Gandhi, Bill Clinton, Martin Johnson, Richard Branson, Nelson Mandela and Margaret Thatcher are six famous people, who are generally acknowledged as *leaders.* What is it that makes them leaders?

Introduction

The subject of leading and influencing is the core theme of this whole unit. In this session we will explore some preliminary ideas about the fundamental differences between leadership and management.

Leadership is a subject area that has been of interest throughout history. In the context of business and management, leadership is considered essential if an organisation is to consistently achieve its objectives. In this session you will explore some different perspectives on the nature of management and leadership.

Session learning objectives

The session learning objectives will firstly consider the wide area of management and leadership, and then ask you to consider them in the context of the supply chain. After completing this session you should be able to:

1.1 Assess and compare some preliminary ideas about the differences between 'management' and 'leadership'.
1.2 Give examples of good and bad management and leadership behaviour.
1.3 Distinguish between 'management' and 'leadership' in an organisational context.
1.4 Compare and contrast 'management and leadership' in a supply chain context.

Unit content coverage

This study session covers the following topics from the official CIPS unit content document.

Learning objective

1.1 Critically evaluate the fundamental differences between leadership and managing.

- The role of a leader and the activity of leadership
- The leader as a visionary and direction-setter and manager, the person who gets things done
- The key traits of a leader that differentiates from a manager
- What leaders actually do, using Adair's model of action-centred leadership
- The close relationship between leadership and management
- The need for a leader to be a good manager too

- The roles of leadership in a purchasing function including the chief purchasing officer/head of purchasing, the purchasing council and a PLT

Prior knowledge

We are not assuming any prior knowledge for this unit other than your previous studies on the CIPS programmes. However, this unit and the unit on strategic supply chain management are closely interlinked and you should consider the impact of strategy on leadership and vice versa at all times.

Timing

You should set aside about 6 hours to read and complete this session, including learning activities, self-assessment questions, the suggested further reading (if any) from the essential textbook for this unit and the revision question.

1.1 The leader as visionary and direction setter, and the manager, who gets things done

Learning activity 1.1

Refer to the six famous people at the beginning of this section. Are they managers or leaders? Justify your answer.

Feedback on page 13

Definitions

There are literally hundreds of definitions of *management* and *leadership* in the literature.

Among the many definitions of **management** are:

> 'The process through which efforts of members of the organisation are co-ordinated, directed and guided towards the achievement of organisational goals. The clarification of objectives, planning, organising, directing and controlling other people's work.'
>
> Mullins (2005: Glossary)
>
> 'The art of getting things done through people.'
>
> Mary Parker Follet (1924)
>
> 'Getting things done with the aid of people.'
>
> Stewart (1967)

Among the many definitions of **leadership** are:

'Leadership is the process of motivating other people to act in particular ways in order to achieve specific goals.'

Hannagan (2005)

'A relationship through which one person influences the behaviour or actions of other people.'

Mullins (2005: Glossary)

'Leadership is the activity of generating effort and commitment towards meeting objectives. It includes influencing and motivating other people to work in support of the plans.'

Boddy (2005)

Management and *leadership* can also be compared and contrasted:

'Management implies leadership, and in fact the success or failure of managers can be judged on their leadership qualities.'

Hannagan (2005)

When considering these definitions some key ideas emerge, which you should think about:

- Process – essentially process is how things are actually achieved in an organisation. This considers how resources are acquired, and allocated in daily workplace activities. Resources include materials, equipment, money, people and time.
- Organisational goals – are what the organisation is trying to achieve over time. Timescales can be long, medium or short term.
- Planning, organising, directing and controlling – are recognised as the traditional roles of management (Fayol, 1914).
- Relationship – signifies that a lot of variables are interacting with each other and that therefore a degree of complexity is involved.

Figure 1.1: A simple model of the organisation in its business environment

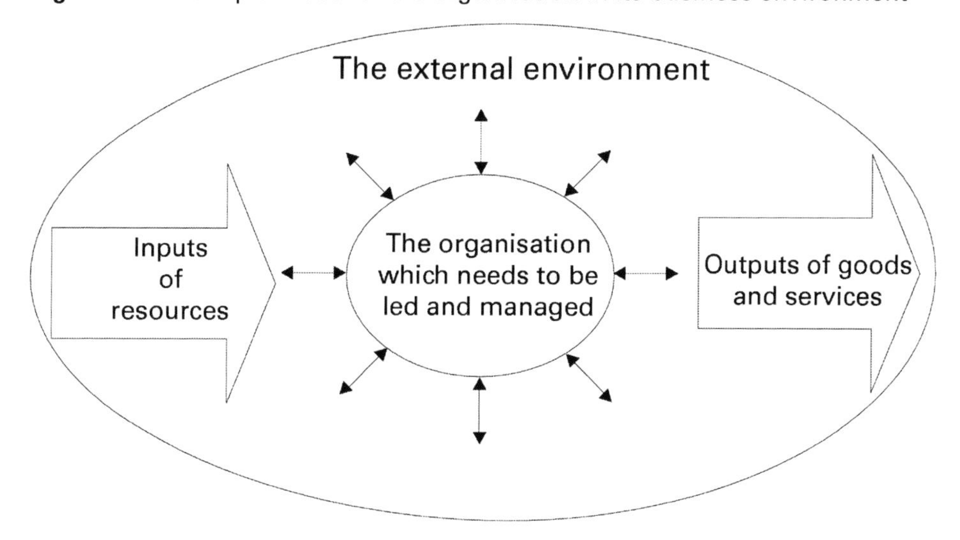

Figure 1.1 captures some of the complexities which are involved, and sets the context within which leadership and management is practised. Any

organisation can be considered in this way, and it is useful for you to think how this could be applied to your own workplace, or to organisations with which you are familiar.

Most of the literature suggests that there is a distinction between the roles of leadership and management.

- Leaders set the major objectives and strategies of the organisation. They take a long-term view, and are concerned with the big issues. This is often referred to as visionary thinking, being able to look ahead to the future, and developing a strategy which will take the organisation forward. You could consider this as the viewpoint of 'elephants and helicopters' – being able to raise yourself above the forest and look down for the main issues (the elephants) which need to be recognised and addressed.
- Managers transmit and enforce the objectives, or implement strategies initiated by leaders. They make sure that the long-term view and big issues are translated into daily activities. This is akin to working on the forest floor, and being surrounded by trees, it is hard to see the whole picture so you need the leader to give clear guidance and support. At the same time, the leader needs the managers to make the vision happen.

Figure 1.2: The strategy hierarchy

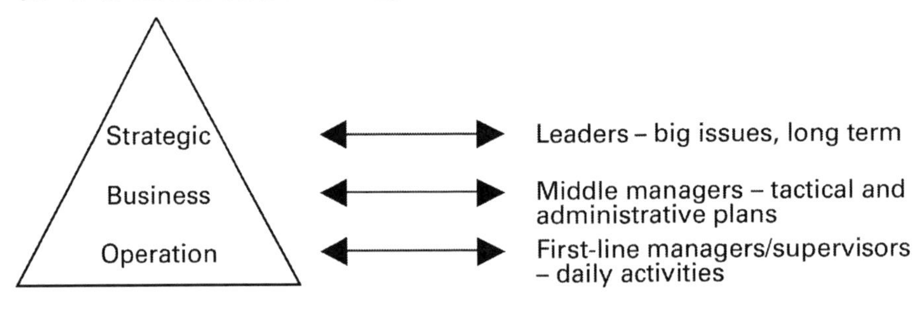

Figure 1.2 shows where these different activities fit into an organisational strategy, and the interactive role of leadership and management, within the strategy.

The thinking about leadership and management is constantly evolving over time, and while a certain consensus may be popular for a while, there has been a range of concepts about which there is a constant debate, without a clear agreement being reached.

Self-assessment question 1.1

List the key differences between the work and roles of leaders and managers.

Feedback on page 13

1.2 Leadership traits

The traits approach

Having spent some time trying to distinguish between leadership and management, a logical question to consider is: are there any specific physical, intellectual or personality characteristics that distinguish leaders from others (that is, **leadership traits**)? This is often referred to as the 'traits' approach to leadership.

Mostly this has involved the study of so-called successful leaders, examining in detail their physical, intellectual or personality characteristics, and then trying to identify themes and patterns which could be common to all of them. Having identified the characteristics it then becomes a simple matter of copying those characteristics, and you can be a leader too!

Learning activity 1.2

> 'Research by the Chartered Management Institute (CMI, 2001) indicated that the quality of leadership in UK organisations is lacking. Over a third of all managers in their survey of 1500 practising managers (and almost half of junior managers surveyed) rate the quality of leadership in their organisations as "poor".'

Reflect on the above statement and consider examples of 'poor' leadership from your own experience. Why was the leadership 'poor'?

Feedback on page 14

In various circumstances and at various times, good leadership has been shown to link strongly to:

- physique
- technical knowledge
- intelligence
- perception and caring
- position in the organisation
- subjective assessment by subordinates
- peer assessment
- length of service in an organisation
- persistence
- courage and risk-taking
- innovation and creativity.

The weakness of this approach is that leaders seem to display such a wide range of traits that it becomes almost impossible to generalise.

In an attempt to try and make leadership more measurable, Cattell and Kline (1977) identified a 'big five' of personality factors as follows:

- extroversion/introversion
- agreeableness/hostility
- conscientiousness/heedlessness
- emotional stability/instability
- open-minded/closed-minded, in terms of intellect.

They attempted to develop various continuums along which leadership traits could be assessed. In contrast, Brown (1986) has observed: 'Some of the most successful leaders in history have been neurotic, epileptic, humourless, narrow-minded, unjust and authoritarian', implying that not all leadership traits necessarily manifest themselves in positive actions. Indeed the traits identified by Brown explicitly suggest that some very unpleasant leadership characteristics can also be successful!

1.3 Differentiating leaders and managers

Much of the above discussion may be appear to be largely indeterminate, and hard to synthesise in that there hardly ever appear to be any clear and discernible themes and patterns to distinguish leaders and managers in terms of traits. So why bother with inherent traits? Maybe you need to look at what leaders and managers actually do, in their actions.

Peters and Waterman (1982) developed a model which may help you to make a distinction between managers and leaders. They developed and elaborated on the '7-S framework' which showed the link between 'hard' and 'soft' skills. Hard technical skills (structure, strategy and systems, the 'icy triangle') were proposed as the distinctive competence of managers. The soft, people-oriented skills (skills, style and staff) were proposed as more distinctive in leaders. What linked them both were the 'shared values' (figure 1.3).

Figure 1.3: The McKinsey 7-S framework

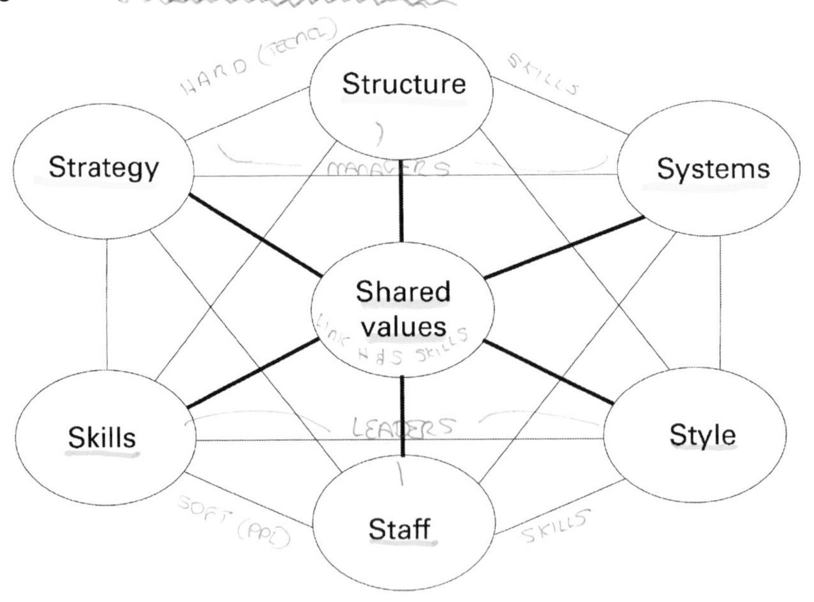

What leaders actually do – action-centred leadership

John Adair considered the things that leaders actually do, and focused on three main areas:

- achieving the task – making sure that tasks, goals, objectives and targets are actually achieved within their stated parameters (usually quality, cost and time);
- building and maintaining a team which is capable and willing to achieve the task;

- developing individuals, so that their needs are satisfied within the constraints of team and task. Its often quoted that 'there is no I in team', but there is a 'me'.

Figure 1.4: Action-centred leadership

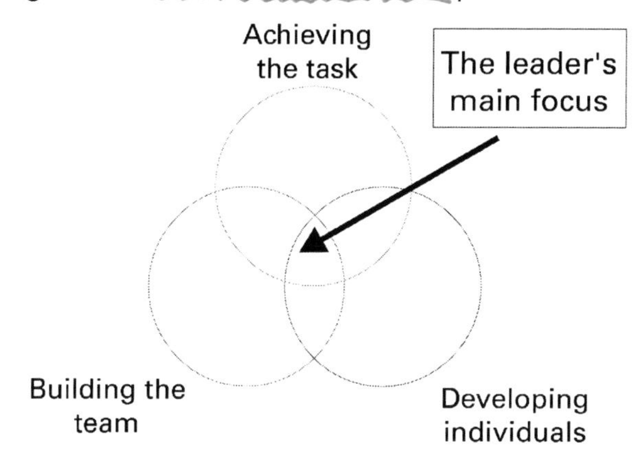

Source: adapted from Adair (1997)

In the model (figure 1.4) it is where the circles all overlap (highlighted by the arrow) that real leadership is happening, and all the various 'needs' are being fulfilled.

In the context of the overlapping needs, the role of the leader involves both hard and soft skills:

- defining the task
- planning
- briefing
- controlling
- evaluating
- motivating
- organising
- providing an example.

Self-assessment question 1.2

The case below is real, but the name of the organisation has been changed to maintain anonymity.

In 1999, Fulchester City Council established its Leadership Charter, based on seven key areas in which managers should demonstrate effective leadership. The Charter requires that managers:

- provide vision and direction
- manage performance
- plan and review activities
- develop people
- develop themselves
- communicate effectively
- demonstrate integrity and commitment.

(continued on next page)

Self-assessment question 1.2 *(continued)*

Consider the main components of the Charter. Do the seven principles adequately address the leadership needs of the organisation?

Feedback on page 14

The link between leadership and management

There are a number of writers who have focused not on differences between leaders and managers, but on the similarities between both activities. Indeed they suggest that all leaders have to have some management attributes and skills, and all managers have a leadership role to play. It is really a question of degree and emphasis. Many of the possibilities which this opens up will be considered in detail later in this course book.

Figure 1.5: The balance between leadership and management

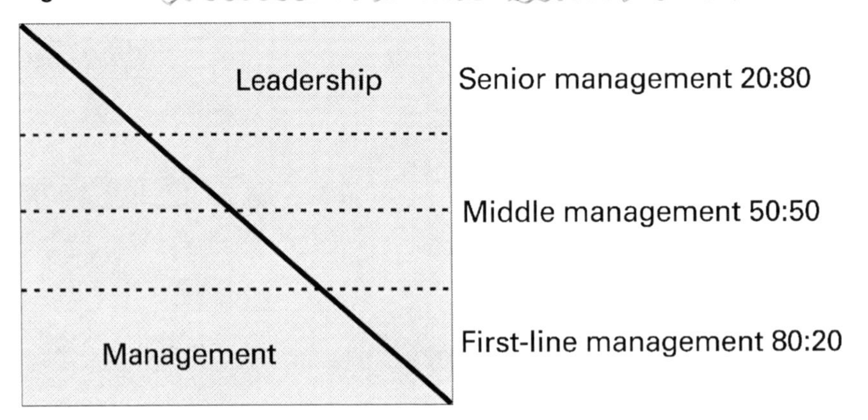

Modern approaches to business recognise the need for a leader to be a good manager too. The soft and hard skills need to be combined for best effect.

Learning activity 1.3

Refer to figure 1.5 and think about the leadership/management attributes that might be needed by a junior manager as opposed to a senior one.

Feedback on page 14

Now that you have completed the learning activity, see if you can answer this question.

Self-assessment question 1.3

Case study

June has just taken over as a department manager in the 'Sparks Electrical' store in a local city – her first managerial role since her graduation. In this branch, there are 12 full-time staff (including June) and a large number of part-timers. Most of the full-time staff have been with the organisation less than two years. June's predecessor, Dave, is being moved on to a role in Head Office.

(continued on next page)

Self-assessment question 1.3 *(continued)*

Before Dave left, she shadowed him for a week, but she has found that the experience raised more fears than it allayed. Some of the things that she is finding out about Dave's style of management have given her grave cause for concern.

Alan is one of the longer-serving members of staff in the department. He has had some supervisory training and has responsibility for one small part of the store. What really concerned June was the way that Dave treated Alan. In his weekly staff meeting anything that Alan said was immediately ridiculed by Dave, even though they were potentially quite reasonable contributions.

Dave has also been monitoring Alan's work very closely for the past 12 months, with daily meetings, which none of the other section heads required their staff to do. Apparently there was a mistake in the pricing arrangements in last year's sale which involved some financial loss to the company. To some extent this may have been due to poor communications from Head Office – the same thing happened in two other stores – but Alan took the blame for it. Dave has not let the matter rest since. Looking at Alan's personnel file the written warning that he received at the time is just about to go 'out of date', and there are no records of any problems since.

Alan is a very hard-working and conscientious individual, and he has clearly found Dave's approach very distressing. He has taken to working late to make sure that everything is absolutely 'first-rate' on this section, which it was anyway as he does his job very well – the problem is that he has become used to Dave giving him a dressing-down, often in public, for the smallest thing, real or imagined. To a lesser extent, Dave applies a similar approach to all the staff with the exception of two men of his own age who are also golfing friends out of work hours. At lunchtimes, these three eat in Dave's office with the door closed.

Informally, June has asked Dave about Alan, and questioned him as to his treatment of Alan. Dave actually took this quite well and said: 'Well you've done a management course – haven't you heard of "bounce-back" theory? If Alan is any good he'll be able to bounce back by himself!'

The situation is having an impact on staff relations and June has noticed that, compared to other branches, the 'atmosphere' is quite different here. What is significant is that the 'bad atmosphere' in her new department seems to be having a negative effect throughout the store.

1. How would you describe Dave's leadership approach?
2. From Monday, the situation will be in June's hands. What can she do to contribute to the restoration of morale in this branch generally, and to address the situation with Alan in particular? What leadership theories might help her with her transition?
3. How should she approach the matter of managing Dave's 'golf chums'?

Try to use the models discussed in the session to help you structure your response.

Feedback on page 14

SEE NOTES 4 S2

1

1.4 Leadership in the purchasing function

A context for purchasing and supply

In this section you are going to explore the general concepts that have been introduced to date and to focus more narrowly on your actual work environment.

Figure 1.6: The purchasing and supply chain model

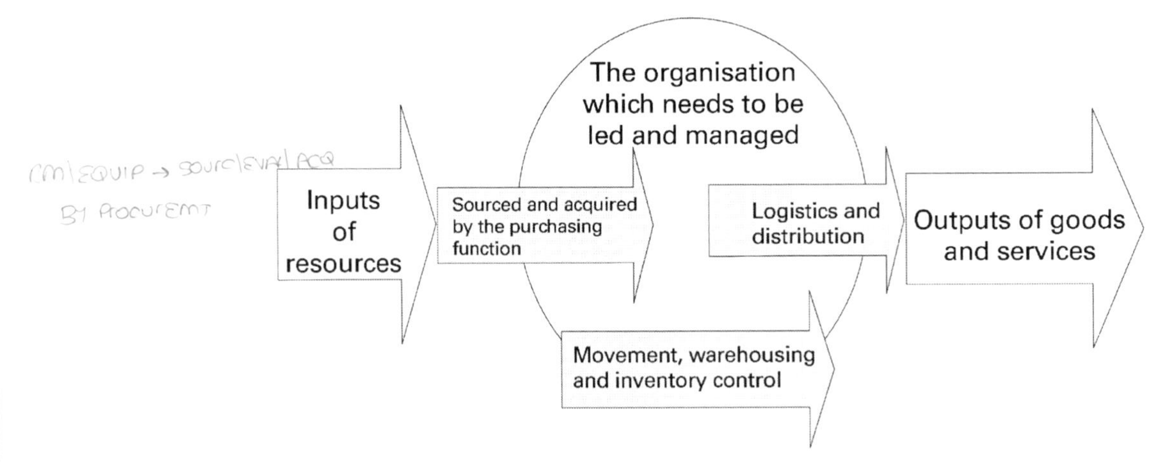

Figure 1.6 develops the simple model from figure 1.1, and incorporates the various elements of the purchasing and logistics function.

- The purchasing function is the key interface in terms of the supply market into the organisation. Raw materials, equipment and knowledge is sourced, evaluated and acquired by the purchasing function.
- Inside the organisation, and this can apply equally to large complex organisations, the purchased items are moved, stored and worked on during daily activities. This inventory needs to be managed, monitored and controlled.
- Finished goods and services then need to be taken to market. This can be through the traditional routes of physical distribution (for example road, rail, air), or electronically via email or the internet.

All of these activities need leadership and management.

Figure 1.7: A strategy hierarchy for purchasing and supply chain

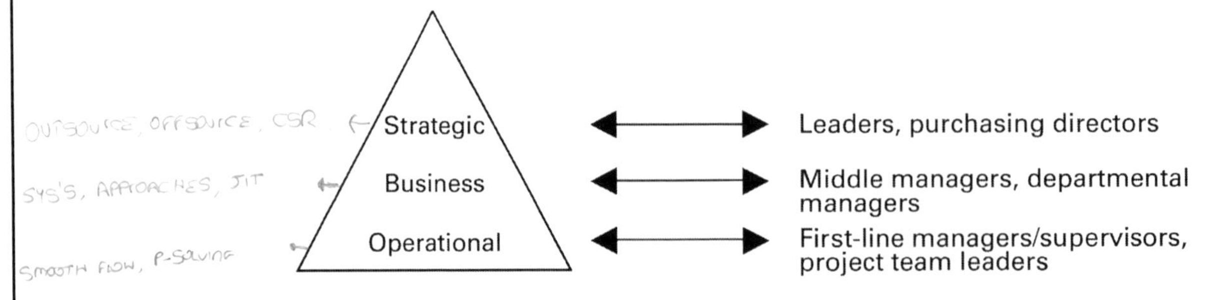

At the strategic level (figure 1.7(), purchasing directors determine and define the strategic approach of the purchasing function. They contribute

to developing long-term views about supplier relationships, outsourcing and offshoring, and how the organisation will compete within a complex and ever-changing business environment. In an era of low inflation and intense competition, purchasing has become of critical strategic importance. Externally there has been the trend, from environmental conservation and corporate social responsibility, for organisations to take a more 'responsible and ethical' approach, which is impacting on this strategic level.

At the business level, departmental purchasing managers, often working together as a cross-departmental purchasing council, develop particular approaches for each department. This goes into the meticulous detail of relationships with suppliers, methods of materials management and systems of inventory control – weighing and evaluating the pros and cons of a variety of business options, making decisions and solving problems in line with the strategic objectives of the organisation.

At the operational level, project team leaders, working within teams, and interacting externally with suppliers and internally with other functions, ensure a smooth flow of materials, equipment, information and knowledge. Most of all, they react and solve the myriad of day-to-day issues which can interrupt that smooth flow.

Learning activity 1.4

To support councils in the process of leadership development, the Improvement and Development Agency (2005, http://www.idea.gov.uk) has highlighted five *competencies* considered to be crucial in leading public sector organisations. These are:

- vision for the community and strategy
- change management
- motivation
- innovation and creativity
- alliance building.

The above is a view for public sector organisations. Evaluate what you consider to be the five competencies for leadership in the purchasing function in your own organisation. Explain why they are the same as, or different from, the public sector.

Feedback on page 15

Leadership skills in purchasing and supply

In traditional purchasing and supply chain approaches the function was largely regarded as administrative. Time spent on each activity:

Activity	Time
Strategy	10%
Supplier development	10%
Administration	80%

Modern approaches suggest the balance is changing dramatically:

Strategy	20%
Supplier development	70%
Administration	10%

If the nature of the work is changing, what new skills need to be acquired and developed in order to lead and manage in purchasing and supply?

Self-assessment question 1.4

Consider a specific example of good or poor practice from a leader in your purchasing and supply area.

What were the implications of the good or bad practice on the performance of the organisation?

What would a good leader and a good manager have done that would have been different?

Try and spend some time thinking about this example in some detail.

Feedback on page 15

Revision question

Now try the revision question for this session on page 297.

Summary

In this session you have started to explore the nature of leadership and management and:

- considered a range of definitions which have enabled you to see some similarities and differences between leadership and management;
- related these definitions to examples of management and leadership from the contemporary world. Leadership and management are required at all levels of the organisation – senior, middle and supervisory management levels;
- begun to relate to generic ideas about leadership and management, and to assess their applicability to the purchasing and supply function.

Suggested further reading

Adair (1979) provides the definitive exposition of action cantered leadership, on which most of the textbooks rely, so it is useful for you to read his own discussion.

Brown (1986) has developed a detailed critique of human relations in the workplace from a social psychology perspective.

Follett (1924) makes interesting reading.

Hannagan (2005) provides an alternative treatment of leadership and management in an HR context.

Mullins (2005). The essential text for this unit, Mullins provides a good introductory discussion in Chapter 8.

Wickens (1995 and 1998) provides a very readable discussion of leadership and how that contributes to the development of staff, which is applied to the context of a major international manufacturing organisation.

Feedback on learning activities and self-assessment questions

Feedback on learning activity 1.1

There is no clear agreement on a correct answer, but among the different emphases which you should have considered are the following:

Management – 'How will we get there?'

- Planning
- Organising
- Directing
- Monitoring
- Controlling.

Leadership – 'Where are we going?'

- Influencing
- Encouraging others
- Involving others
- Communicating
- Motivating.

You should probably note more 'leadership' behaviours in our group of six.

Feedback on self-assessment question 1.1

Not exhaustive but should include:

Leaders

- Setting the vision
- Articulating the vision
- Setting values by example
- Innovation and creativity
- Motivating staff
- Setting behaviours (culture) by example
- Figurehead, spokesperson

Managers

- Planning admin. systems
- Reward and recognition systems

- Scheduling and programming
- Problem solving
- Clarification
- Interface between leaders and staff
- Training
- Appraisal and feedback
- Role model to staff

Feedback on learning activity 1.2

There are no real textbook answers here, but you should be giving examples which are specific to your own experience, which provide evidence in terms of actions and behaviours.

Usually 'poor' leadership will be because one of the essential requirements for good leadership is absent.

Feedback on self-assessment question 1.2

Your considerations should aim to be structured and broad-ranging. You should be defining some of the key concepts in the Charter, and then using a model of leadership from your reading, to see if the seven principles are applicable. It is likely that the seven principles do provide a good example of leadership principles in a public sector context. If we were to be critical of the principles, perhaps they are not sufficiently time-bound or specific enough.

Feedback on learning activity 1.3

Junior managers mostly involved with management with a smaller element of leadership activities. For example, in a buying department the junior manager would be mostly involved in the daily activities of making sure that deliveries have arrived as scheduled, checking that invoices are correct and that onward movements of materials into the operation happen smoothly. They may only be involved periodically in strategic reviews and strategic negotiations with suppliers. Senior managers are mostly involved in leadership activities, with a smaller element of management activities. In a buying office their work is mostly about strategic policies with regard to sourcing and cost reduction, and less on the daily details.

Feedback on self-assessment question 1.3

1. There seems to be some bias against Alan, and Dave is being very dictatorial with him, and yet treats other staff quite differently. There seems to be very little basis for Dave's attitude to Alan, and Alan seems to be doing a good job.
2. Action-centred leadership can help with all the staff and Alan in particular. Communication, trust and openness will all imply a less dictatorial and more democratic and consultative style.
3. Golf chums need careful handling – she does not want to alienate them, but needs to keep them involved and supportive. In this case it

is probably wise to clearly set out the roles and responsibilities of all concerned and stick to them scrupulously.

Feedback on learning activity 1.4

- Vision for the organisation and strategy – purchasing has a strategic contribution to make to the overall success of the organisation, so a clear vision is needed.
- Change management – much of the admin. tasks can now be facilitated by technology; supplier development needs to be the main focus.
- Motivation – fundamental, along with communication.
- Innovation and creativity – a fast-changing environment requires innovative responses.
- Alliance building – complexity requires more complex and yet flexible networks.

Feedback on self-assessment question 1.4

Did you identify any evidence or lack of 7-S framework behaviour, or action-centred leadership? What were the effects of the poor leadership on people, systems, practices? How did staff respond?

Contrast with good leadership behaviour and actions, and how this can affect performance positively.

Study session 2

Successful leaders: are they born or made?

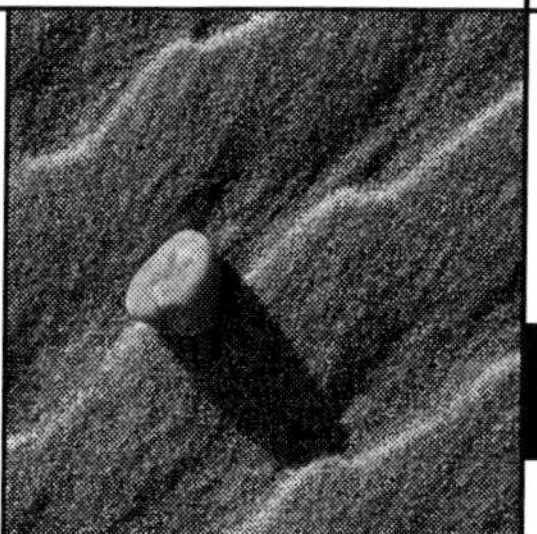

2

If successful leaders are only born, then there would not be any point in trying to teach 'leadership'. But if leadership can be taught, then anyone can aspire to be a leader.

Introduction

This session develops further the preliminary consideration from study session 1. Study session 1 largely examined the *characteristics* of leaderships to assess their replicability.

Study session 2 tries to look at *behaviours* of leaders, what they actually do, as a guideline to increase your understanding of leadership in action. From understanding leadership behaviour in others, you can then develop and enhance your own leadership skills.

Session learning objectives

These session objectives attempt to assess several of the key components of effective leadership. After completing this session you should be able to:

2.1 Describe and assess the role of the visionary in leadership.
2.2 Define the terms 'directive' and 'facilitative' and describe and assess these styles of leadership.
2.3 Describe the key components of emotional intelligence and outline the strong link with leadership skills.
2.4 Describe the role of integrity and values within leadership.
2.5 Critically assess the behavioural traits of successful leaders.
2.6 Identify key communication skills for leadership (including promotional, influencing and persuasion, and inspirational).

Unit content coverage

This study session covers the following topics from the official CIPS unit content document.

Learning objective

1.2 Critically assess the behavioural traits of successful leaders.

- The role of the visionary in leadership
- The terms 'directive' and 'facilitative' and their styles of leadership
- The key components of emotional intelligence (Goleman) and the strong link with leadership skills
- The role of integrity and values within leadership
- Key communication skills for leadership, including promotional, influencing and persuasion and inspirational

Prior knowledge

Before attempting this session you should have completed study session 1.

Timing

You should set aside about 6 hours to read and complete this session, including learning activities, self-assessment questions, the suggested further reading (if any) from the essential textbook for this unit and the revision question.

2.1 The role of the visionary in leadership

One of the key roles of the leader is to communicate explicitly the purpose of the organisation. By explicitly we mean that this communication is formalised through written as well as verbal communication. The leader is not just the vehicle of rhetoric, they also have to ensure that there is some clear substance throughout the whole organisation and also with the external environment (figure 2.1).

Figure 2.1: A communication hierarchy

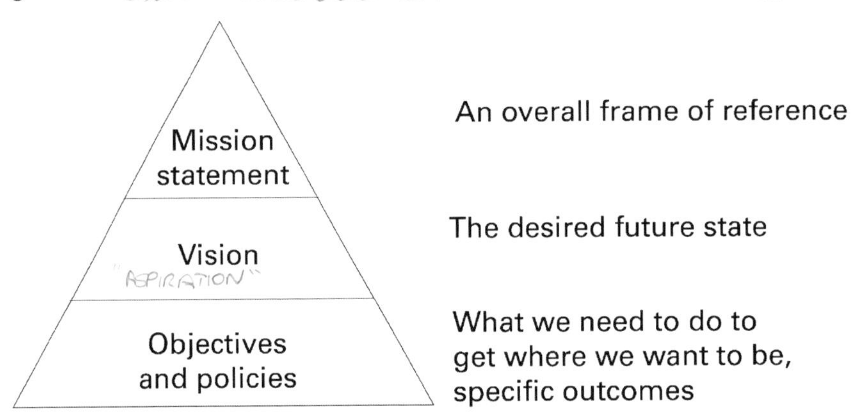

Johnson and Scholes (2004) define **vision** as 'a desired future state of the organisation. It is an aspiration around which a strategist, perhaps the chief executive, might seek to focus the attention and energies of members of the organisation.'

So vision is where we want to be, but remember the caveat that the future is uncertain, so we need to be constantly reviewing and reassessing the communication hierarchy of the organisation. I like the concept of vision as 'knowing what a good day looks like, and being able to communicate that to others' (Franco, 2004).

Most famous of all the visionary statements is the following:

> 'I have a dream that one day all the nations will rise up and live out the true meaning of its creed.'
>
> Martin Luther King, 20/8/1963, Lincoln Memorial, Washington DC

Learning activity 2.1

See table 2.1 from Johnson and Scholes (2004). Fill in some detailed examples from your own organisation in the blank column.

Table 2.1

Term	Definition	Your organisation
Mission	Overriding purpose of the organisation, in line with stakeholder expectations	
Vision	Desired future state	
Goal	General statement of aim	
Objective	Quantification of the goal with more precision	
Unique resources and core competence	Resources, processes or skills which produce a competitive advantage	
Strategies	Long-term direction	
Control	How we monitor the steps above, stay on track or modify	

Source: Johnson and Scholes (2004)

Feedback on page 25

Self-assessment question 2.1

Provide some specific examples of 'visionary' leadership from your own experience. What effect did it have on you?

Feedback on page 25

2.2 'Directive' and 'facilitative' styles of leadership

Background thinkers

Table 2.2 Some key writers on management and leadership

Writer	Theory	General ideas
Frederick Winslow Taylor	Scientific management	Managers know 'the one best way' and can develop relevant strategies for the organisation
Henri Fayol	Prime management functions	Planning, organising, coordinating, commanding and controlling
Peter Drucker	Tasks, responsibilities, practices	Satisfying goals, focus on productivity, social responsibility
Henry Mintzberg	Managerial roles, what they do!	Interpersonal, informational, decision-making

Table 2.2 above provides a brief summary of the thinking of some of the key thinkers on management in the twentieth century. You are strongly advised to read the authors' work in more detail. All of them have written extensively and are widely quoted in the main textbooks on management.

Leadership schools of thought

Table 2.3 Leadership schools of thought

Idea	Writers	Main concept
Trait theories (see study session 1)	Stodgill et al, Bennis and Nannis	Personal leadership characteristics, logical thinking, persistence, interpersonal skills
Behavioural theories (see this session)	Ohio Studies, Blake and Mouton	What leaders actually do, leadership style
Situational theories (see study session 3)	Hersey and Blanchard	Leadership in a context, which may change and therefore requires change from the leader

Table 2.3 provides a brief summary of the main schools of thought about leadership styles in the twentieth century. You are strongly advised to read their work in more detail. All of them have written extensively and are widely quoted in the main textbooks on management.

Main behavioural thinkers

The Ohio and Michigan schools of thought both focused on what became known as the concern for task/concern for people matrix (figure 2.2), after Blake and Mouton (1964).

Figure 2.2: The Blake and Mouton managerial grid

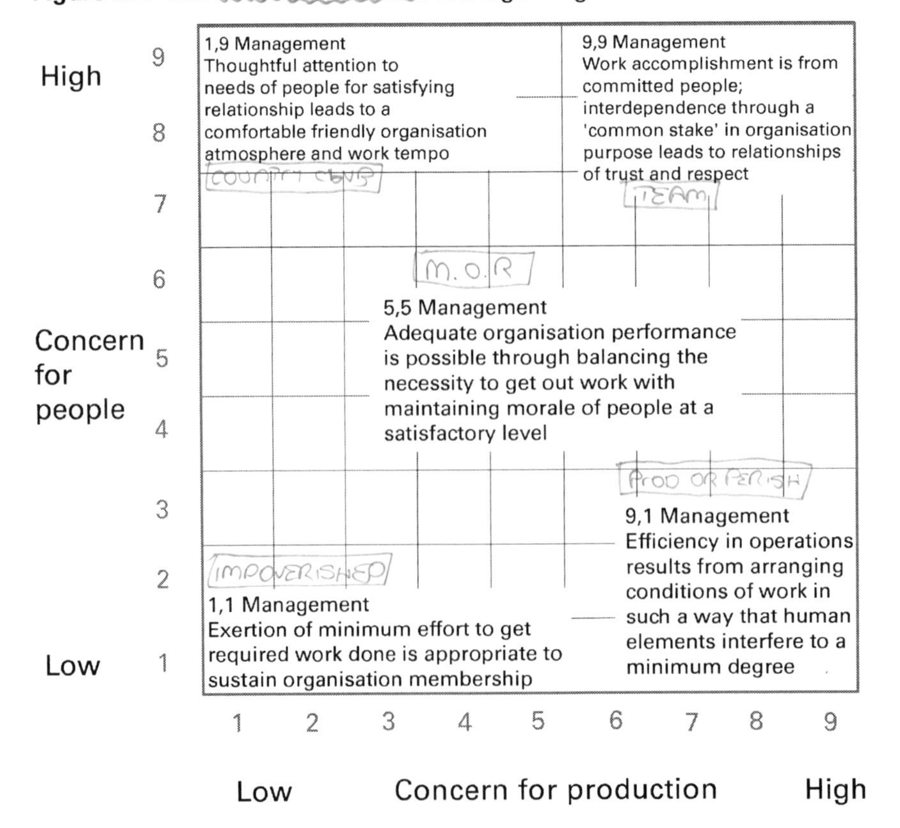

The main categories as per the grid were colloquially described as follows:

- 1,1 the impoverished style
- 1,9 the Country Club style
- 9,9 the team style
- 9,1 the produce-or-perish style
- 5,5 the middle-of-the-road style.

The idea of a continuum of styles and bipolar thinking was developed by a number of thinkers, principal of whom were Tannenbaum and Schmidt (1973).

Tannenbaum and Schmidt (1973) developed a style continuum which had as its extremes autocratic (directive) and facilitative (laissez-faire) thinking (figure 2.3).

Figure 2.3: Leadership style continuum

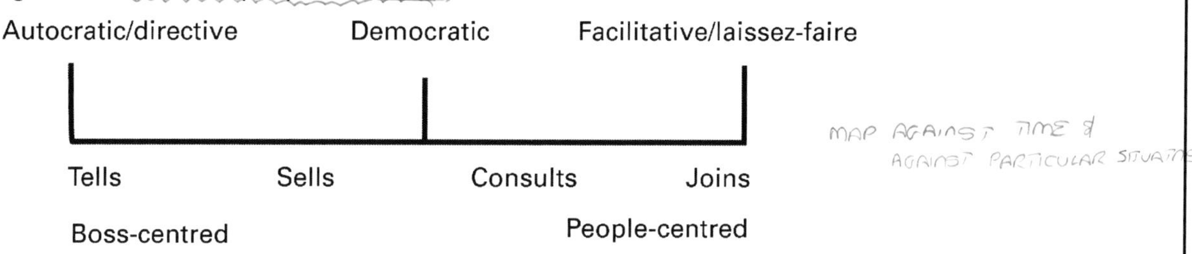

Source: adapted from Tannenbaum and Schmidt (1973)

They defined leadership as 'the behaviour of leaders towards subordinates, the manner in which tasks and functions of leadership are conducted'. Where you were on the continuum could be mapped against time and against particular situations.

Learning activity 2.2

Consider the following mini-scenarios:

- Jorma Ollila of Nokia – He is extremely ambitious and extremely demanding. He gives authority to people to do things, but he demands performance in return. The main risk he sees is complacency. He talks of a 'daily, continuous fight against bureaucracy and against becoming an incumbent, stable institution. People easily move into their comfort zones and don't ask chilling enough questions of themselves, or of their environment'. (*Financial Times*, December 2000)
- Lesley Macdonagh of Lovells – 'My position is an elected one: I have been elected and re-elected three times. You've got to be convincing. But being adamant about the direction we should go is a card I will play only sparingly, so people are prepared to listen when I do feel something passionately. The only time I would get very resolute would be if I felt someone was taking advantage of the firm or not pulling their weight.'

Compare and contrast the leadership approach of these two very successful leaders.

Feedback on page 25

Self-assessment question 2.2

Go back to the leaders mentioned at the beginning of study session 1, and now consider the leadership styles of our 'famous six'. Suggest another famous six, who display different leadership styles. Place them all on the Tannenbaum and Schmidt continuum and the Blake and Mouton grid.

Feedback on page 25

2.3 Emotional intelligence and leadership skills

Psychologists have long explored aspects of cognitive and non-cognitive intelligence:

- Thorndike (1937) considered the social aspects of intelligence;
- Wechsler (1958) considered rational thinking, within a person's own personal external environment;
- Gardner (1983) developed ideas about people having 'multiple intelligences' across the senses;
- Salovey and Meyer (1990) coined the term '**emotional intelligence**' as 'a form of social intelligence that involves the ability to monitor one's own and others' feelings and emotions. To be able to discriminate amongst them and to use this information to guides one's own thoughts and actions.'

Goleman (1995) crystallised thinking about emotional intelligence into what he termed five domains:

- self-awareness, recognising feelings when they occur;
- managing emotions, being able to handle feelings so we are not overcome;
- self-motivation, using feelings to achieve goals;
- recognising emotions in others;
- handling relationships by managing the emotions of others.

Moreover Goleman's research suggested that emotional intelligence is not innate (in contrast to IQ), but can be learned, and therefore can be taught to others.

Learning activity 2.3

Consider the five domains of Goleman and demonstrate where they are relevant to ideas about good leadership.

Feedback on page 26

Self-assessment question 2.3

How does emotional intelligence relate to leadership in supply chain function? What potential benefits could be derived?

Feedback on page 26

2.4 Integrity and values within leadership

Learning activity 2.4

Why are integrity, values and corporate social responsibility now of concern to supply chain professionals? Discuss or reflect on this question and try to provide examples from your own experience.

Feedback on page 26

Self-assessment question 2.4

What potential conflicts do integrity and values create when you are trying to 'get the job done'?

Feedback on page 26

2.5 Behavioural traits of successful leaders

In study session 1 a long list of traits was suggested, which at various times have been identified. The list is repeated to refresh your memory:

- physique
- technical knowledge
- intelligence
- perception and caring
- position in the organisation
- subjective assessment by subordinates
- peer assessment
- length of service in an organisation
- persistence
- courage and risk-taking
- innovation and creativity.

Are some traits more essential than others? It is difficult to see any evidence of unanimity. Mullins (2005) suggests 'attempts at identifying common personality, or physical and mental characteristics … have met with little success'. *Management Today* (1999), cited in Mullins (2005) in a study of women leaders, concluded that 'women leaders wield the kind of power and influence that defies stereotypes'.

Learning activity 2.5

Prepare a table of critical/desirable/nice-to-have leadership traits.

Feedback on page 26

Self-assessment question 2.5

Identify and justify the critical traits for the supply chain function.

Feedback on page 27

2.6 Key communication skills for leadership

Modern approaches to leadership suggest the multifaceted nature of leadership. Mullins (2005) suggests 'leadership is related to motivation, interpersonal behaviour and the process of communication'.

Mullins (2005: 318) cites as an example the definition of **communication** by the Autoglass company: 'the ability to create openness and trust by sharing information widely, listening and encouraging free dialogue'.

Learning activity 2.6

Define each of the key communication skills.

Feedback on page 27

Self-assessment question 2.6

Provide examples of your definition in action.

Feedback on page 27

Revision question

Now try the revision question for this session on page 297.

Summary

In this session you have considered a variety of the critical factors which are considered essential for successful leaders:

- A wide range of traits has been identified, but there is little conclusive evidence of a consensus about which traits are essential.
- Leadership most definitely requires clear forward-thinking skills, often referred to as 'visionary thinking'.
- A wide range of leadership styles is identified along a continuum from directive to facilitative.
- Emotional intelligence has a strong link to leadership skills, as does integrity and values.
- A number of key communication skills for leadership have been briefly considered.

Suggested further reading

Blake and Mouton (1964), figure 1, page 10. Blake and Mouton are the originators of the idea of the Managerial Grid, so reading them is useful.

Goleman (1995) developed thinking on emotional intelligence in this classical text.

Johnson and Scholes (2004). Read the section on vision and mission.

Mullins (2005). Read the sections on leadership and management.

Feedback on learning activities and self-assessment questions

Feedback on learning activity 2.1

You should undertake some research in your own organisation to see what information is available.

Feedback on self-assessment question 2.1

Was the example specific? Did you move from descriptive to analytic? How did the 'vision' impact on you? You should be trying to identify how the leadership vision impacted on your behaviour.

Feedback on learning activity 2.2

The former seems quite autocratic, and the latter more democratic.
But both demonstrate the willingness and an ability to change with the situation.

Feedback on self-assessment question 2.2

Assess according to criticality demonstrated, and to the evidence produced in support.

Feedback on learning activity 2.3

You should be able to see a strong link between the five domains and the soft skills of leadership (7-S framework).

Feedback on self-assessment question 2.3

You can relate these broad theories to the supply chain function. There is a clear link to many of the commercial relationships, such as negotiation and developing relationships with suppliers and customers.

Feedback on learning activity 2.4

Consider issues of corporate responsibility of relevance to supply chain and purchasing:

- ethical sourcing
- sustainability
- offshoring and outsourcing
- fairness in dealing with developing countries.

All of the above require organisations to make business decisions, where integrity and values are increasingly required to be demonstrated.

> 'Corporate social responsibility is an ever-increasing subject which must be borne in mind when dealing with suppliers, although the extent of the breadth and depth of its impact will vary across sectors.'
>
> http://www.cips.org/BigPage.asp?PageID=872&CatID=205

Feedback on self-assessment question 2.4

Access http://www.cips.org where you will find an interesting discussion on the principles of corporate social responsibility and the relevance for supply chain professionals.

Feedback on learning activity 2.5

Table 2.4

Trait	Critical	Desirable	Nice to have
Physique			
Technical knowledge			
Intelligence			
Perception and caring			
Position in the organisation			
Subjective assessment by subordinates			
Peer assessment			
Length of service in an organisation			
Persistence			
Courage and risk-taking			
Innovation and creativity			

There are no definite answers to this activity (table 2.4). But be prepared to justify your answers.

Feedback on self-assessment question 2.5

Saunders (1997) suggested that new traits are required for the supply chain function:

- commercial awareness
- appreciation of the integrative nature of logistics
- effective communication
- planning and organisation
- creativity
- ability to develop partnerships
- strategic leadership
- performance measurement
- programme management
- negotiation
- awareness of total quality management
- benchmarking
- analytical abilities
- structured framework for supplier assessment.

Feedback on learning activity 2.6

Promotion: The ability to clearly set out your particular point of view in a way that is understood by subordinates.

Influencing: The ability to communicate in a way that succeeds in getting others to act in the way that you desire.

Persuasion: The ability to get others to change their attitudes and behaviours in line with your wishes.

Inspiration: The ability to motivate 'hearts and minds' in others so that they would wish to emulate what you are suggesting, because of the effect that you have inspired in them by your words and deeds.

Feedback on self-assessment question 2.6

Mullins (2005) suggests that the key communication skills for leaders are:

- Promotion: the ability to clearly set out your particular point of view in a way that is understood by subordinates.
- Influencing: the ability to communicate successfully so that others act in the way that you desire.
- Persuasion: the ability to get others to change their attitude and behaviour in line with your wishes.
- Inspiration: the ability to motivate others so that they wish to emulate what you are suggesting because of the effect that you have inspired in them by your words and deeds.

You should have related these to supply chain activities.

Study session 3

Different ways of leading effectively: styles and approaches

Introduction

There is no 'one best way' to provide leadership. There have been many different leaders throughout history and they have been successful through a variety of leadership approaches.

This session considers a variety of approaches that leaders can practise to provide effective leadership. This will assist you to assess why leaders are effective or ineffective in different organisational contexts, and why leadership styles and approaches can vary.

Leadership as a function of direction, influence and motivation:

> 'Leadership is the art of getting someone else to do something you want done because he wants to do it.'
>
> Dwight D Eisenhower

Contrast the above with a quiet and unobtrusive approach to leadership:

> 'A leader is best when people barely know he exists. When his work is done, they will say: we did it ourselves.'
>
> Lao Tzu

Session learning objectives

These learning objectives consider different styles of leadership and their appropriateness in different situations. Implicit in this is the question which considers whether we can change our approach, or are we bound by nature? Finally we look at different approaches in a strategic context. After completing this session you should be able to:

3.1 Distinguish between a range of leadership styles.
3.2 Consider and assess which leadership approach is most appropriate in certain cases or situations.
3.3 Assess whether we can change our leadership style.
3.4 Critique the difference between transactional leadership and transformational leadership.
3.5 Explain the relevance of leadership to 'strategic' thinking.

Unit content coverage

This study session covers the following topics from the official CIPS unit content document.

Learning objectives

1.3 Develop a range of leadership styles and judge when best to use them.

- The three main classifications of leadership styles: authoritarian, democratic and laissez-faire

- McGregor's Theory X and Theory Y
- A continuum of different leadership styles from facilitative through to directive
- The contrasting methods of tell and sell and the other two broad categories of leadership style: consult and join
- The merits of a situational approach to leadership
- The four main stages in Hersey's model of situational leadership and when each stage is appropriate to use in a purchasing context
- Transactional leadership and transformational leadership

1.4 Critically evaluate strategic leadership approaches:

- Strategy
- Human assets
- Expertise
- Control
- Change

Prior knowledge

Before attempting this session you should have completed study sessions 1 and 2.

Resources

Internet access is required for self-assessment question 3.3.

Timing

You should set aside about 6 hours to read and complete this session, including learning activities, self-assessment questions, the suggested further reading (if any) from the essential textbook for this unit and the revision question.

3.1 A range of leadership styles

Mullins (2005), in the chapter on the nature of leadership, defines **leadership style** as: 'the way in which the functions of leadership are carried out, the way in which the manager typically behaves towards members of the group'.

In terms of the definition above, style is about behaviour, what leaders actually *do* (actions), not simply what they say (rhetoric). Interestingly Mullins suggests that leadership is an inherent part of any manager's job, and implies that this is applicable not only to senior managers, but also to middle and first-line managers.

Tannenbaum and Schmidt

Tannenbaum and Schmidt (1973) developed a style continuum which has as broad classifications autocratic (often referred to as directive), democratic and facilitative behaviours (figure 3.1). They defined leadership as 'the behaviour of leaders towards subordinates, the manner in which tasks and functions of leadership are conducted'. Your behaviour as a leader or manager could be mapped against time and against particular situations, and placed along the continuum.

Figure 3.1: Leadership style continuum

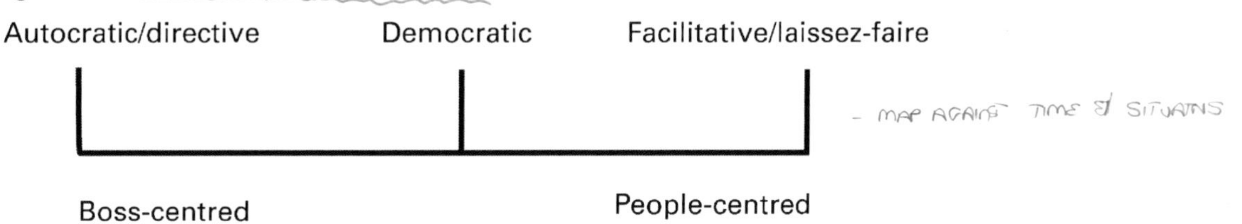

Source: adapted from Tannenbaum and Schmidt (1973)

The autocratic (also referred to as directive) style is demonstrated by some of the following behaviours:

- Leader makes decisions without reference to anyone else, because they have the authority to do so.
- There is a high degree of dependency on the leader. Staff are not encouraged to make suggestions or allowed any degree of autonomy.
- This can create demotivation and alienation of staff because they are tightly constrained by the autocrat's style.
- This may be valuable in some types of business where decisions need to be made quickly and decisively.
- This may be acceptable in some cultures which expect leaders to be authoritative and make the decisions.

The democratic style is demonstrated by some of the following behaviours:

- The leader encourages discussion and debate throughout the group before decisions are actually made. Who makes the decision will depend on the degree of democratic style being used.
- Decision making emerges from a consideration of different perspectives – leadership may be emphasised throughout the organisation.
- Consultative approach: is a process of consultation before decisions are made in order to ensure that a consensus will emerge.
- Persuasive approach: leader makes the decision and then seeks to persuade others that the decision is correct before proceeding.
- This approach may well help motive all the staff because they are involved in decision making.
- Staff can feel ownership of and commitment to the decisions that emerge.
- This can improve the sharing of ideas and experiences within the business.
- But consultation can delay decision making, or lead to decisions that are a compromise between differing views, which is not always ideal.

The laissez-faire style is demonstrated by some of the following behaviours:

- 'Let it be' – the leadership responsibilities are shared by all, and the leader leaves it to the group.
- This approach can be very useful in businesses where creative ideas are important, and a lack of authority facilitates this.

- This can be highly motivational as people have control over their own working life, without 'restrictions' from authority.
- But this can make coordination and decision making time consuming and lacking in overall direction, since there is a lack of control.
- This approach relies absolutely on good teamwork and on good interpersonal relations between the group.

Since Tannenbaum and Schmidt developed this model, a number of authors have extended the continuum with further subdivisions:

- Paternalistic leadership, by a father figure who exerts firm but benign control from a position of authority based on experience. Thus paternalism supplies needs for those under its protection or control. Much of this approach is inherent in traditional Eastern philosophical approaches.
- Servant leadership (Greenleaf, 1970). The essential idea is that the leader serves the people he or she leads. This implies that people are an end in themselves and that this approach leads directly to benefits which can be realised in terms of an organisational purpose or bottom line. This supportive style of leadership has also been developed in the writings of Peters and Waterman (1982) and Drucker (1999).

Learning activity 3.1

Find examples from current sources (articles, newspapers, and so on) of 'leadership styles' in real life. And then select one of them and study in more detail to get a deeper understanding of leadership styles in action.

Feedback on page 41

3.2 McGregor's Theory X and Theory Y

McGregor (1960) set out two very broad approaches to human nature which he termed Theory X and Theory Y (see table 3.1). McGregor very much believed that how people were managed affected their work behaviour and attitudes. He strongly supported *participative/consultative* approaches to management as a way to encourage Theory Y behaviour among staff.

Table 3.1 Theory X and Theory Y

Theory X assumptions	Theory Y assumptions
People inherently dislike work and are lazy	People view work as being as natural as play and rest, and just as potentially enjoyable
People must be coerced or controlled to do work to achieve objectives	People will exercise self-direction and self-control towards achieving objectives they are committed to
People prefer to be directed	People learn to accept and seek responsibility
Motivating is achieved only through pay and basic rewards	Motivation can also come from challenges, responsibility and self-esteem needs

Source: Mullins (2005)

You could also usefully explore the idea of Theory Z, a Japanese-style approach proposed by Ouchi (1981), which outlines some of the people-focused strategies practised by Japanese organisations.

3.3 The choices available to leaders and managers

Tannenbaum and Schmidt extended their three broad approaches to leadership into four practical styles of behaviour (figure 3.2).

Figure 3.2: Leadership methods

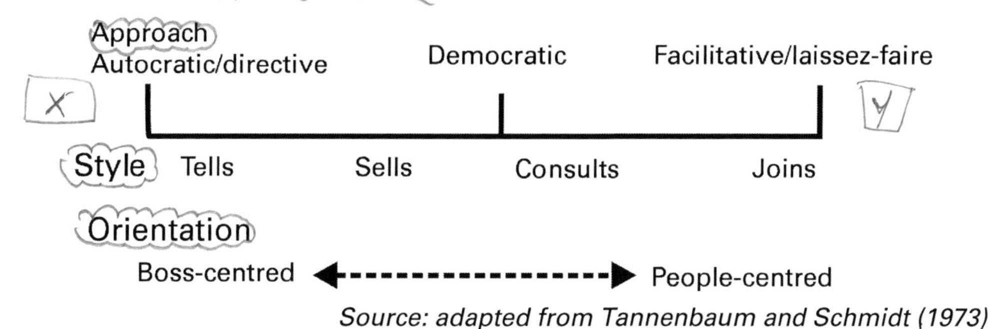

Source: adapted from Tannenbaum and Schmidt (1973)

Tells – the manager identifies a problem, chooses a solution and announces this to staff. Staff are then expected to implement this solution, as directed by the manager. This is often referred to as a top-down approach.

Sells – the manager identifies the problem, chooses a solution, but recognises that a bold announcement may encounter resistance from staff. He or she therefore attempts to persuade staff to accept the decision by spending some time explaining the rationale behind the decision-making process that has been followed.

Consults – the manager identifies the problem, but consults staff before making a decision. The consultation involves listening to the advice and options proposed by staff, and taking those views into consideration when making the decision.

Joins – the manager defines the problem, and most likely sets some constraints within which the solution is bound (quality, cost and time). The group is then given the responsibility and authority to make decisions. The manager may or may not be available in an advisory role as needed.

The 'tell' and 'sell' approaches are very much to the autocratic-directive end of the continuum, and are underpinned by a 'boss-centred orientation', based on the responsibilities of the leader. The 'consult' and 'join' approaches are very much more at the democratic and facilitative end of the continuum. The orientation here is very much more people focused. Clearly a link can be made between the work of Tannenbaum and Schmidt and McGregor, with Theory X to the left of the continuum and Theory Y to the right.

Self-assessment question 3.1

1. Select one of the leaders that you identified in learning activity 3.1 above and consider the approach of your chosen leader in terms of their approach to individuals (Theory X and Theory Y). Provide specific examples to justify your views.
2. In what way could they have improved as leaders?

Feedback on page 42

3

Hersey's model of situational leadership

Hersey (1984) and Hersey et al (2000) followed on from a number of previous writers (table 3.2) to develop the model of situational leadership.

Table 3.2 Contingency theory authors

Author	Main emphasis of leadership
Fielder (1967)	Effectiveness based on organisational performance
Vroom and Yetton (1973)	Effectiveness based on quality of decision making, the acceptance by staff of the decision, and how long it takes to make a decision
Vroom and Jago (1988)	Added many other contingency variables: quality requirements, commitment requirements, leader information, problem structure, commitment probability, goal congruence, subordinate conflict, subordinate information, time constraints, geographical dispersion, motivation time and development
House (1971), House and Dessler(1974)	Interaction between the performance of staff and the behaviour of the leader in satisfying their expectations

Source: adapted from Mullins (2005)

Their approach identifies the *situation or circumstance* as the key factor in determining which leadership style is most relevant and appropriate (figure 3.3). It is a key skill of leadership to recognise what is going on, and then select the best behaviour or style to deal with that situation effectively.

Figure 3.3: Situational leadership model

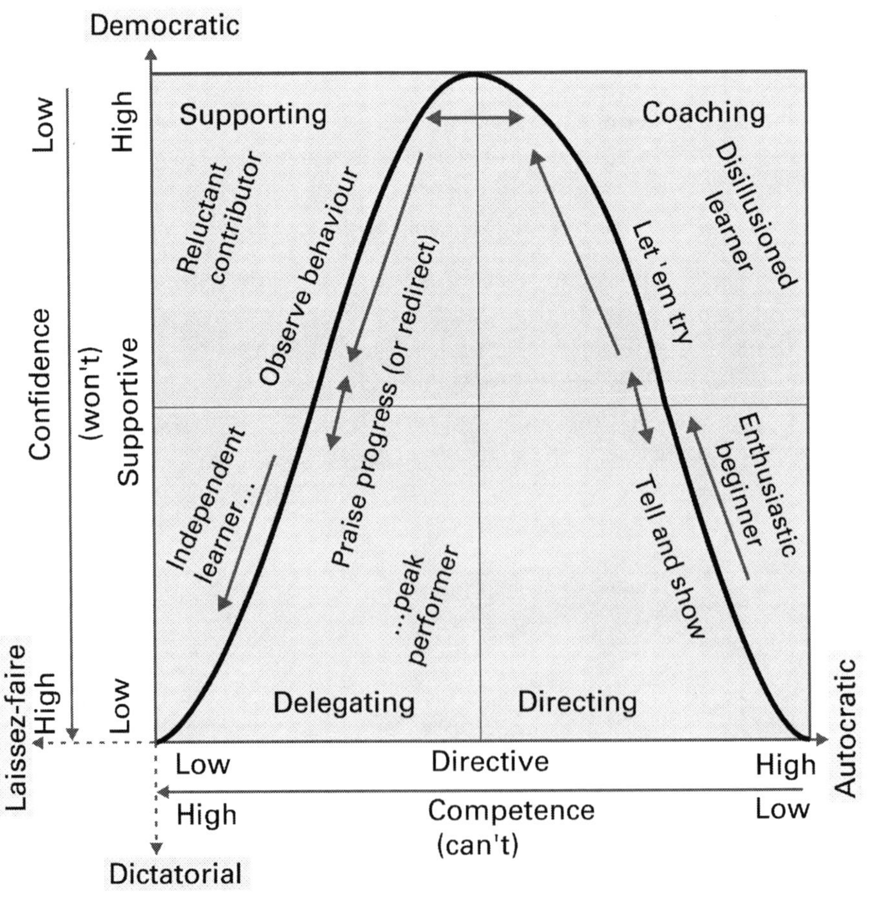

Source: adapted by JE Chamberlin from Mullins (2005: 302)

In order to assess the best behaviour or style that is appropriate the leader has to consider the 'state of readiness' of staff that the leading is attempting to influence. Readiness is a combination of ability, willingness and resources.

- Ability refers to skills, knowledge and so on.
- Willingness is attitudes – wanting to perform.
- Resources are those tangibles which actually provide assistance such as equipment, money, information and other people.

Managers and leaders therefore have to develop their people in all of the three dimensions in order to have effective staff. In essence hard and soft skills are equally important.

Hersey et al identified four general states of readiness:

R1 – low follower readiness, unable, unwilling, uncommitted and demotivated;

R2 – low to moderate follower readiness, unable but willing and motivated;

R3 – moderate to high follower readiness, able but unwilling and insecure;

R4 – high follower readiness, able, willing and confident.

Depending of the state of readiness, four corresponding leadership styles are proposed:

S1 – telling – requires a lot of guidance on the specific tasks to be completed;

S2 – selling – high guidance on the task and two-way communication;

S3 – participating – requires a lot of two-way communication, but less focus on task since the follower is capable;

S4 – delegating – little direction or support needed because the follower is able and motivated.

Learning activity 3.2

What are the pros and cons of the situational leadership model?

Feedback on page 42

Now that you have some appreciation of the situational leadership model, you should try and answer the following question.

Self-assessment question 3.2

A brief reminder of the four main Hersey categories of situational leadership:

(continued on next page)

Self-assessment question 3.2 *(continued)*

S1 – telling

S2 – selling

S3 – participating

S4 – delegating.

Provide specific examples of circumstances in a supply chain environment, where each of the styles would be appropriate.

Feedback on page 42

The merits of a situational approach to leadership

Learning activity 3.3

How do you evaluate whether a theory is of any use?

Feedback on page 43

Mullins (2005), in the section on the Leadership Relationship, makes the point: 'Leadership is a dynamic form of behaviour and there are a number of variables which affect the leadership relationship.'

McGregor (1960) in Mullins (2005) identify four major complex and interrelated variables in the leadership relationship:

- leadership characteristics – honesty, visionary, clear communication, inspirational and so on;
- the attitudes, needs and other personal characteristics of followers;
- the nature of the organisation, purpose, structure, tasks and so on;
- the external environment.

All of the first three factors are within the remit of the leader to control. The external environment is largely outside the leader's control, but good leaders will be able to steer a path through the uncertain external environment because they have clearly aligned the first three factors.

A good theory?

Questions to ask yourself about situational leadership:

Is it easy to understand? It is based on the premise that leaders are only as good as the quality of their followers.

Is it easy to use? It is based on the premise that the leader can train, support and develop the skills, attitudes and behaviours of followers, which is action based.

Does it make sense? It does provide a systematic framework which links the needs of followers to the actions of leaders.

Is it sustainable? It appears to have stood the test of time. For at least 25 years it has been a prominent part of management and leadership training.

> 'There is nothing so practical as a good theory.'
>
> Kurt Lewin (1951)

Self-assessment question 3.3

The LEAD questionnaire

The LEAD questionnaire describes 12 situations, and offers four possible leadership responses, one representing each of the four situational leadership styles for each situation. There are two versions of the LEAD questionnaire, the LEAD-self and the LEAD-other.

Style range score: The participant's style range is determined by the number of times he or she selected each of the four styles: telling, selling, participating or delegating. If a style is selected three or more times, it is considered part of the participant's leadership profile.

Effectiveness score: The participant's effectiveness score is determined by how closely his or her choices matched 'the right answer' for the situation. Choosing the preferred leadership style for a situation yields a +2, whereas the second choice is worth a +1. The other choices are worth -1 and -2, respectively. The highest possible score is therefore +24 and the lowest possible score would be -24.

The LEAD questionnaires were introduced in *The 1976 Annual Handbook for Group Facilitators* and in the third edition of Hersey and Blanchard's (1977) *Management of Organizational Behavior.* Situational Leadership and the LEAD questionnaire were widely used in management training in the 1980s and 1990s (Zorn and Violanti, 1993), and are still used by many organisations today.

Hersey and colleagues at his Center for Leader Studies argue that the measure was designed for training purposes, and have published information about the development and reliability of the instrument.

The LEAD questionnaire and other situational leadership materials are available from the Center for Creative Leadership, at http://www.ccl.org/leadership/assessments/LEADOverview.aspx?pageId=71.

What is your natural leadership style? Try and obtain a copy of the Hersey/Blanchard LEAD questionnaire, fill it in, see the results and assess the results for yourself.

Can you change your natural style? How do you change from style a to style b?

Feedback on page 43

3.4 Transactional leadership and transformational leadership

Transactional leadership

There is a contrast between transactional leadership and transformational leadership. **Transactional leadership** is based on legitimate authority within the bureaucratic structure of an organisation. The emphasis is on clear goals and objectives, and the resultant tasks, outcomes and rewards for staff are clearly aligned to achievement of goals. The transaction is based on mutual self-interest, and mutual dependence. Essentially it is based on a trading of mutual benefits. The leader provides direction for the group and the group provides a status to the leader by accepting his or her authority. Generally this approach works well in a stable environment where matters are proceeding smoothly.

Transformational leadership

This approach has evolved because the traditional stable business environment is largely a thing of the past. Leaders now have to find ways of revitalising and transforming the organisation in light of a rapidly changing business environment, where the transactional approach is not sustainable (Burns, 1978). Consider this explanation of **transformational leadership** from Mullins (2005):

> 'Transformational leadership, by contrast is a process of engendering higher levels of motivation and commitment among followers. The emphasis is on generating a vision for the organisation, and the leader's ability to appeal to higher ideals and followers, and creating a feeling of justice, loyalty and trust. In the organisational sense, transformational leadership is about transforming the performance or fortunes of a business.'

Components of transformational leadership

Bass (1985) motivates followers to exceed expectations by the leader doing a variety of things: generating greater awareness of organisational purpose and task outcomes, getting people to focus on the needs of the organisation at the expense of self-interest, activating higher-level (self-esteem and self-actualisation) needs.

Taffinder (1995) suggested that these two approaches could be combined into the concept of a 'renaissance leader'.

Learning activity 3.4

Bass (1985) describes four basic components of transformational leadership:

- idealised influence
- inspirational motivation
- intellectual stimulation
- individual consideration.

(continued on next page)

Learning activity 3.4 *(continued)*

Using the guidelines provided by Bass (1985), provide examples of each of these in your own organisation.

Feedback on page 43

And having completed this activity, you should attempt the following question yourself.

Self-assessment question 3.4

Are there particular circumstances where the transactional and the transformation approach work best?

Feedback on page 44

3.5 Strategic leadership

Johnson and Scholes (2004) suggest that strategic leadership is directly linked to the management of change in an organisation, and that managers at all levels have the ability to influence change.

Senior managers

At senior levels in an organisation a number of different areas can be emphasised as a route to achieving change. Which approach will be dependent on situation or contingencies and circumstances. Maybe in these cases situational leadership in the general sense becomes, more particularly, situational *strategic* leadership?

Learning activity 3.5

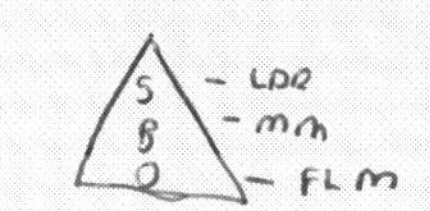

Show in a model the links between leadership and strategy, in a way which makes sense to you.

Feedback on page 44

Table 3.3 Strategic leadership approaches

	Focus of attention	Behaviour	Role of others	Implications for change
Strategy	Analysis and formulation	External scanning	Daily operations	Change delegated to others
Human assets	Developing people	The right people and a common culture	Devolved strategy development	Local strategy through the right people
Expertise	Disseminated	Via systems and procedures	Managing expertise	Via expertise
Control	Procedures and measures	Monitoring against standards to reduce variation	Perform to a standard	Carefully monitored and controlled

(continued on next page)

Table 3.3 *(continued)*

	Focus of attention	Behaviour	Role of others	Implications for change
Change	Continual change	Communicating and motivating change	Change agents	Change is critical

Source: Farkas and Westlaufer (1996) cited in Johnson and Scholes (2004)

Middle managers

With a top-down approach to strategic change, there is a role for middle managers, since they are often the implementers of strategy:

- making sure that resources are allocated appropriately;
- monitoring performance;
- monitoring behaviour of staff;
- communicating the strategy.

There are however some divergent views as to the role of middle managers.

Peters and Waterman (1982) have argued that middle managers often resist and block change because they feel their position is threatened by the delayering, restructuring and downsizing that accompanies strategic change. They argue that therefore middle managers add little value and should be trimmed and cut as much as possible.

Floyd and Wooldridge (1996) argue that middle managers have a positive role to play in implementing and controlling strategy. They also reinterpret the strategy on a daily basis by their relationships with key stakeholders of the organisation. They are the key interface between senior management and the staff in both directions. They act as advisers to senior managers because they are close to the implementation and can more easily see potential problems at close quarters.

Nonanka and Tageuchi (1995) argued that the positive role of middle managers was so important that middle managers were the actual heart of 'knowledge creation' in an innovative organisation, and as such were indispensable.

Outsiders also are potentially important as potential change agents. This will be considered in detail in a later session.

Self-assessment question 3.5

Using the generic ideas in table 3.3, assess the relevance of strategic leadership approaches to the supply chain by providing examples relevant to your own organisation.

Feedback on page 44

Revision question

Now try the revision question for this session on page 297.

3

Summary

Key learning points in this session:

- You should now be aware of a range of leadership styles, against a continuum of the three main classifications of leadership styles, and able to assess when best to use them.
- You should now be able to evaluate the relevance of leadership style and Theory X and Theory Y.
- You have undertaken an evaluation of the merits of a situational and contingent approach to leadership.
- You should now have a preliminary appreciation of the complexities of organisational change and the challenges this poses for leadership throughout the organisation.

Suggested further reading

Johnson and Scholes (2004). Chapter on managing strategic change.

Mullins (2005). Chapter on the nature of leadership.

Students are encouraged wherever possible to try and access the original texts where they can explore the discussions in full. Amongst the most influential are:

Bass (1985).

Burns (1978).

Drucker (1999).

Floyd and Wooldridge (1996).

Hersey (1984).

Hersey, Blanchard and Dewey (2000).

McGregor (1960).

Nonanka and Tageuchi (1995).

Ouchi (1981).

Peters and Waterman (1982).

Tannenbaum and Schmidt (1973).

Feedback on learning activities and self-assessment questions

Feedback on learning activity 3.1

The list is wide-ranging and some examples are suggested below. It is good practice for you to study leaders in some depth, so that you have examples which you can draw on in some detail, while appreciating the wide range of leaders that abound.

Autocratic style: for example Hitler, Rupert Murdoch, Margaret Thatcher.

Directive style: for example Tony Blair, George W Bush, Richard Branson.

Democratic style: for example Clive Woodward, Rudi Giuliani.

Facilitative style: for example Bill Gates, Anita Roddick.

Paternalistic style: for example Lord Sieff of Marks & Spencer, the Sainsbury family, the Cadbury family, Nelson Mandela.

Servant style: for example Gandhi and other knowledge leaders (the sort of leaders who provide leadership because of their innate deep knowledge of an area, or because most of their staff possess knowledge skills which need to be freed and liberated by an enlightened and flexible (even casual) style) (maybe Bill Gates again?).

Feedback on self-assessment question 3.1

1. You should ensure that your examples try and mirror some of the description in table 3.1.
2. Can improvements be attributed to moving along the continuum in some way? Either more or less autocratic, or more or less facilitative, and so on.

As an example you could consider the Prime Ministerial career of Margaret Thatcher. At the beginning of her career she needed the support of colleagues and adopted a strong but consultative style of leadership. Over the years it was suggested that she became increasingly authoritarian, almost bullying. Why do you think that change in leadership came about?

Feedback on learning activity 3.2

Pros

- Easy to understand.
- Easy to use.
- Provides a clear guideline to leaders.
- Provides clear support mechanism to staff.
- Is sustainable.

Cons

- Is it about leadership or management?
- Leadership about inspiring people, not decision making.
- Too focused on change and not about routine day-to-day activities.
- Excess focus on the leader.
- Situational leadership is a truism.

Feedback on self-assessment question 3.2

S1 – telling. Appropriate at induction for new staff, or in the first instance that a member of staff encounters a new situation. Example: evaluating a supplier for the first time, or a first supplier visit.

S2 – selling. Appropriate to be shadowed by a member of staff during a supplier visit, followed by a detailed debrief of what went well or badly and why that was so. Low risk for them, but you are involving them in your experiences and discussing this with them.

S3 – participating. They now are competent in the technical task of supplier audit. They are expected to do the visit themselves. In advance of the visit you discuss carefully some of the main issues and encourage them to suggest options, before confirming a plan of action.

S4 – delegating. They do supplier audits as a normal part of their job and keep you routinely informed. They may consult and seek guidance only in exceptional circumstances (back to S3).

Feedback on learning activity 3.3

See below for some of the key questions that you could have asked.

- Is it easy to understand?
- Is it easy to use?
- Does it make sense?
- Do organisations use it?
- Can it be adapted for specific circumstances?
- Does it explain reality?

Feedback on self-assessment question 3.3

The ideal leadership profile would be 1-2-3-4, the four-style profile. Most leaders have a two-style profile, although three-style profiles are not uncommon. Within the Western culture it is suggested that the 2-3 profile is the most common profile because Western culture places a lot of emphasis on the supportive role of leaders. Hersey and Blanchard suggest that you may well have a natural disposition towards a particular style of leadership, but that a good leader should be able to adapt and change their style to suit the situation which they are facing.

Feedback on learning activity 3.4

Compare your answers against a brief set of descriptions using Richard Branson and the Virgin Group as an example.

- Idealised influence – charismatic leadership and respect from followers, for example Richard Branson and Virgin.
- Inspirational motivation – behaviour of the leader which provides challenges to followers, for example Branson's adventures in power boats and balloons.
- Intellectual stimulation – leader solicits novel approaches and creative solutions from staff, for example entry into airlines, cola, personal finance sectors.
- Individual consideration – growth and development of followers, for example Virgin graduate recruitment programme.

Feedback on self-assessment question 3.4

Transactional leadership works better when there is:

- stable environment
- highly regulated industry sector
- stable organisational structure and culture
- relatively stable competitive situation.

Transformational leadership works better when there is:

- unstable external environment
- highly deregulated or growing industry sector
- fluid, delayered organisational structure
- highly competitive situation
- high level of technological innovation.

Feedback on learning activity 3.5

See the discussion on the strategy hierarchy in study session 1 (figure 3.4).

Figure 3.4: The strategy hierarchy

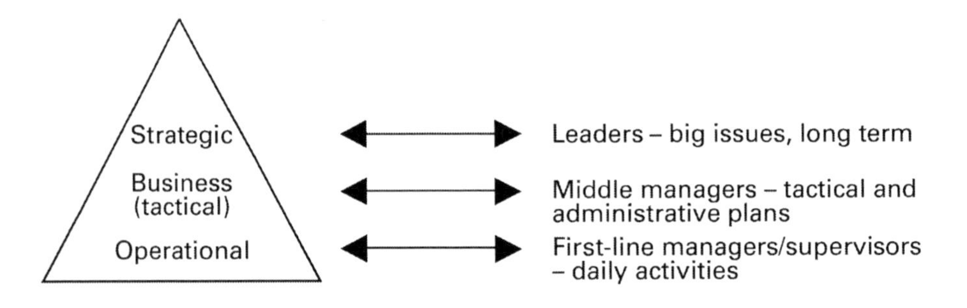

Feedback on self-assessment question 3.5

The feedback provided directs you to real-world examples, which you are encouraged to research for yourself.

Table 3.4

	Example	Focus of attention	Behaviour	Role of others	Implications for change
Strategy	Classical strategic planning at General Motors – reference Alfred Sloan	Analysis and formulation	External scanning	Daily operations	Change delegated to others
Human assets	KPMG – the global accountancy company	Developing people	The right people and a common culture	Devolved strategy development	Local strategy through the right people
Expertise	The approach of ISO 9000 quality system	Disseminated	Via systems and procedures	Managing expertise	Via expertise

(continued on next page)

Table 3.4 *(continued)*

	Example	**Focus of attention**	**Behaviour**	**Role of others**	**Implications for change**
Control	Six-Sigma Methodology	Procedures and measures	Monitoring against standards to reduce variation	Perform to a standard	Carefully monitored and controlled
Change	The Honda Effect – a classic case study by Richard Pascale about Honda cars in the USA in the 1970s	Continual change	Communicating and motivating change	Change agents	Change is critical

Study session 4

Influencing and power in the supply chain

Introduction

Influence and power will be explored in this session. Can you have influence without power, or power without influence, or are they two sides of the same coin?

Following on from the sessions on leadership and management, we now begin to examine how managers and leaders actually use their knowledge, skills, attitudes and behaviours to achieve the organisations objectives within the supply chain context. This session is where theory starts to be put into action, in real-world situations.

Supporting reading about this session can be found in Mullins (2004), sections on Leadership and Improving Organisational Performance. Relevant reading can also be found in Johnson and Scholes (2005), sections on Expectations and Purposes, and Managing Strategic Change.

Session learning objectives

After completing this session you should be able to:

4.1 Explain some of the key concepts relating to 'influencing' in the supply chain.
4.2 Create stakeholder maps, and use them to make decisions about stakeholder strategy.
4.3 Describe key methods of influencing local suppliers and global suppliers.
4.4 Appraise concepts of 'power' and where they can be used effectively.

Unit content coverage

This study session covers the following topics from the official CIPS unit content document.

Learning objectives

2.1 Continually influence stakeholders within the supply chain through using models of influence.

- Collaboration and how this may differ from competition, adversarialism and/or accommodation
- What is meant by influencing
- The difference between influencing and negotiation
- The importance of rapport when influencing and the key components in creating rapport
- Interpersonal sensitivity and its importance in managing key stakeholders
- Appropriate stakeholder map for a given purchasing activity and how power and dependency issues are identified
- Key methods of influencing

2.2 Critically assess how the different sources of power are legitimate and acceptable when leading and influencing areas of the supply chain.

- Five sources of power and applying them to the purchasing context
- Coercive power
- Referent power
- Expertise power

Prior knowledge

Before commencing this session you should have completed study session 3.

Resources

Internet access is required for self-assessment question 4.2.

Timing

You should set aside about 6 hours to read and complete this session, including learning activities, self-assessment questions, the suggested further reading (if any) from the essential textbook for this unit and the revision question.

4.1 Influence

Learning activity 4.1

Before we commence this session, make an attempt at defining the following common terms:

- influence
- power
- collaboration
- competition
- negotiation
- conflict.

Feedback on page 58

The relevance of influence

Mullins (2004) states that 'the most important point is the nature of the leadership relationship and the manner in which the leader *influences* the behaviour and actions of other people'.

In other words, leadership is only relevant when it results in other people being influenced and behaving and acting accordingly. It is the reactions of the followers which actually determines whether influence is being exerted by the leader.

Stannack (2003) defines **influence** 'as the apparent ability to use power'. He suggests also that influence has a number of facets:

- social influence when people change their behaviour in response to actions of others;

- indirect influence based on reputation or perceptions of the people being influenced.

Using influence to achieve objectives

Stannack (2003) suggests a number of objectives which can be achieved through the use of influence:

- compliance – in response to requests;
- obedience – in response to orders;
- conformity – in order to adhere to norms or standards;
- commitment – in response to the creation of a shared vision.

Implicit in all the above is the underpinning power or authority which adds weight to and underpins the request, order, and so on. Real influence is exercised when the underpinning authority is not needed to be made explicit. In other words, wisdom, knowledge, expertise and good communication skills ensure influence is real, without the authority having to be emphasised based on status, position or power.

Rapport as a source of influence

As a leader, it is vital to communicate and work with others in ways that suit them. Remember that communication is 7% words, 38% tone of the voice and 55% body language. When you have a good feeling with someone you probably have rapport. Building rapport is a technique described and practised in neuro-linguistic programming (NLP), which is the study of what works in thinking, language and behaviour.

What is rapport?

Rapport is the process of building and sustaining a relationship of mutual trust and understanding. It is the ability to relate to others in a way that makes people feel at ease. When you have rapport with someone you feel at ease, conversation flows and silences are easy. It is the basis of good communication *and is a form of influence*. It is a major component of listening, when the whole body indicates interest in what the other person is saying.

Creating rapport

First you have to be aware of yourself. Then make a conscious effort to match as many of the other person's characteristics as possible. This is often referred to as 'mirroring':

- Posture – look at and match the position of the body, legs, arms, hands and fingers, and how the head and shoulders are held.
- Expression – notice and match the direction of the look and movement of the eyes. Ensure that you make and keep eye contact.
- Breathing – match the way the other person is breathing. People will breathe either fast or slow, from their chest or their abdomen.
- Movement – notice if their movements are fast or slow, steady or erratic. Make your movements the same.
- Voice – think about the pace, volume and intonation of their voice. Listen to the type of words being used. Try to use a similar voice and words.

Rapport, pacing and leading

Pacing is about respecting the feelings or style of others. If someone is feeling anxious, to pace him or her is to show an understanding of that anxiety. If someone is having fun, to pace him or her is to join in the fun. When we talk about someone's excitement or enthusiasm being infectious, we are really talking about our ability to pace and join in.

When you can match and pace you can also, with practice, lead and influence. You might lead from a subdued lethargic mood into an exciting energetic mood, or lead from speaking quietly to speaking loudly.

You might want to use matching, pacing and leading with individuals or groups:

- when someone is angry, to help calm them down;
- when someone is tense, to help them relax;
- when things feel slow, to speed them up and create a feeling of energy.

Source: http://www.modern.nhs.uk (2005)

Building trust and relationships

If you have a good relationship and mutual trust between yourself and those you are working with, you are more likely to find them receptive to the new ways of thinking and the improvement methods you want to introduce.

What is trust?

Trust requires two things: competency and caring. Competency alone or caring by itself will not create trust. Scholtes (1988) suggests that if I think someone is competent, but I do not think they care about me or the things that are important to me, I will respect them but not necessarily trust them. On the other hand, if I think someone cares about me but I do not feel they are competent or capable, I will have affection for that person but not necessarily trust them to do the job in hand (figure 4.1).

Building trust

Figure 4.1: Competence/Care Matrix

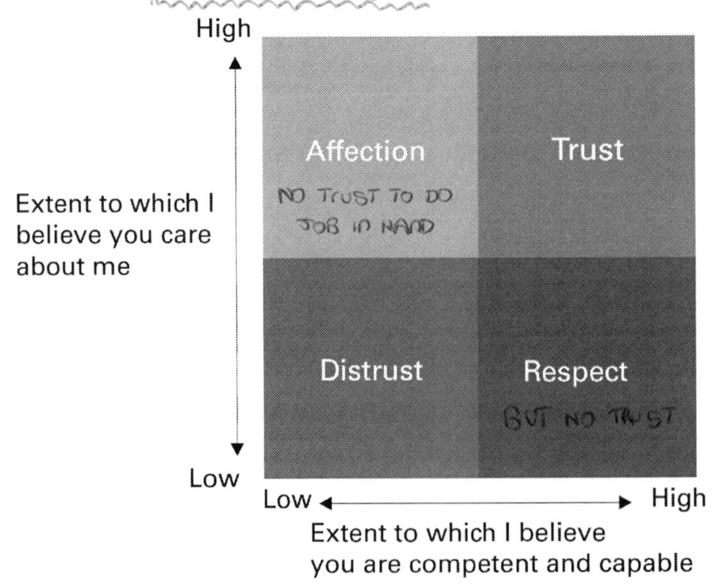

Source: adapted from Scholtes (1988)

Trust and relationships

You can encourage trust if you:

- do what you say you will do and do not make promises you cannot or will not keep;
- listen to people carefully and tell them what you think they are saying. People trust others when they believe they understand them;
- understand what matters to people. People trust those who are looking out for their best interests.

You can encourage good relationships with people if you:

- are able to talk to each other and are willing to listen to each other;
- respect each other and know how to show respect in ways the other person wants;
- know each other well enough to understand and respect the other person's values and beliefs;
- are honest and do not hide your shortcomings. This may improve your image but does not build trust;
- do not confuse trustworthiness with friendship. Trust does not automatically come with friendship;
- tell the truth!

Other relevant concepts

It is beyond the scope of this session to go into significant detail, but you should be aware of the following concepts which are tactical developments of relationship building in individual or organisational settings. These are areas which will be explored in more detail in later sessions.

Collaboration is essentially individuals or organisations working together for mutual benefit. There are a whole range of reasons and contexts where collaboration can usefully occur.

Competition is essentially the normal state of business between organisations in a free market economy. It is believed that the free market is the best way to ensure efficient utilisation of resources through market forces in competition with each other.

Adversarialism is more or less the norm in competitive situations. Win–lose is largely the 'rule' under which business is undertaken. At the same time there is often a logic in making accommodations with competitors for mutual benefit, or where competition could be harmful or excessively costly.

Self-assessment question 4.1

Place some of the following behaviours which have been introduced in this section onto the appropriate quadrants of figure 4.2:

(continued on next page)

Self-assessment question 4.1 *(continued)*

Figure 4.2

	My organisation: Win	My organisation: Lose
Your organisation: Win		
Your organisation: Lose		

Cooperate

Accommodate

Competition

Adversarialism

Feedback on page 58

4.2 Stakeholders and stakeholder mapping

Stakeholder mapping

Johnson and Scholes (2004) define **stakeholder mapping** as 'identifying stakeholder expectations and power to help understand political priorities'.

What they are suggesting is that when organisations and individuals are thinking about taking actions or developing policies and objectives, they should take careful note of the people who will be affected by those resulting actions, policies and objectives. In taking note they should carefully assess:

- how interested each stakeholder is in the proposed actions, policies and objectives;
- how much power and influence they can exert on the proposed actions, policies and objectives.

Learning activity 4.2

Fill in table 4.1 for three key stakeholders to a project which your organisation is currently undertaking.

Table 4.1

Stakeholder assessment	Stakeholder 1	Stakeholder 2	Stakeholder 3
Stakeholder name			
What are their goals?			
How have they reacted to similar projects in the past?			
What are they likely to do with this project?			
What effect will the project have on them?			
What strategy are we going to initiate to get their support or compliance?			

Feedback on page 58

Mendelow (1991) developed the concept of a power/interest matrix (figure 4.4) as a useful tool to map stakeholders and their importance. On the basis of the results of the mapping, organisations can then take appropriate actions to *manage* stakeholder expectations and reactions.

- *Key players* are of major importance because they are interested and powerful. We need therefore to ensure that they are on our side, or at the very least they are not against us.
- *Keep satisfied* the stakeholders who need to be kept satisfied. They are powerful, but not that interested at this stage. We need to make sure that they stay that way, since if they were to be upset they could use their power to make life difficult.
- *Keep informed* applies to stakeholders who are interested but not very powerful. Let's keep them informed so they stay happy and supportive. They may become powerful in the future, so we do not want to antagonise them.
- *Minimal effort* is applied to low-power, low-interest stakeholders. They are not important and not interested particularly. Let's do nothing to antagonise them and they will stay uninvolved.

Figure 4.4: Power/Interest Matrix

Power \ Level of interest	Low	High
Low	A Minimal effort	B Keep informed
High	C Keep satisfied	D Key players

Source: Mendelow (1991) in Johnson and Scholes (2004)

Using stakeholder mapping

Stakeholder mapping helps you to address a number of issues in a more structured way.

Is the range of stakeholders that have been identified appropriate for the sort of business sector within which your organisation is operating? Consider, in particular, issues of corporate governance and the influence of your organisation towards community interests.

Who are likely to be the main resisters and supporters of your actions, policies and objectives, and what can you do to influence or persuade them?

Would you wish to reposition any stakeholders?

Remember that stakeholder attitudes may change over time. You therefore need to re-map stakeholders regularly to see if anything has changed, and what actions you then need to take.

4.3 Methods of influencing

Self-assessment question 4.2

Read the article on Global Citizenship at HP on the weblink

(continued on next page)

Self-assessment question 4.2 *(continued)*

http://www.hp.com/hpinfo/globalcitizenship/gcreport/publicengage/stakeholder.html.

Read from the heading 'Stakeholder engagement' including 'Our main stakeholder groups and how we engage', the 'Feedback on HP's 2004 Global Citizenship Report' down to the end of the quotation 'This needs to be brought out more to show the ways it is a leader in the field.'

The report concludes with external evaluation and quotes – you should try and map the divergent views offered within a Strategic Priorities Assessment for HP – see table 4.2 in Feedback section.

Feedback on page 58

The Kraljic matrix as an example of power and influence

Figure 4.5: Kraljic matrix

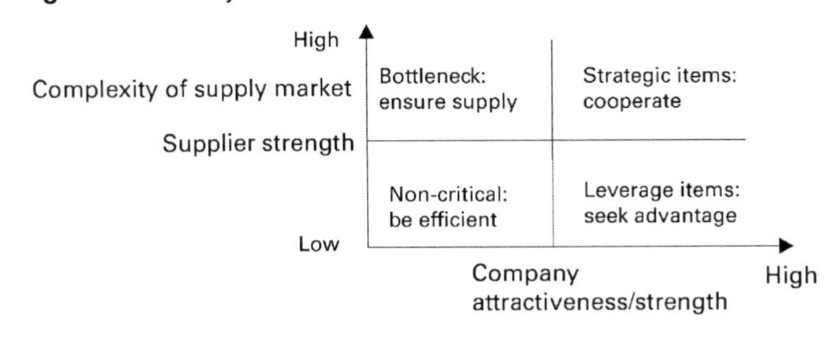

Source: Kraljic (1983)

The Kraljic matrix (figure 4.5) is a very common sourcing assessment tool, which has an interesting application in a similar vein to stakeholder mapping.

As a sourcing tool it suggests the sorts of sourcing strategies that organisations should adopt for effective and efficient purchasing. Clearly, a comparison of the relative strengths of the supply market against our company strength has implications for power and influence calculations, which can be used for short-term benefit, or more strategically.

In this model the matrices to be compared are the complexity of the supply market and strengths of suppliers, and the strength of our organisation vis-à-vis the supply market.

Four basic strategies are identified:

- Non-critical – where both the supply market and our organisation is relatively weak and the product to be purchased is non-critical. In this scenario we should purchase as efficiently as possible, seeking the best way to purchase under the best terms that we can. An example would be the purchase of low-value items of a generic nature.
- Leverage – where we are a key purchaser and the market is relatively weak, because there is plenty of competition. In this situation we should use our buying power to get the best prices and most advantageous terms. An example would be the way the large supermarket chains in the UK use their power to leverage best prices from farmers who are mostly small-scale and in fierce competition with each other.

- Bottleneck – where the market is controlled by few very strong suppliers, and we are relatively weak. We could be put at a serious disadvantage if we do not ensure supply, so we seek continuity by entering into long-term contracts or paying premium prices. An example is almost any organisation who deals with Microsoft.
- Strategic – is the situation where we are strong and so are key suppliers to the market. Essentially we need each other, so it is to mutual advantage that we cooperate with strategic partnerships over the long term. An example of this would be the mutual dependency of the major branded products to retail supermarkets. Nestlé and Tesco need each other so they seek a cooperative relationship for mutual benefit.

Learning activity 4.3

Assess some of the items that your organisation purchases, using the Kraljic matrix. Are you positioning your approach with the suppliers of those items appropriately? Would you seek to reassess the way you deal with some of your suppliers?

- Non-critical
- Leverage
- Bottleneck
- Critical

Feedback on page 59

Self-assessment question 4.3

Using table 4.3, critically evaluate a variety of influencing styles that you adopt, and the relevant situations where they are applied:

- Cooperation
- Accommodation
- Competition
- Adversarialism

Table 4.3

Influencing style adopted	Situation	Outcome

Feedback on page 59

4

4.4 Five sources of power

Definitions of power

According to Johnson and Scholes (2004), **power** is 'the ability of individuals or groups to persuade, induce or coerce others into following certain courses of action.'

According to Mullins (2005), 'At a broad level, power can be interpreted in terms of control or influence over the behaviour of other people with or without their consent.'

Stannack (2003) captures it neatly: 'In actual fact power is neutral. Power is the ability to expand and/or reduce the choices available to an individual or a group.'

Power per se is neither good nor bad; it is how it is used that can have positive or negative consequences.

French and Raven

French and Raven (1959) should give some structure to considerations of power. They identified five main sources of power as follows:

- Legitimate power. The target of influence perceives the legitimacy of power due to position or status of the holder of the power. For example, middle managers and first-line managers have authority because of their position within the formal structure of the organisation. This is often referred to as position power.
- Reward power. Authority to use organisational resources for rewards or recognition as perceived by the follower. For example, pay, promotion, increased responsibility, perks.
- Coercive power. Threat of sanctions or punishment and the ability to carry them through. For example, the withholding or delay of pay, promotion, increased responsibility, perks.
- Referent power. Ability to identify with and be influenced by the manager. Based on the perception of attractive personal traits in the manager – charisma.
- Expertise power. Authority based on the perception of skill, competence, expertise and/or experience of the manager. Based on credibility and clear evidence of expertise in previous situations.

In recent times there have been additions to the above list:

- Finlay (2000) adds personal power, based on the trust and support of colleagues; and
- connection power based on personal and professional access to people and information. This is often based on 'networking ability'.

Learning activity 4.4

Apply French and Raven (1959) to sources of power in the purchasing context.

(continued on next page)

Learning activity 4.4 *(continued)*

Legitimate:

Reward:

Coercive:

Referent:

Expertise:

Feedback on page 59

Now attempt the following self-assessment question.

Self-assessment question 4.4

In the UK, there has been a trend recently to move away from the transactional approach of purchasing, based on power, in favour of long-term relationships based on trust and mutual benefits. Is the concept of power therefore no longer relevant? Discuss the main issues in no more than 250 words.

Feedback on page 59

Revision question

Now try the revision question for this session on page 297.

Summary

This session has clarified the concept of influence, and some related terms associated with influence.

You have also been introduced to stakeholders, and the importance of recognising who they are, and what you do with them.

Power and its various sources have also been considered.

Several tools and techniques of analysis have been considered:

- power/interest matrix
- competence/care matrix
- Kraljic matrix.

Suggested further reading

In addition to Mullins (2005) and Johnson and Scholes (2004), Stannack (2003) in the CIPS study guide on Commercial Relationships, provides useful contemporary insights into the practical aspects of leadership in developing and managing relationships with suppliers and other stakeholders. Scholtes (1998) is a useful practical guide on hints and tips for effective leadership.

4

Feedback on learning activities and self-assessment questions

Feedback on learning activity 4.1

There is no specific feedback at this stage; just try and capture the terms with as much precision as you can. Compare what you have noted with the definitions which follow in this session.

Feedback on self-assessment question 4.1

Figure 4.3

		My organisation: Win	My organisation: Lose
Your organisation	Win	Cooperate Accommodate	Competition Adversarialism
	Lose	Competition Adversarialism	Cooperate Accommodate

Please note the possibilities (figure 4.3):

In win–win and lose–lose situations it is sensible for both sides to cooperate and seek accommodations with each other. Even if both sides are losing, it is sensible to cooperate and accommodate to minimise the losses! Obviously it would be better still to find ways to win–win, and they may well emerge.

In win–lose and lose–win situations, you are likely to find competitive and adversarial behaviours. Arguably these situations are untenable and create at best short-term outcomes.

Feedback on learning activity 4.2

Check your assessment against the explanation which follows in the next section.

Feedback on self-assessment question 4.2

From the perspective of stakeholders identified above, a number of issues will emerge, against which the current performance of HP can be assessed using table 4.1. What do you think are the priorities for HP in the future? Justify your view.

Table 4.2

Issues	Current performance	Priorities

Feedback on learning activity 4.3

Key points

Appropriateness – your supplier strategy should be appropriate to the complexity of the supply market and supplier strength, against your organisation's relative strength.

Re-assessment – as with stakeholder mapping, suppliers can be repositioned on the matrix. For example, an up-and-coming supplier may be relatively new, but you can see that they have great potential in the future. Rather than use your current power to leverage, you may well wish to enter into strategic cooperation at an early stage, so that when they are stronger in the future, they are already locked in to a positive relationship with you.

Feedback on self-assessment question 4.3

A quality answer will produce evidence of a variety of influencing styles, used in appropriate situations. You should question your approach if you only use one method of influencing in most situations.

- cooperate
- accommodate
- competition
- adversarialism.

Does your organisation use a variety of influencing styles? It should.

If the outcomes sought by your organisation were not achieved, could another approach have worked better?

Feedback on learning activity 4.4

Legitimate: Purchasing director as the chief purchasing officer.

Reward: Purchasing departmental head, who conducts your periodic appraisals.

Coercive: Purchasing departmental head who sets tough personal objectives, perhaps linked to disciplinary action in the event of non-achievement.

Referent: The negotiator who has achieved a spectacular outcome, through developing new relationships.

Expertise: The technical skills of contract formation from the legal experts, who come up with well-formed contracts.

Feedback on self-assessment question 4.4

You should present a reasoned argument setting out the pros and cons of both approaches before assessing, on balance, which approach you favour. Or does it depend on the situation and the contingent factors? Concentrate on the quality of the argument rather than the giving of an opinion.

Study session 5

Leading and influencing in four directions

So far we have explored management, leadership and influencing from a general perspective. Now you know about leadership in theory, but how do you do it in the work environment?

Introduction

As a manager and leader, you are involved in a dynamic and turbulent business environment, where there are many demands on your time and attention, and there can often be a tendency to feel that you are being pulled in many directions simultaneously. Leaders, at whatever level, ensure that they are not at the beck and call of events and competing demands, but that they influence the situation in an active rather than a reactive manner. Managing in four directions is a key leadership skill that needs to be appreciated and practised in practical ways so that effective performance is enhanced.

This session develops strategies that can be used to lead and influence in all four directions. This session considers specific ways of leading and influencing, which are applicable to project and normal working scenarios. This enables you to put the theory into a realistic work-based setting.

Session learning objectives

After completing this session you should be able to:

5.1 Explore different ways of 'managing upwards'.
5.2 Explore different approaches to consider in 'managing the team'.
5.3 Explore different ways to 'manage across' the organisation.
5.4 Demonstrate an understanding of external stakeholders and how to influence them.

Unit content coverage

This study session covers the following topics from the official CIPS unit content document.

Learning objective

2.3 Lead and influence effectively in four different directions.

- Manage your manager and identify key methods for managing upwards
- A range of influencing styles for leading direct reports and teams, and understanding what is meant by the term readiness in relation to individuals being led (Hersey & Blanchard)
- A range of influencing styles for cross-functional leadership, both within and outside the bounds of formal teams
- The range of external stakeholders (including suppliers, customers, collaborators and other third parties) and effective influencing styles

Prior knowledge

Before commencing this session you will need to have completed study session 4.

Timing

You should set aside about 6 hours to read and complete this session, including learning activities, self-assessment questions, the suggested further reading (if any) from the essential textbook for this unit and the revision question.

5.1 Lead and influence in four directions

Managing in four directions

Essentially managers need to appreciate that they can and should influence in four different directions to be really effective in the workplace. We will consider each of these directions (figure 5.1) in turn.

Figure 5.1: Managing in four directions

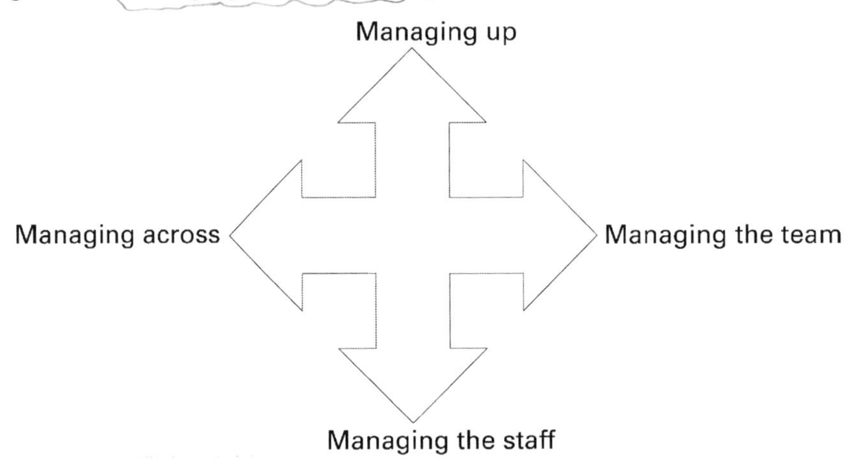

Managing upwards

Middle and first-line managers often claim that a lack of top management support is one of the most common reasons why they cannot work effectively and they run into difficulties. They need senior management support to help solve problems, to provide resources or to show a sense of ownership towards project or normal day-to-day activities.

Couzins and Beagrie (2003) attempt a definition of the concept of managing upwards:

> 'As well as influencing direction, effectively *managing upwards* can help to alleviate pressure on both sides, by managing and aligning expectations, and reducing the incidence of management by interference.'

A good starting point is to have a thorough understanding of your manager, and their raison d'être. Appreciate what motivates, disheartens or frustrates them, and this will help you to understand their priorities and their working style. Put yourself in their shoes and try to get under their skin. Be clear what they want and this will enable you to successfully meet and surpass their requirements and expectations.

Learning activity 5.1

Consider some practical ways that you could 'manage up' with your senior manager.

Feedback on page 72

Buchanan and Boddy (1992) suggest that good communication with senior management shows that you are capable of:

- political awareness in identifying potential coalitions, and in balancing conflicting goals and perceptions within a complex organisational setting;
- demonstrating clear influencing skills – to gain commitment to your plans and ideas from potential sceptics and resisters;
- a helicopter perspective – to stand back from the immediate task and take a broader view of priorities.

Figure 5.2: Managing up

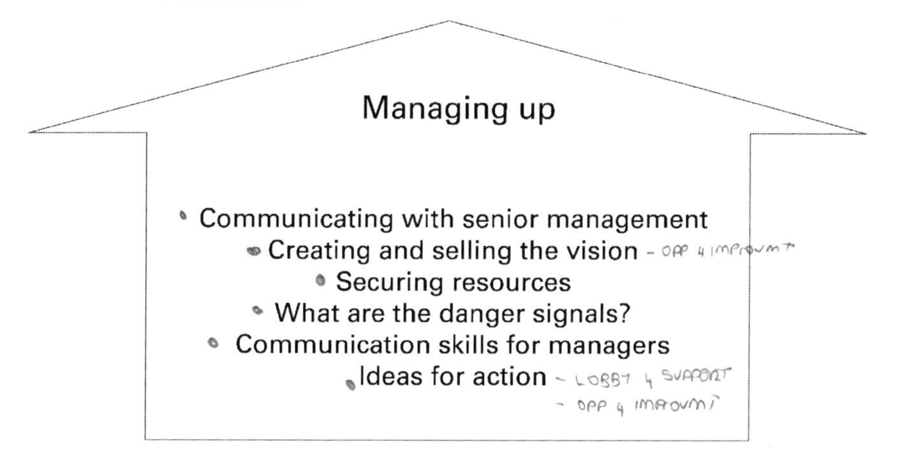

Creating and selling the vision is critical to managing upwards (figure 5.2). Often ideas for improvements or new innovations can start with middle and first-line managers. These ideas often begin in a loose and unstructured way. Someone has an idea, sees a possibility and determines an opportunity for improvement. Through a process of trying out the idea on colleagues, discussing how it might work, lobbying for support, and so on, some shape starts to emerge. It is probably still tentative – for example, a feasibility study or a review of options. An influential manager who is active at this stage can ensure that the idea is translated into a clear vision of what the possibilities are, and has a clear set of objectives (figure 5.3). This then needs to be communicated upwards to senior managers, whose support is required to take this forward.

Figure 5.3: Creating and selling the vision

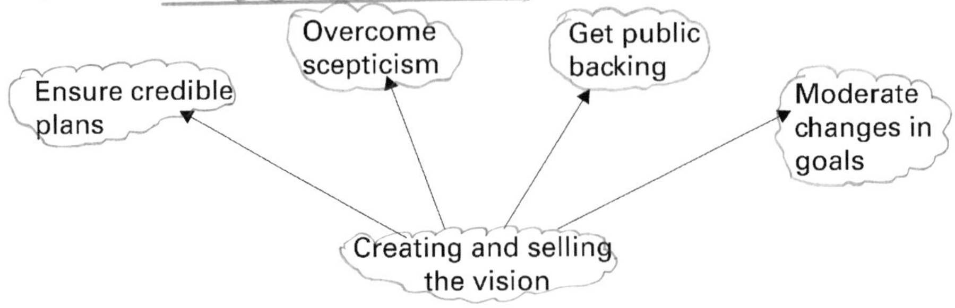

Overcome scepticism
Get public backing
Ensure credible plans
Moderate changes in goals
Creating and selling the vision

Source: adapted from Meredith and Mantel (2000)

Figure 5.4 shows some of the main benefits which can ensue if we manage upwards effectively. Our idea manages to secure adequate resources, and thus results are achieved.

Figure 5.4: Securing resources – the benefits

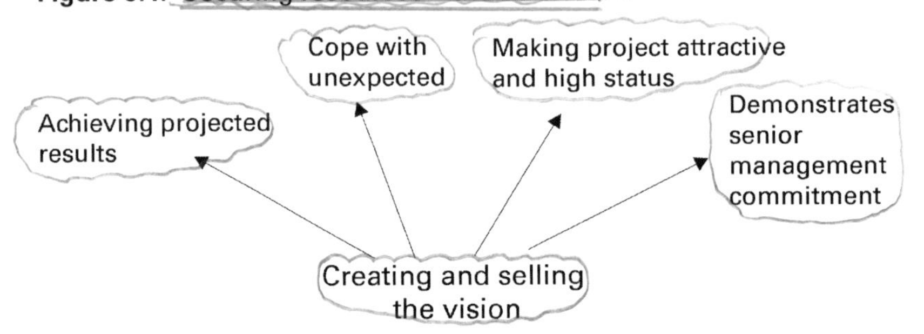

Source: adapted from Meredith and Mantel (2000)

If managing upwards is not working as well as it should, what are the danger signals? There are visible danger signals, which give early warning to middle and first-line managers of possible trouble with senior management:

- when senior managers interfere without consultation;
- when support is not provided when needed, or in diminished quantity;
- when communication seems poor;
- when the promises or commitment does not materialise.

The communication skill for managing up is the common communication process. Most people are too optimistic about the communication process and assume too much. Although writing and speaking are relatively easy, achieving understanding is much more difficult (figure 5.5).

Figure 5.5: Model of the communication process

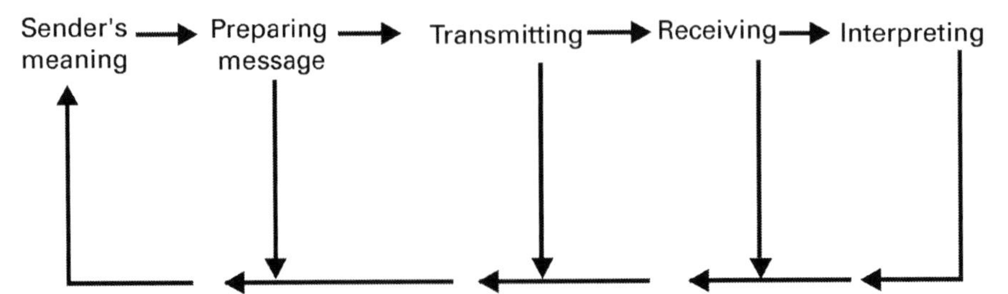

What are the most common barriers to effective communication?

- Noise – the clamour of a busy environment which makes it difficult to hear communications.
- Selective and biased perceptions – hearing what we want to hear.
- Language and tone – distort the message.
- Lack of feedback – not checking that the message has been clearly received and understood.

> 'We can be careless coders and lazy listeners. What might at first appear to be a simple process can be highly error-prone. Some of the main barriers to communication concern: power differences, gender differences, physical surroundings, language and cultural diversity.'
>
> Huczynski and Buchanan (2001)

Self-assessment question 5.1

What benefits could be achieved by 'managing upwards' successfully?

Feedback on page 72

5.2 Managing the team

Readiness

In study session 3 we examined Hersey's model of situational leadership, and how the leadership style adopted was based on an assessment of the best style to adopt in relation to the 'state of readiness' of the follower. It may be useful to go back to that session and remind yourself briefly of the details.

Managing the team is how you as a manager cannot just respond to the state of readiness, but how you can influence your team members to make improvements in attitudes, behaviours and performance, to achieve improvements in readiness.

Learning activity 5.2

Consider the following scenario as a basis for analysis.

You are in charge of a small cross-functional team that is involved in sourcing materials for a new product which is regarded as vital to future growth of your organisation. You do not have enough team members who have been allocated to the product-sourcing group and are struggling to meet the deadlines agreed in the sourcing plan. The team is composed of a number of technical experts, all of whom are seconded to your team

(continued on next page)

5

Learning activity 5.2 *(continued)*

for 20% of their time. John is the software developer, Jim is the engineer, Jack has been promoted from the factory floor, Sid is the cost accountant and Fred is a sales executive, while you are the contract manager. You do not really know each other very well and have only three months before production is scheduled to start. You do not really understand the complexity of the new product and the research and development department have provided you with an extensive list of requirements, but are not members of the sourcing team. The rest of the team are keen to get on with their areas of technical expertise but look to you to source the material requirements.

What team issues do you identify as requiring attention?

Feedback on page 72

Managing the team

Figure 5.6: Managing the team

Managing the team

- Building an effective team
- Providing a focus for the work
- Driving the work forward
- Making the most of diversity
- What are the danger signals?
- Team-building skills for managers
- Ideas for action

Middle and first-line managers need help, provided by a group of people to work with them during project and daily activities (figure 5.6). Where the business environment is novel, uncertain and relatively open-ended, success depends on bringing a deliberately diverse group of people together, and working to bring them into a committed and enthusiastic team (figure 5.7).

Figure 5.7: Benefits of an effective team

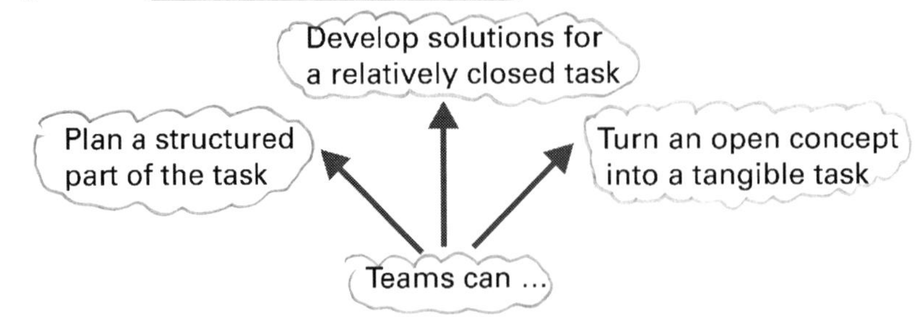

Source: adapted from Meredith and Mantel (2000)

We will consider in more detail, ideas on teams, teamwork and what makes an effective team in a later session.

Figure 5.8: The three agendas of managing the team

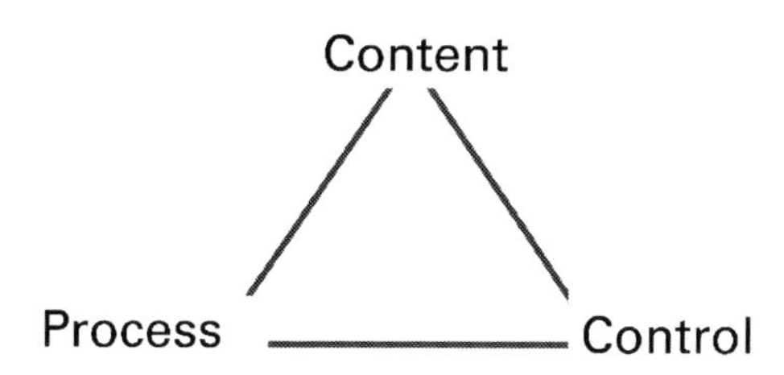

Making the most of diversity is achieved by a well-balanced team, comprising members who, as a group, can deal with the three agendas of change (figure 5.8).

The content agenda

- Expertise in payment systems, planning systems and new technology of whatever it is that the project or day-to-day activities concern;
- policy awareness as the ability to link the work to the wider policies and strategies of the organisation;
- operating knowledge of how the relevant part of the enterprise works.

The process agenda

- Team-building skill to help the disparate members of the team learn to work together;
- awareness of process is being conscious that the way things are done matters as much as what is done; both within the team itself, and in its relations with others;
- time and commitment, a willingness and ability to give the time needed to be an effective team member, and that their boss accepts this.

The control agenda

- Helicopter view – manager who is able to see the broader picture, within which the work fits;
- time-keeping – not necessarily in the literal sense, but simply someone aware of how the work is progressing, and how that relates to expected completion or delivery dates;
- administrator – manager with a knack for keeping records and documents in shape, who ensures that work and the relevant reports are done on time.

Self-assessment question 5.2

Refer back to the scenario in learning activity 5.1 above and consider some practical ways that you could 'manage the team'.

Feedback on page 73

5.3 Managing the staff

Figure 5.9: Managing the staff

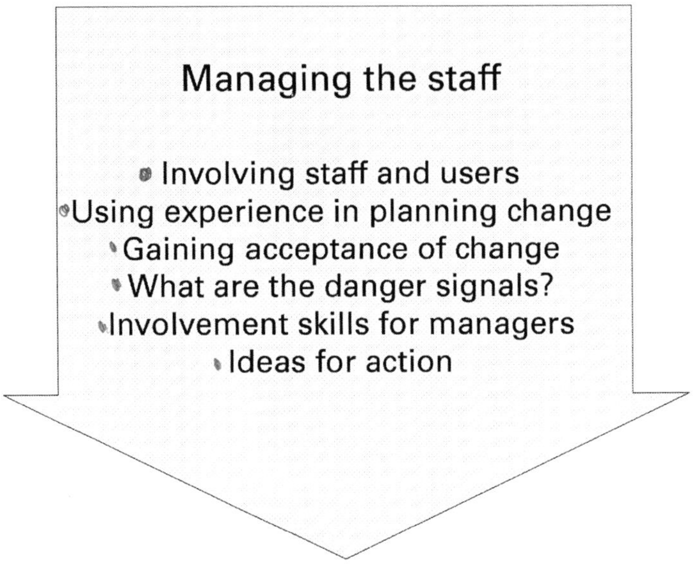

Managing the staff

- Involving staff and users
- Using experience in planning change
- Gaining acceptance of change
- What are the danger signals?
- Involvement skills for managers
- Ideas for action

Effective managers have to bring people along with the changes they are making (figure 5.9). Changes could be just small adjustments to daily activities, or significant projects to deliver dramatic changes. A sense of involvement has to be created among those who will be working together or using the new systems and procedures, for example. The most visible group are the people whose work is directly altered by the new ideas and who will be living with the results in their daily work. They have to set up the system, and run it thereafter.

Using the experience of your staff in planning changes to work means having staff who will participate as fully as practicable in the design and implementation of the work. Good management of the staff must ensure that they are involved fully in a way that is relevant to the practicalities of their daily work. All the issues making up the 'content' agenda need to be handled.

Gaining acceptance of change is complex. A good rule of thumb is that a change imposed from above will not be accepted as readily as one to which staff have contributed.

Learning activity 5.3

Refer back to the scenario in learning activity 5.1 above.

In addition to the team issues you have considered, your boss has also asked you to communicate with the operations department about the introduction of the new product, and the operational requirements that will ensue. The production supervisor who has been designated to run the new production line is not very up to date with the new technology, and feels there will be real difficulties with 'this new-fangled product'. He sends you an email

(continued on next page)

Learning activity 5.3 *(continued)*

suggesting that it is impossible for his department to be ready to start production in three months. What are some of the indicators which suggest that people could be resistant to new ways of working?

Feedback on page 73

Involvement skills for effective managers are the active seeking out of ways to enable other staff to participate fully in the new ways of working which emerge, as follows.

Change

Staff briefed in a consultative format.

Staff actively take part in demonstration of new systems.

Demonstration designed to highlight not just features, but benefits for staff.

Contrast

Staff able to discuss in small groups what change might mean.

Staff able to express personal anxieties about the change.

Staff given degree of choice over when or whether they personally had to be part of the change.

Surprise

Implementation staff present at meetings, to ensure accurate information is passed out.

Staff told in advance about surveys, visits from consultants, deliveries of equipment, and so on.

Staff given significant influence over working methods and aspects of change design.

Self-assessment question 5.3

Consider some practical ways that you could 'manage the staff'.

Feedback on page 73

5.4 Managing stakeholders

Stakeholder mapping and appropriate actions were addressed in a previous session.

5

Figure 5.10: Managing stakeholders

Managing across

- Stakeholder mapping
- Ensuring consistent planning and implementation
- Creating a sense of ownership
- What are the danger signals?
- Negotiating skills for managers

A key management skill is to create a sense of ownership in your stakeholders (figure 5.10). Remember that stakeholders can be inside or outside your organisation. Stakeholders need to 'own' the issues that you are addressing before they will be willing to invest time and effort into making a change work. The manager must build a sense of ownership among other departments and external stakeholders towards the new ideas, so that it is not seen as someone else's problem. The manager also expects and needs support from other departments to meet deadlines set, come up with ideas to overcome difficulties and generally to support the new work publicly. This will only happen if the staff in the respective functions and stakeholders feel a sense of ownership and responsibility towards the new ideas.

A significant skill which managers must develop is the ability to *negotiate effectively*. This will be addressed in a later session.

Learning activity 5.4

Refer back to the scenario in learning activity 5.1 above.

Before you meet with the production supervisor, you want to see if you can contact a few key stakeholders to enlist their support. You send an email to several key players and get the following responses:

- Your boss responds by saying that you are fully capable and he has every confidence in your ability to deal with the production supervisor.
- The finance director has a number of projects to attend to and cannot see you for at least four weeks.
- The customer who has ordered the new product says that the contract is agreed and he will activate penalty clauses if the product is not available on time.
- The union representative says he will support his production staff, who are not happy with changes to working conditions.

What are the danger signals, which indicate that stakeholders are resistant to new ideas or systems? Note also that different stakeholders have different

(continued on next page)

Learning activity 5.4 *(continued)*

needs and interests. Contrast also stakeholder attitudes towards projects and significant changes, compared to normal day-to-day activities.

Feedback on page 74

The key management skill in managing stakeholders is to be able to identify ways of influencing the key players and integrating with a range of inside and outside stakeholders, so as to align their interests within the new ideas which you wish to promote. You will need to:

- find out whose commitment you need;
- decide what benefits can be offered;
- involve others in the work;
- build good relationships.

Self-assessment question 5.4

Apply the model and ideas of 'managing in four directions' to a work situation in which you have been involved. Provide concrete examples of where this model provides useful insights for managers.

Feedback on page 74

Revision question

Now try the revision question for this session on page 297.

Summary

This session has produced a framework for middle and first-line managers to influence and provide effective leadership in situations where they need to promote and manage relationships in order to effect productive changes to work, or to initiate new ideas and ways of working.

Key skills that are explored are the ability to appreciate that management is a multi-directional activity. Managing in four directions provides an analytical tool to integrate the various perspectives that need to be on board for work to be effective.

Suggested further reading

Boddy (2002).

This session is based to a significant degree on the work of Buchanan and Boddy (1992), which is suggested as essential reading for this session.

Couzins and Beagrie (2003) provide useful insights on managing upwards.

Huczynski and Buchanan (2001).

Johnson and Scholes (2004). Section on organisational goals.

Meredith,and Mantel (2000) provide a wide-ranging treatment of the broader aspects of project management, within which leadership is involved.

Feedback on learning activities and self-assessment questions

Feedback on learning activity 5.1

The key strategy for communicating with senior management successfully is to build credibility. Some tactics which help achieve this are outlined below:

- Create the communication links so that there is a mechanism to access senior managers in an effective way.
- Get the procedure right so that roles, responsibilities and levels of control over resources are appropriate.
- Plan how you will report progress in a way that effectively presents information in a way that is easily understood.
- Positive impressions are then created which enable you to manage effectively and efficiently, with senior management support.

Refer to the section which follows for more detailed guidance.

Feedback on self-assessment question 5.1

It is estimated that you will have upwards of 20 managers during your career. Mastering the art of managing upwards will probably result in you avoiding many of the barriers and stresses that prevent effective work. Career challenges and upwards career progression are the long-term reward. The short-term reward is better performance for you and your team. Through careful upwards management by you, your senior manager understands what you are trying to achieve, and how you intend to go about it.

Feedback on learning activity 5.2

This is not an exhaustive list, but consider:

- not enough team members;
- different professions or national backgrounds;
- different operations or ways of operating;
- staying within the relative comfort of technical expertise, rather than seeking openness and creativity in solving joint problems;
- unable to cope with speed and intensity or the unpredictable nature of work;
- not 'team players' – withdraw, rather than come forward;
- geographical separation – communication problems;
- ineffective working;

- opposing coalitions;
- competing demands.

Feedback on self-assessment question 5.2

Ideas for action:

- choose the right people if you can;
- negotiate time for the team;
- generate excitement;
- 'What's in it for me?' – be sure there are individual benefits for members;
- face up to disagreements;
- publicise and celebrate success;
- keep looking outside, do not become insular;
- use high-performance methods (HPM).

Feedback on learning activity 5.3

This is not an exhaustive list, but consider:

- refusing to use the equipment or system;
- deliberate misuse of the system;
- using the system as rarely as possible;
- making no effort to learn how to use it;
- excessive fault-finding and criticism;
- bringing other interest groups into the discussion, delaying agreement;
- delaying other changes necessary for the system to work;
- endless discussion and requests for more information;
- missing meetings about the change;
- not releasing staff for training;
- maintaining old procedures;
- suggesting new features, which make the change more complex.

Feedback on self-assessment question 5.3

In terms of the content agenda make sure that you address:

- rewards
- anxieties about ability
- training
- security of jobs and status
- budgets
- quality of jobs
- power changes.

In terms of the process agenda:

- ask staff for ideas;
- encourage secondment to the your team;
- questionnaires, seminars and focus groups;
- individual discussion;

- use newsletters and modern technology (videos or video-conferencing).

Feedback on learning activity 5.4

The following danger signals could have been included in your list:

- distancing of previous allies (why have stakeholders who supported you in the past become less enthusiastic?);
- giving low priority to the project;
- recalling previous failures;
- political obstacles being raised.

Feedback on self-assessment question 5.4

In considering this question, did the situation you are assessing result in a successful outcome and if so did the practical guidelines in this session offer any useful insights (figure 5.11)?

Figure 5.11

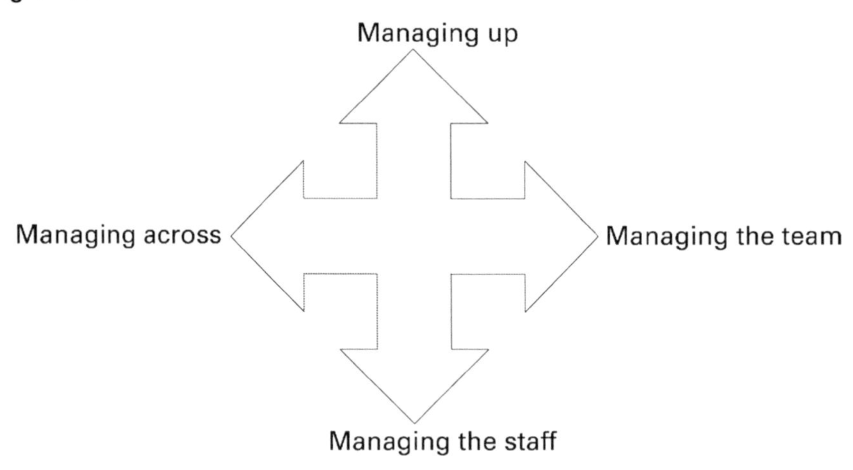

Study session 6

Influencing the supply chain: tactics

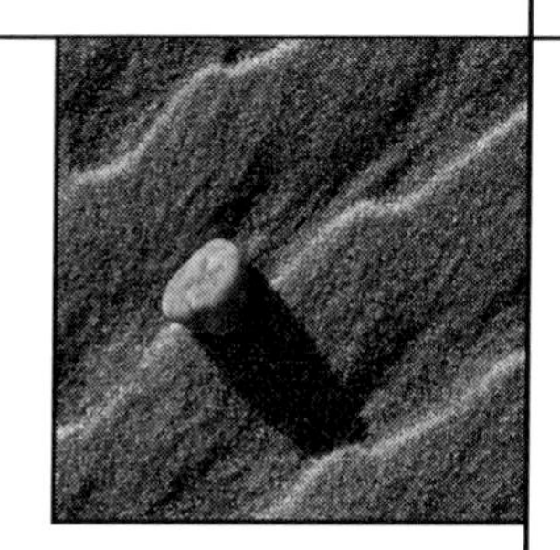

Introduction

We have considered the complexities of power and influence in previous sessions. This session explores how power and influence work at the tactical and operational level of an organisation. There are a variety of tactics available to leaders; which are most effective?

How does all the 'theory' that we have covered relate to the supply chain? How can we translate the theory into the daily operations of supply chains?

Session learning objectives

After completing this session you should be able to:

6.1 Demonstrate an understanding of 'tactics' and where they link to strategy and operations.
6.2 Explain different methods of influencing.
6.3 Assess the 'effectiveness' of each of the alternative tactics listed in learning objective 2.4.
6.4 Understand the relative merits of escalation as a means of influencing.

Unit content coverage

This study session covers the following topics from the official CIPS unit content document.

Learning objectives

2.3 Lead and influence effectively in four different directions.
- The relative merits of escalation as a means of influencing

2.4 Develop a range of tactics and definitions to effectively influence the supply chain.
- Rational persuasion
- Inspirational appeal
- Consultation
- Ingratiation
- Exchange
- Personal appeal
- Coalition
- Legitimating
- Pressure

Prior knowledge

Before starting this session you will need to have covered study sessions 4 and 5.

6

Resources

Internet access is required for learning activity 6.1 below.

Timing

You should set aside about 6 hours to read and complete this session, including learning activities, self-assessment questions, the suggested further reading (if any) from the essential textbook for this unit and the revision question.

6.1 Tactics, strategy and operations

You should be familiar with the strategy hierarchy (figure 6.1) by now.

Figure 6.1: The strategy hierarchy

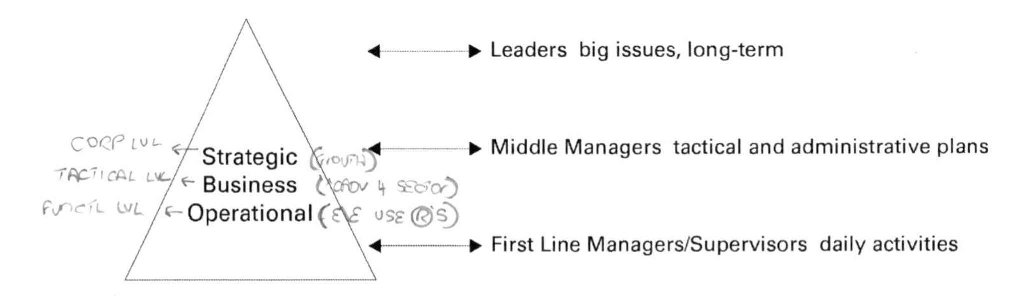

- Strategic level is also referred to as the *corporate level* of strategy. This describes the company's overall direction in terms of its general attitude towards growth and management of its various business and product areas.
- Business strategy is also referred to as the *tactical level* of strategy. This usually occurs at the departmental or product level. The main focus is to emphasise and focus on finding ways to improve the competitive position of the organisation in the specific market sector where the department operates.
- Operational strategy is also referred to as *functional strategy*. The focus is on the day-to-day operation, and how it contributes to the achievement of strategic and tactical objectives, by efficient and effective use of resources.

The key point to be aware of is that organisations must seek to achieve a seamless interlinking of strategic, tactical and operational levels of strategy, in order to achieve sustainable competitive advantage. An innovative and visionary corporate strategy is useless unless the organisation has the capability to deliver the strategy at a tactical and operational level. Likewise, excellent tactical and operational capability is useless unless the organisation has a clear strategic direction over the long term.

Learning activity 6.1

You now need to access the website of *The Guardian* newspaper: http://www.guardian.co.uk. In the Search box enter 'Sainsbury' and 'profits'

(continued on next page)

Learning activity 6.1 *(continued)*

and use filters Guardian Unlimited, 2005 and November to restrict your search. Read the article by Mark Tran dated 16 November 2005, about Sainsbury's, a leading UK retail supermarket. The headline is 'Sainsbury's upbeat over recovery'. Identify the main issues at each of the three strategic levels.

Feedback on page 83

Self-assessment question 6.1

How would you develop a strategy for the supply chain in your own organisation? Saunders' model (figure 6.2) may assist your analysis. Saunders (1997) suggests a model for the development of a supply chain strategy framework.

Figure 6.2: Supply chain strategy framework

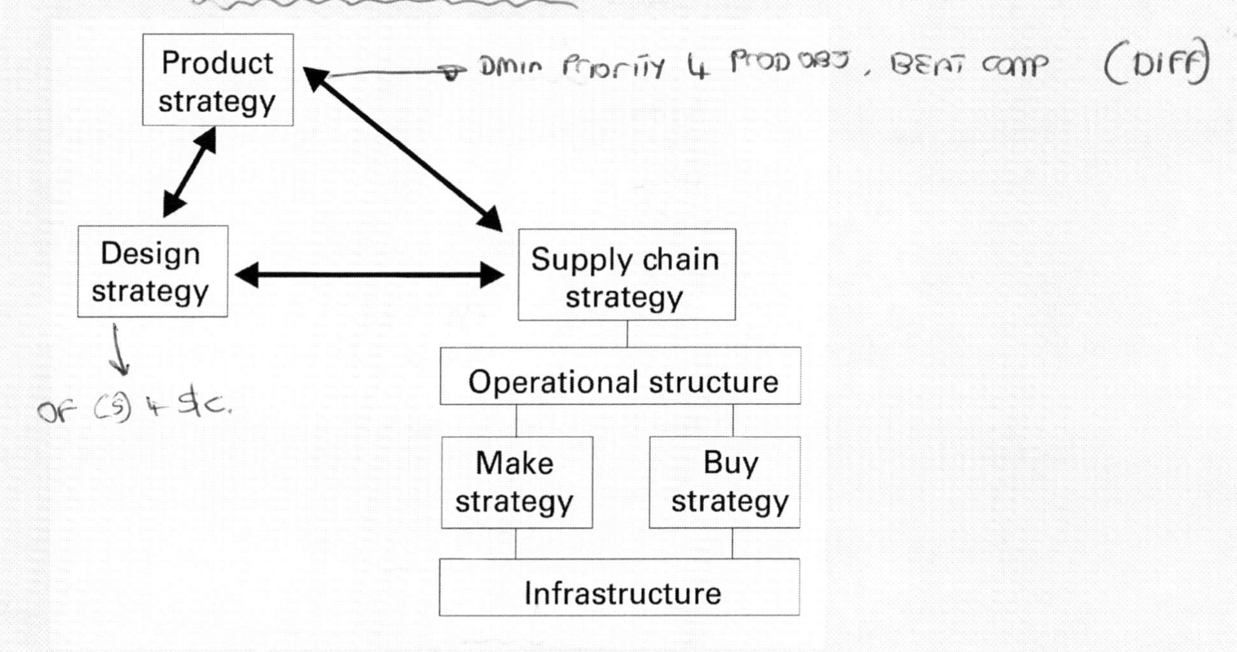

Source: Saunders (1997)

Feedback on page 84

6.2 Methods of influencing at the tactical level

Yukl (2006) suggests that influence is at the heart of leadership: 'To be effective as a leader, it is necessary to influence people to carry out requests, support proposals and implement decisions.'

We have considered the complexities of power and relationships in previous sessions. This session explores how power and influence work at the tactical and operational level of an organisation. A variety of tactics which leaders can employ are considered. As we proceed, try and assess the effectiveness of these various approaches, from your experience.

Yukl (2006) identified three generic types of influence, according to the primary purpose intended to be achieved:

- Impression management tactics are intended to influence people to like the person who is doing the influencing.
- Political tactics are used to influence any decisions to gain benefits for you or your group.
- Proactive influence tactics have a task focus, such as ensuring changes will happen via support, assistance or other proactive responses by the person or group who have been influenced.

Based on a variety of research programmes a number of specific types of influencing tactics were identified as being commonly used. The list below is based on work by Yukl and his colleagues (2001).

Rational persuasion: uses logical arguments and facts

Apprising: explains the benefits for the person being persuaded

Inspirational appeal: appeals to values, ideals or emotions

Consultation: invites participation from the person being persuaded

Collaboration: offers resources and assistance

Ingratiation: uses praise and flattery

Personal appeal: appeals to friendship or loyalty, or asks a personal favour

Exchange: offers some reward in return for support

Coalition tactics: gets other supporters to help persuade

Legitimating tactics: attempts to establish authority of the persuader

Pressure tactics: includes demands, threats and reminders.

Learning activity 6.2

Give examples from your own experience of each of the 11 tactics of influence listed above.

Feedback on page 84

Rational persuasion involves use of explanations, logical arguments and factual evidence to demonstrate that a request or suggestion is feasible and relevant to the task at hand. The degree of influence exerted often depends on how much evidence is produced, how detailed the explanation, and how much time and effort is expended in getting support. This tends to work best when objectives are shared, but staff are unclear about how the objective is to be achieved. They know the what, but are uncertain about the how.

Apprising involves the leader explaining the benefits to staff as to why they should support the leader. It appeals to the 'what's in this for me?' attitude which some staff may have. This tends to work best if the leader actually has the credibility to deliver the benefits which are being proffered.

Inspirational appeal involves an emotional and value-laden appeal, intended to focus on the emotions of staff, rather than the logic of rational persuasion. The intention is to elicit enthusiasm and commitment by appealing to the instinctive emotions of staff.

Consultation occurs when staff are invited to participate in planning how to implement a proposed action or proposal. Their input can be useful at a technical level, but also it is likely that consultation achieves commitment and support from staff, and a drive to ensure that the idea achieves its intended outcome.

Collaboration involves an offer to provide resources if staff agree to carry out the request of the leader. The underpinning idea is to reinforce the mutual nature of the activities. Staff have work to undertake, the leader helps and supports by providing resources that help them to do the task successfully.

Ingratiation attempts to influence staff's attitude, and get them to be more positive about the leader. The leader gives compliments, does favours, praises and shows respect, such that staff respond appropriately. Sincerity is the key to effective use of this tactic. You have to mean it, staff will see through falseness.

Personal appeal is influence based on friendship or loyalty to the leader. If friendship and loyalty are genuine and strong, then there is a high likelihood that this tactic will be successful.

Exchange involves an explicit or implicit offer of some reward for staff in return for their compliance and support. Exchange is about increasing benefits, such that it is worthwhile for staff to agree. It is very much about finding the appropriate 'carrot', and showing that you are able to deliver the promised reward.

Coalition tactics involve bringing in other people to help influence staff. This may be peers, superiors, subordinates or stakeholders whose views staff respect.

Legitimating tactics involve attempts to establish authority of the leader. For routine issues this is unlikely to be important, but if requests are unusual and appear to be outside your remit, you may have to establish authority through 'proving' that you have it.

Pressure tactics include threats, warnings, assertive behaviour and frequent requests to see if requests have been complied with. A careful balance has to be taken with this approach. Pressure may succeed in achieving compliance, but may engender resentment and a lack of commitment on behalf of staff, because willingness is ignored.

Self-assessment question 6.2

Attempt the following multiple-choice activity. Explain the logic behind your choices.

1. Which influence tactic is most dependent on the agent's reward power?
   (a) Rational persuasion
   (b) Personal appeal
   (c) Legitimating
   (d) Exchange
2. Which influence tactic is used most frequently in organisations?
   (a) Rational persuasion
   (b) Exchange
   (c) Consultation
   (d) Personal appeals
3. Which influence tactic is most likely to result in target commitment?
   (a) Exchange
   (b) Personal appeal
   (c) Consultation
   (d) Ingratiation
4. Which tactic is more likely to be used in a follow-up influence attempt than in an initial influence attempt?
   (a) Ingratiation
   (b) Consultation
   (c) Personal appeal
   (d) Pressure

Feedback on page 84

6.3 How effective are each of the influencing tactics?

Effectiveness is very difficult to assess in all circumstances, it always depends on the purpose and context in which any particular influencing tactic is used.

Various research studies have examined how a leader's use of tactics varies depending on the direction of influence (see section 6.). At the same time it is highly likely that a number of tactics will be used at the same time and in combination. So the key consideration in this section is how effective are different influencing tactics, either alone or in combination (see table 6.1)?

Various factors affect the effectiveness of influencing tactics:

S • relative status of the leader and staff;
U • the normal use of the particular tactic within the prevailing culture of the organisation;
P • sufficient power in the leader to reinforce the tactic;

- how much resistance is encountered;
- cost/benefits of particular tactics.

Table 6.1 Effectiveness of influencing tactics

Tactic	Direction mainly used	Stage mainly used	How used	Effectiveness
Rational	All directions	At first stage	Alone and in combination	High
Apprising	Down	–	In combination	Medium
Inspirational	Down	No particular stage	In combination	High
Consultation	Down and lateral	No particular stage	In combination	High
Collaboration	Down and lateral	–	In combination	High
Ingratiation	Down and lateral	At first stage	In combination	Medium
Personal	Lateral	At first stage	Alone and in combination	Medium
Exchange	Down and lateral	After first request	Alone and in combination	Medium
Coalition	Lateral and up	At late stage	Alone and in combination	Low–medium
Legitimating	Down and lateral	After first request	In combination	Low
Pressure	Down	At late stage	Alone and in combination	Low

Source: adapted from Yukl (2001)

Learning activity 6.3

What does 'effectiveness' in terms of 'influencing' mean for your organisation? How would it be different in another sector?

Feedback on page 84

Self-assessment question 6.3

Instructions: This exercise consists of three influence situations that commonly occur in organisations. Please describe in detail what the agent in the scenario should say and do to influence the target person. If you believe that more than one type of influence tactic is appropriate, indicate how the tactics should be sequenced.

Scenario 1

The product manager wants to assign a new task to a specific subordinate who has the skills to do it well. The task is to conduct a study on ways to improve customer service, and it is important for the product manager to get this information. The subordinate is reluctant to do the task because it is only distantly related to his job, and the other job responsibilities are already overwhelming. What should the manager say to influence the subordinate to carry out the task in an effective way?

(continued on next page)

Self-assessment question 6.3 *(continued)*

Scenario 2

The research and development manager is trying to complete a project to develop a new type of diagnostic instrument for medical laboratories. This project is important because the new instrument could be a major source of future profits for the company. To keep the project on schedule, the R&D manager needs the information services department to prepare a report earlier than initially expected. The R&D manager has no direct authority over the IS manager. What should the R&D manager say to influence the IS manager to complete the report quickly?

Scenario 3

The production manager has an innovative idea for a change in procedures to reduce costs and increase profits, but implementation of the idea would involve purchasing some new equipment as well as hiring and training two operators. To make the change requires the approval of the immediate boss, the production vice-president, who is usually reluctant to make risky decisions. What should the manager say to influence the production VP to approve the proposed change?

Feedback on page 84

6.4 The relative merits of escalation as a means of influencing

Escalation can be defined as a raising of intensity of activity in response to circumstances and situations.

If you refer to table 6.1, Yukl (2006) implies that effectiveness of the influencing tactic reduces the more escalation is increased.

> 'The success of a manager depends greatly on the manner in which power is exercised. Effective leaders are likely to use power in a subtle, careful fashion that minimises status differentials and avoids threats to the target persons' self-esteem. In contrast, leaders who exercise power in an arrogant, manipulative, domineering manner are likely to engender resentment and resistance.'

Yukl is arguing that rational persuasion, apprising, inspirational appeal, consultation and collaboration are not reliant so much on power as on rationality, and as such are more likely to be effective and gain the support of staff.

Escalating the argument by increasing the use of pressure and even coercion, is likely to create a response that becomes counter-productive over time, in that the influencing effort required is likely to create a strong response such as resentment and resistance.

A lot will depend on the circumstances and situation so it is hard to generalise completely about Yukl's suggestions. Indeed on the other hand it could be argued that escalation of an issue by the manager sends out a clear signal that you are serious about the issue, and that you intend to be forceful in pursuing your point of view in a rigorous manner. This may indeed then result in compliance from the staff, because they realise that resistance is unlikely to be effective.

Revision question

Now try the revision question for this session on page 297.

Summary

This session has focused on influence. Successful leadership is largely dependent on how influence is exercised at the tactical level of the organisation. Influence involves using power in a subtle, careful way. The intention is to enhance cohesion with staff through a focus on the soft aspects of influence, rather than the hard exercise of power.

Research suggests that the most effective tactics are rational persuasion, consultation, collaboration and inspirational appeals. Selection of tactics is situational and also depends on the status of the people involved.

Suggested further reading

The Guardian newspaper: http://www.guardian.co.uk

The chapter on leadership in Mullins (2005) introduces ideas on influencing.

Saunders (1997) relates influencing tactics to the supply context, and Yukl (2006) is the originator of much of the theoretical underpinnings on power and influencing tactics, and the situations where each type can work most effectively.

Feedback on learning activities and self-assessment questions

Feedback on learning activity 6.1

Corporate

- The profits were essentially flat.
- Maximising the opportunities presented by the changing competitive environment.
- Trying to make up ground on Tesco and Asda.
- The supermarket group appeared to be growing faster than the overall economy.
- Customers were seeing improvements from the Making Sainsbury's Great Again plan.

Tactical

- Reported a 2.1% rise in sales in the six months to October.
- Our offer is massively better than it was a year ago.
- Concentrated on fresh produce in an effort to differentiate itself from rivals.

- Sold more than half of all British Cox apples in the UK after a marketing campaign linking them to sausages and sage.

Operational

- Sainsbury's has been gradually rectifying problems in its supply chain by tackling IT difficulties and improving delivery of stock from depots to stores.
- Highlighted seasonal products such as Jersey Royal new potatoes, asparagus and strawberries.
- One negative note saw increased provisions for bad and doubtful debts pushing Sainsbury's Bank into a loss.

Feedback on self-assessment question 6.1

Have you been able to apply the model in a meaningful way to your own organisation? There should be some evidence and analysis in all of the boxes in figure 6.2!

Feedback on learning activity 6.2

See explanations in the section which follows learning activity 6.2.

Feedback on self-assessment question 6.2

1. (d) exchange
2. (a) rational persuasion
3. (c) consultation
4. (d) pressure.

Feedback on learning activity 6.3

Assess the various tactics listed in the text and particularly in table 6.1. Seek to find a clear definition for 'effectiveness'.

Effectiveness will depend on:

- relative status of the leader and staff – in terms of power and influence;
- the normal use of a particular tactic and how it is accepted within the prevailing culture of the organisation. Is this a normal and acceptable tactic?
- sufficient power in the leader to reinforce the tactic;
- how much resistance is encountered;
- cost/benefits of particular tactics.

Feedback on self-assessment question 6.3

Scenario 1

- Collaboration would be useful to help the subordinate do the assignment (for example, offer help on other tasks, offer to postpone or reassign some tasks).

- Rational persuasion would be useful to clarify the importance of the assignment for the organisation.
- Apprising may be useful to help clarify how the assignment would further the subordinate's career.
- Consultation may be useful to involve the subordinate in determining how the assignment could be done.
- Ingratiation may be useful to increase acceptance of the assignment (say that the subordinate is uniquely qualified to do it).
- An inspirational appeal may be useful if the assignment can be linked to values, such as concern for customer service, or loyalty to the organisation.
- Exchange may be useful if it is feasible to offer an incentive (bonus, promotion) for successful performance of the assignment.

Scenario 2

- Rational persuasion would be useful to clarify why the report is needed sooner than initially expected.
- Consultation may elicit ideas about possible ways to speed up the report.
- Collaboration may be useful if there is some way to help the IS manager do the report (for example, provide additional resources or assistance, postpone another assignment to make time).
- An inspirational appeal may be useful if successful completion of the project can be linked to target values.
- Exchange may be useful if there is something the R&D manager can offer that is sufficient to motivate compliance by the IS manager.
- A personal appeal may be helpful if the R&D manager has a close friendship with the IS manager.

Scenario 3

- Rational persuasion would be useful to make a strong case why the proposed change is feasible, desirable and involves low risk.
- A coalition involving other department managers would be useful to show the production VP that there is widespread support for the change.
- Inspirational appeals may be feasible if it is possible to link the proposed change to the production VP's values and aspirations.
- Collaboration may be useful if there are things the production manager can do to make it easier for the production VP to implement the proposed change.

Study session 7

Influencing the supply chain successfully

This is the final session in the section that considers leading and influencing in the supply chain. How can leadership and influence be effective and result in successful achievement of the intended outcomes?

Introduction

We have explored leadership and influencing in some depth over study sessions 4 to 6. Study session 7 will attempt to focus you so that you will appreciate the relative worth of some of the approaches that have been considered.

Session learning objectives

After completing this session you should be able to:

7.1 Describe and contextualise the concept of internalisation.
7.2 Explore the rationale behind the concept of compliance as a tactic of influencing the supply chain.
7.3 Describe and contextualise the concept of resistance.
7.4 Critically assess the outcomes and relative merits of attempts to influence the supply chain.

Unit content coverage

This study session covers the following topics from the official CIPS unit content document.

Learning objectives

2.5 Critically assess the outcomes of attempts to influence the supply chain.

- Internalisation
- Compliance
- Resistance

Prior knowledge

Before starting this session you will need to have completed study session 6.

Resources

Internet access is required for self-assessment question 7.1 below and self-assessment question 7.4 below.

Timing

You should set aside about 6 hours to read and complete this session, including learning activities, self-assessment questions, the suggested further reading (if any) from the essential textbook for this unit and the revision question.

7.1 How do we assess whether influence has been successful?

Put very simply, attempts at influence can be assessed as to how far the outcome is what was intended by the leader. In other words, did the outcome match the intention in the first place? As with all attempts at influence, the outcomes can achieve the desired effect, they can exceed the desired effect, or they can fail to achieve the effect to the degree expected.

Kelman (1958) looked at the psychological variables involved in this complex process. What are the motives and intentions of the people doing the influencing compared to those being influenced? What is the context in which the influencing occurs?

Influence processes

Kelman (1958) identified three broad types of influence processes:

- *Instrumental compliance*. The subordinate carries out the request in exchange for a reward or to avoid some punishment. The only reason for compliance is to gain some benefit and it is likely that the actions of the subordinate will be the minimum necessary to achieve the required outcome. Compliance suggests implicitly that support is somewhat reluctant.
- *Internalisation.* The subordinate becomes committed to support the request because, to a greater or lesser extent, they actually support what is asked of them. The request appears to be desirable and correct from the subordinate's perspective. The subordinate in this situation does not really consider benefits in a tangible sense, but supports the request because they think it is a good idea in itself.
- *Personal identification* is when a subordinate supports requests in order to obtain the approval of their leader, and thus gain self-esteem by doing so. Approval from the leader signifies that the subordinate is doing a good job and thus enables the subordinate to identify with the success of the outcomes.

It can be appreciated that these three processes all may result in the same outcome in that a task is done by the subordinate, but suggests quite different motives and perceptions underpinning the attitude of the subordinate.

Learning activity 7.1

Reflect on what internalisation means, and how it can be used in the supply chain context.

Feedback on page 94

Now that you have reflected on the context of internalisation within the organisation, try this self-assessment question to develop a wider context.

Self-assessment question 7.1

Consider ideas about 'partnership sourcing' by visiting http://www.pslcbi.com/ – a joint initiative set up by the Confederation of British Industry (CBI) and the Department of Trade and Industry (DTI) in 1990 to promote the concept of partnering in business. Partnership sourcing focuses on both the public and private sectors covering all industry sectors, manufacturing and services, working with small, medium and large enterprises.

What are the main principles which drive the approach of partnership sourcing?

Feedback on page 94

7.2 Outcome of influence attempts

Yukl (2006) suggests: 'one useful basis for evaluating the success of an influence attempt is whether the immediate outcome is what the agent intended'. He identified three distinct outcomes:

- *Commitment.* Subordinates agree with a request from the leader, and make every effort to do what has been asked of them. Commitment is usually regarded as the most desirable outcome from influence tactics.
- *Compliance.* Subordinates are willing to do what is asked of them, but are not always enthusiastic and positive. Behaviour has been influenced, but attitudes have not. Compliance may be enough to achieve relatively simple tasks, but if the task is complex and difficult then it may not be sufficient.
- *Resistance.* Subordinates are opposed to the request, and actively try and avoid doing it. Resistance can be more or less significant depending on the strength of feeling involved.

Learning activity 7.2

Is the supply chain environment for your organisation currently more or less susceptible to compliance tactics? At present in the private sector there seems to be a great emphasis on cost cutting, supplier rationalisation and outsourcing or offshoring. In the public sector the emphasis seems to be on cost cutting, structural integration and working with partnership organisations. What impact does that have on your staff in your workplace?

Feedback on page 95

Now that you have considered the changing workplace environment, try and answer the following question.

Self-assessment question 7.2

Consider and evaluate how far your own organisation is affected by 'compliance' issues. What actions does it take as a consequence?

Feedback on page 95

7.3 Resistance

Resistance to influence tactics can vary tremendously. A lot will depend upon the strength of feelings and relative power of leader and subordinates.

Yukl (2006) describes the tactics of resistance as forming a continuum from 'refusal' at one end of the continuum to 'agree but sabotage' at the other end, with 'excuses', 'request changes', 'appeal to higher authority' and 'delay' being found between the two extremes.

Outright refusal is an extreme situation when the subordinate feels do strongly about a situation that will not do what is asked of them. This clearly is a challenge to the authority of the leader, who will then need to assess carefully what response to make.

Excuses are often used to explain or justify why a request cannot be carried out. Rather than refusal, some explanation is offered by the subordinate as to why the request cannot be done. There can be legitimate excuses, such as contravention with, say, legal or health and safety requirements, or insufficient resources such as money or time. Excuses can also be less legitimate, and here again leaders need to assess and respond accordingly.

Subordinates can often request changes to the request as an attempt to modify it, or even to withdraw it altogether.

If the request is regarded as unreasonable, subordinates can appeal to higher authority as a means to change or annul a request. This 'going over the head' of one's manager is often used by subordinates, and creates yet another dynamic to the situation which poses issues for all concerned.

Delay can be used in various ways. For example subordinates delay in the hope that the manager forgets and therefore the request can be put aside and not completed. Or delay can send clear signals that the request is unreasonable or unrealistic within the resource constraints set by the manager.

Finally they can agree to the request. In effect they pretend that they are compliant, but actually they then attempt to sabotage things by doing the request wrongly to a greater or lesser degree.

Learning activity 7.3

You should try and describe specific examples of resistance in the supply chain. Evaluate how these have impacted on organisations.

Feedback on page 95

Now attempt the following question which requires you to do some research of your own.

Self-assessment question 7.3

Often, creating value requires significant change. John P Kotter concluded in his book *A Force for Change: How Leadership Differs from Management* (1990) that there are eight reasons why many change processes fail:

- allowing too much complexity;
- failing to build a substantial coalition;
- not understanding the need for a clear vision;
- failing to clearly communicate the vision;
- permitting roadblocks against the vision;
- not planning and getting short-term wins;
- declaring victory too soon;
- not anchoring changes in corporate culture.

Find references to Kotter's work and describe his 'eight steps to successful change'.

Feedback on page 95

7.4 Relative merits of influence tactics

A number of studies have been performed in the area of the assessment of the relative merits of influence tactics, but not specifically in supply chains.

Dunphy and Stace (1993) looked at corporate change in Australia and came up with a useful matrix (figure 7.1) which compared the style of change (influence and power) and the degree of change (from small change to major transformations). They were mainly interested in mergers and acquisitions and found that, in two-thirds of cases, successful influences were either coercive or dictatorial. They suggested that where influence needed to be successful and the situation was complicated and difficult, then it was better to be forceful. Interestingly, while they emphasised clear forceful influencing at the outset, they also suggested that to embed influence over the long term it was advisable to then switch quickly to a more consultative and collaborative style of management.

Figure 7.1: Dunphy Stace Matrix

Fine-tuning incremental modular corporate style of change

Change	Transformation	Management
Participative evolution	Charismatic transformation	Collaborative Consultative
Forced evolution	Dictatorial transformation	Directive Coercive

Source: adapted from Dunphy and Stace (1993)

Charbonneau (2004) examined the association between four influence tactics known to be effective in generating commitment to a task and perceptions of transformational leadership, and found strongly in favour of rational persuasion and inspirational appeals as effective influence tactics. To quote from the abstract to his research:

> 'Eighty military personnel were rated by 181 peers on four influence tactics and four transformational leadership factors. The influence tactics of rational persuasion, inspirational appeals, consultation and collaboration were expected to differentially predict idealized influence (behaviour), inspirational motivation, intellectual stimulation and individualized consideration. Results show that rational persuasion significantly contributed to the variance in all four transformational leadership factors. Inspirational appeals made significant contributions to the variance in idealized influence and inspirational motivation. Consultation and collaboration did not significantly contribute to explaining the variance in any of the four transformational leadership factors. These results suggest that training in rational persuasion and inspirational appeals may increase perceptions of transformational leadership style.'

Farrell and Schroder (1999) assessed the relationship between power bases and influence strategies in an organisational buying situation, the selection of the services of an advertising agency. They concluded that power and influence were relevant:

> 'The study has contributed to theory by demonstrating the relationship between the power bases of individuals and corresponding behavioural influence strategies. For practitioners, results suggest that influential individuals should be targeted with appropriate information that is relevant to both their power bases and the corresponding influence strategy.'

Noypayak and Speece (1998) conducted studies with managers in Thailand and used the 11 influencing tactics originally suggested by Yukl (1990). Their conclusion in the Abstract:

> 'A typology for assessing managerial roles was used to explore Thai managers' self-reported use of influence tactics with subordinates. In-depth interviews were conducted with 16 Thai managers in the

> Siam Cement Group. Managers who viewed themselves as vision setters tended to use rational persuasion, consultation, and pressure most. Motivator managers used rationality and ingratiation. Analyzer managers used pressure. Task masters used rationality and pressure. However, all types of manager sometimes used other tactics besides the most common ones. Much of this behavior is similar to how managers in studies from the USA behaved. However, Thai managers showed some orientation toward "softer" methods, whether or not the managerial role is typically associated with "soft" or "hard" methods.'

A contingent conclusion in that influence tactics used are based mostly on the dominant natural style of the manager.

Lam (1997) used the Yukl (1990) 11 influencing tactics in the context of Hong Kong and found that:

> 'Front-line workers responded best to exchange and upward appeals tactics, assertive tactics receiving the lowest score. Managers were more responsive to rational persuasion and consultation tactics and less to assertive and exchange tactics.'

Learning activity 7.4

Track down the articles quoted in section 7.4 (see the suggested further reading section at the end of this session) and read the findings in more detail. Try also to find other research in the area of most effective influencing tactics.

Feedback on page 96

Self-assessment question 7.4

Go to http://www.anneriches.com.au/article-ct3.html and read the article down as far as:

'4. The final stage

When employees **commit** to the change, they start focussing on the future instead of dwelling on the past. They have a clear sense of their roles and where they are going.'

Now tackle this question. When you are planning and implementing change, what actions would you take to overcome each of these behaviours and emotions which subordinates feel?

Feedback on page 96

Revision question

Now try the revision question for this session on page 298.

Summary

There is an evolving literature in the area of which influencing tactics are likely to be most successful. Internalisation, compliance and resistance are broad outcomes which are relevant and may guide your thoughts. This session should be useful in helping you to appreciate that there is a wide debate as to the relative merits of influencing tactics, and yet hard evidence is very sparse. You need to assess the context of the purchasing and supply chain function and appreciate which approach is most relevant.

Suggested further reading

Dunphy and Stace (1993) provide a practical model, backed by solid empirical research, to suggest ways to achieve change by different styles of management.

Kelman (1958) is worth reading as many of the ideas on successful change and the attitudes which are needed are based on his seminal ideas.

More scholarly empirical research on Yukl's typologies of influence tactics can be accessed in the articles by Charbonneau (2004), Farrell and Schroeder (1999) and Noypayak and Speece (1998).

Feedback on learning activities and self-assessment questions

Feedback on learning activity 7.1

Both instrument compliance and personal identification suggest some *transaction* is taking place. Leader wants to achieve something; subordinate wants some tangible or intangible benefit in return.

Internalisation seems a preferable response for both the leader and the subordinate as the benefits are mutual because the ideas are what develops a *relationship* between the leader and team members, based on mutual benefit.

In terms of the purchasing and supply chain, you can relate this to the behaviours that you want to develop in the team – relationships imply some win–win and mutual benefit.

Feedback on self-assessment question 7.1

Partnering encourages the building of relationships between organisations in order to add value, deliver benefit and thereby enhance competitiveness. Like most good ideas, the concept of partnering is simple: customers and suppliers working together as a team can drive down total cost, improve quality, innovate and speed products to market far more effectively than in an adversarial relationship. You are encouraged to read examples of successful collaborations in the section Best Practice – Case Studies (see http://www.pslcbi.com/).

Feedback on learning activity 7.2

You should reflect on the current supply chain environment for your industry sector and consider what compliance can mean in respect of:

- supplier relationships
- legal constraints
- cultural issues
- competitive pressures
- globalisation issues
- quality, cost, time issues.

Feedback on self-assessment question 7.2

There should be a range of answers depending on organisation and industry sector context. All of the variables identified in learning activity 7.2 should be considered.

- Supplier relationships – are suppliers able to influence you? (recall the Kraljic matrix in study session 4); is power more relevant now?
- Legal constraints.
- Cultural issues – in dealing with organisations from geographically different areas.
- Competitive pressures.
- Globalisation issues.
- Quality, cost, time issues.

Feedback on learning activity 7.3

A range of examples (table 7.1) from the continuum should be found.

Table 7.1

Resistance type	Example
Refusal	
Excuses	
Request changes	
Appeal to higher authority	
Delay	
Agree but sabotage	

What sort of examples did you identify? What sorts of power and influences were in evidence?

Feedback on self-assessment question 7.3

1. Establish a sense of urgency.
2. Create a coalition.

3 Develop a clear vision.
4 Share the vision.
5 Empower people to clear obstacles.
6 Secure short-term wins.
7 Consolidate and keep moving.
8 Anchor the change.

According to Kotter, it is crucial to follow the eight phases of change in the correct sequence.

Feedback on learning activity 7.4

From your research do you find any consensus on which influencing tactics are most successful?

There is no unanimity from research, but it could be argued that the balance is slightly in favour of softer, more cooperative and collaborative approaches. You can also reflect whether this is necessarily the best method of influencing in supply chain situations.

Feedback on self-assessment question 7.4

Read the second part of the article at http://www.anneriches.co.au/article-ct3.html and see how this fits with your response.

Reflect on how this approach extends on force field analysis (Lewin, 1951).

Study session 8

People factors: individuals and teams

'People are our greatest asset ... Most companies talk the talk, but walking the walk continues to be a problem for some organizations.'
***HR Magazine*, April 2005**

Introduction

This session is the first of six sessions (study sessions 8 to 13) which consider how we develop a culture of productivity through people. Leadership and influence in purchasing can only be effective through the active involvement of people. This session looks at the people factors, at an individual level and also in the context of teams and teamwork.

Session learning objectives

After completing this session you should be able to:

8.1 Assess your own individual 'learning style' and evaluate how appropriate this style is in your work environment.
8.2 Outline and critique team models of the 'solo leader' and the 'team leader'.
8.3 Critically evaluate Herzberg's motivational and hygiene factors for leadership.
8.4 Assess the need to change roles and refresh the status quo on a regular basis.

Unit content coverage

This study session covers the following topics from the official CIPS unit content document.

Learning objectives

3.1 Determine the need for people to work effectively individually and in work-based teams, and justify their development.

- The range of personal preferred styles for working effectively (including introversion and extraversion) and their relative merits in the workplace
- Team models of the solo leader and the team leader
- Herzberg's motivational and hygiene factors for leadership
- The need to change roles and refresh the status quo on a regular basis

Prior knowledge

You need to have studied study sessions 1 to 7.

Resources

Internet access is required for parts of this session, including learning activity 8.1 below and self-assessment question 8.2 below.

Timing

You should set aside about 6 hours to read and complete this session, including learning activities, self-assessment questions, the suggested further reading (if any) from the essential textbook for this unit and the revision question.

8.1 Individual learning and team development

Individual learning

Mullins (2005) defines **learning** as 'change of a relatively permanent kind which may result in new behaviours and actions or new understanding and knowledge gained through a formal process or spontaneously and incidentally through life experiences.'

Let us break this definition down into its main components:

- *Change of a relatively permanent kind* – means the learning only happens when it results in individuals changing their attitudes or behaviours, behaving differently as a result of learning.
- *Formal process or spontaneously* – formal processes (as in a classroom) test and assess *what* has been learned against a formal standard. Spontaneous learning is a continuous and often unconscious process acquired through normal social activities and in the workplace. This is often referred to as experiential learning, and studies suggest this is the principal way that people learn through their lives, and that formal processes, while significant, contribute much less to total learning.

Kolb's experiential learning cycle

Kolb (1984) provides a useful descriptive model of the learning-through-experience process (figure 8.1).

Figure 8.1: Kolb's experiential learning cycle

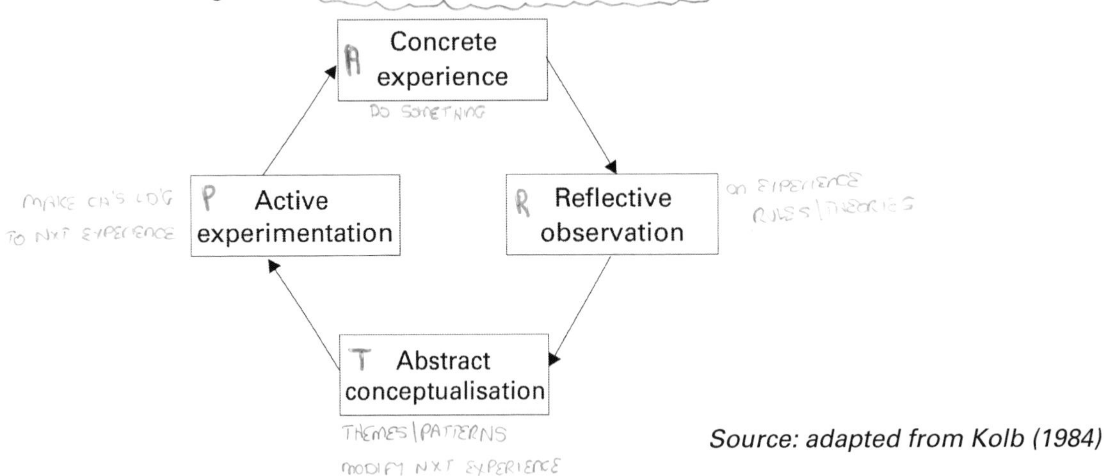

Source: adapted from Kolb (1984)

This suggests that there are four stages which follow from each other.

- *Concrete experience*, we do something, is followed by
- *Reflection*, we think on that experience on a personal basis. This may then be followed by the derivation of general rules describing the experience, or the application of known theories to it, that is
- *Abstract conceptualisation*, can we see any themes or patterns, and hence to the construction of ways of modifying the next occurrence of the experience
- *Active experimentation*, this is when we make changes leading in turn to the next concrete experience.

All this may happen in a flash, or over days, weeks or months.

Atherton (2005) explains the Kolb cycle and considers the psychological processes in more detail – see Further reading section.

Learning styles: which one are you?

Learning activity 8.1

There are a variety of 'learning styles' questionnaires, for example Honey and Mumford, MBTI and so on. Try and obtain a questionnaire to assess what your preferred learning style is.

http://www.ncsu.edu/felder-public/Learning_Styles.html is an online resource which you may find useful.

Feedback on page 106

At an individual level, you do not always have to start with concrete experiences. Depending on your preferred learning style, your approach to learning, you can start at different stages of the learning cycle.

Honey and Mumford (1984) have identified four main learning style preferences. By thinking about your preferred style, you can try and apply this to learning new things. If you are able to use your natural style, you are likely to find learning much easier and quicker.

- *Activists* like to be involved in new experiences. They are open-minded and enthusiastic about new ideas but get bored with implementation. They enjoy doing things and tend to act first and consider the implications afterwards. They like working with others but tend to hog the limelight.
- *Reflectors* like to stand back and look at a situation from different perspectives. They like to collect data and think about it carefully before coming to any conclusions. They enjoy observing others and will listen to their views before offering their own.
- *Theorists* adapt and integrate observations into complex and logically sound theories. They think problems through in a step-by-step way.

They tend to be perfectionists who like to fit things into a rational scheme. They tend to be detached and analytical rather than subjective or emotive in their thinking.
- *Pragmatists* are keen to try things out. They want concepts that can be applied to their job. They tend to be impatient with lengthy discussions and are practical and down to earth.

Most of us have elements of more than one learning style. Think about your strongest style and your weakest style to identify how you learn (figure 8.2).

A full online version of the questionnaire is available from http://www.peterhoney.com on a pay-as-you-go basis. Your results include a full report with suggestions about how to become a more effective learner.

Figure 8.2: Linking the Kolb cycle to learning styles

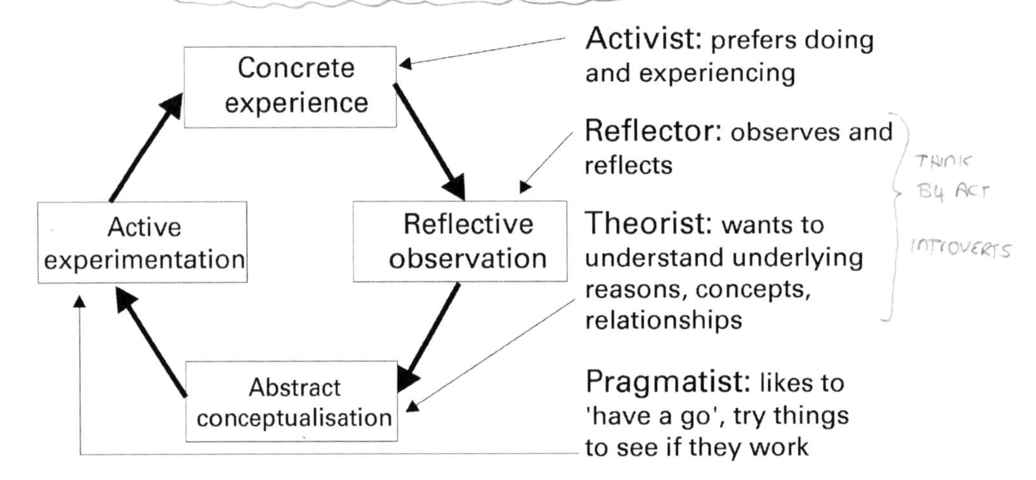

Broadly speaking, theorists and reflectors like to think carefully before they act. They prefer to weigh up the consequences before they commit. This can be called a preference to be introverted in their behaviour and thinking. Activists and pragmatists prefer actions first and then think about what happened as a guide to future actions. They are the extroverts.

Introverts and extroverts

Visit the website (http://www.socionics.com/main/types.htm) where Jung's theory of psychological types is summarised. People can be either extroverts or introverts, depending on the direction of their activity; thinking, feeling, sensing, intuitive, according to their own information pathways; judging or perceiving, depending on the method in which they process received information. This leads to individuals fitting into 16 fundamentally different types.

Extroverts are directed towards the objective world whereas introverts are directed towards the subjective world.

Sensing is an ability to deal with information on the basis of its physical qualities and its affection by other information. Intuition is an ability to deal with the information on the basis of its hidden potential and its possible existence.

Thinking is an ability to deal with information on the basis of its structure and its function. Feeling is an ability to deal with information on the basis of its initial energetic condition and its interactions.

Perceiving types are motivated into activity by the changes in a situation. Judging types are motivated into activity by their decisions resulting from the changes in a situation.

These four opposite pairs of preferences define eight different ways of dealing with information, which in turn result in 16 psychological types.

Self-assessment question 8.1

Reflect on results of your preferred learning style. Think about the implications of different preferences in a workplace context – how will this impact on the organisation.

Feedback on page 106

8.2 Solo leader and team leader

The previous section looked at individual learning and learning styles. This has implications for leadership in that leaders have to manage individuals. At the same time leaders may have their preferred approach.

In study session 2 we explored Tannenbaum and Schmidt's continuum from autocratic to laissez-faire leadership approaches.

Belbin (1993) contrasts two broad leadership styles: the team leader and the solo leader. The solo leader rules in an autocratic manner, is directive, expects compliance from staff and often leads from the front. Belbin suggests that solo leaders can be effective in times of crisis because they act swiftly and decisively, but if they fail this can have serious consequences. Solo leaders clearly have a Theory X view of their people.

In contrast, team leaders act in a much more participative and structured manner. They have a Theory Y view of people and therefore consult, delegate and trust their people to perform well.

Belbin clearly favours the team leadership approach:

> 'We are living in a world of increasing uncertainty where things are changing quite dramatically and often very quickly. One person can no longer understand all of this and provide the direction needed to cover every situation. Team leadership is the only form of leadership that is acceptable in a society where power is shared and so many people are nearly equal. As dictators fall, whether in the state or in industry, people are looking for a type of leadership other than one that comes down from high above.'

Table 8.1 Solo leader and team leader

	Solo leader	Team leader
1.	He knows everything best (interferes)	Chooses to limit his roles and delegates other roles to those who can do better
2.	Conformity – tries to make everybody be the same	Builds on diversity – values the differences in different people
3.	Collects admirers and 'yes men'	Seeks talented people and does not feel threatened by them
4.	Tells subordinates what to do	Encourages colleagues to use their particular strengths in their own way
5.	Management by objectives – makes it clear exactly what everyone is supposed to do	Creates mission – helps to clarify the vision which others act on as they think best.

Source: adapted from Belbin (1993)

Learning activity 8.2

Which leadership style is most evident in your own organisation: solo leader or the team leader?

Feedback on page 106

Belbin and his colleagues at Henley Management Centre went on to undertake extensive research in attempting to understand what makes an effective team and the interaction between individual team roles and team balance.

Table 8.2 Belbin's team roles

Belbin team-role type	Contributions	Allowable weaknesses
Plant	Creative, imaginative, unorthodox. Solves difficult problems.	Ignores incidentals. Too preoccupied to communicate effectively.
Coordinator	Mature, confident, a good chairperson. Clarifies goals, promotes decision making, delegates well.	Can often be seen as manipulative. Offloads personal work.
Monitor evaluator	Sober, strategic and discerning. Sees all options. Judges accurately.	Lacks drive and ability to inspire others.
Implementer	Disciplined, reliable, conservative and efficient. Turns ideas into practical actions.	Somewhat inflexible. Slow to respond to new possibilities.
Completer finisher	Painstaking, conscientious, anxious. Searches out errors and omissions. Delivers on time.	Inclined to worry unduly. Reluctant to delegate.

(continued on next page)

Table 8.2 *(continued)*

Belbin team-role type	Contributions	Allowable weaknesses
Resource investigator	Extrovert, enthusiastic, communicative. Explores opportunities. Develops contacts.	Over-optimistic. Loses interest once initial enthusiasm has passed.
Shaper	Challenging, dynamic, thrives on pressure. The drive and courage to overcome obstacles.	Prone to provocation. Offends people's feelings.
Teamworker	Cooperative, mild, perceptive and diplomatic. Listens, builds, averts friction.	Indecisive in crunch situations.
Specialist	Single-minded, self-starting, dedicated. Provides knowledge and skills in rare supply.	Contributes only on a narrow front. Dwells on technicalities.

Source: http://www.belbin.com/belbin-team-roles.htm

Self-assessment question 8.2

Belbin developed a questionnaire to enable people to determine what their natural team roles are. Try and obtain this questionnaire (http://www.belbin.com) and see which primary and secondary team role applies to you.

Feedback on page 107

8.3 Herzberg's motivational and hygiene factors

Belbin's identification of distinctive team roles poses some interesting questions for leaders. If all these roles exist then how many people do we need in our team? Can people play more than one role at the same time? Can people switch from one role to the other? Is leadership and management only inherent in the chairman role? In short, what can leaders do to ensure productive work from their people in the light of Belbin's work? Many of these questions were answered by Belbin, and your reflection should confirm how well Belbin's ideas are relevant to your workplace.

Herzberg et al (1959) conducted research in motivation and job satisfaction, and developed the 'two-factor' theory of motivation and job satisfaction. People were asked to cite examples of when they felt exceptionally good or bad about work, and what it was that caused those feelings.

Five factors stood out as strong determiners of job satisfaction (the motivational factors):

- achievement
- recognition
- work itself

- responsibility
- advancement.

The determinants of job dissatisfaction (the hygiene factors) were found to be:

- company policy
- administrative policies
- supervision
- salary
- interpersonal relations
- working conditions.

Learning activity 8.3

What are the motivational and hygiene factors in your organisation? Are they as important as Herzberg suggests?

Feedback on page 107

Herzberg's theory thus posits that there are two classes of factors that influence employee motivation: intrinsic factors and the extrinsic factors (figure 8.3).

The intrinsic factors were also called the motivator factors and were related to job satisfaction. The extrinsic factors were called hygiene factors and were related to job dissatisfaction. Motivators (intrinsic factors) led to job satisfaction because of a need for growth and self-actualisation, and hygiene (extrinsic) factors led to job dissatisfaction because of a need to avoid unpleasantness.

By providing motivators and removing hygienes, management can facilitate the growth of employees. This is essential to both the individual and the organisation. Growth makes the employee more valuable to the organisation because of his/her ability to perform higher order duties.

> 'management cannot really motivate employees, it can only create the environment in which the employees motivate themselves.'

(Herzberg et al, 1959)

Figure 8.3: Two-factor theory

Self-assessment question 8.3

Is Herzberg's theory applicable to the supply chain context?

Feedback on page 107

8.4 Changing roles and refreshing the status quo

It is implicit in Belbin's and Herzberg's work on team roles and motivation that competent managers and leaders must manage their people in appropriate ways in a modern organisation.

For Herzberg this meant that job enrichment, job rotation and job enlargement should be the focus by which managers can keep staff motivated and satisfied with their jobs, and thereby more productive and effective.

For Belbin this meant being able to get their people to change roles as required. The ability to change team roles is analogous to Herzberg's ideas on job enrichment, job rotation and job enlargement. Roles and jobs are not naturally fixed; they can and should be changed (refreshed) on a regular basis. The role of the manager, plus appropriate training and development, thus becomes critical in making this happen (figure 8.4).

Figure 8.4

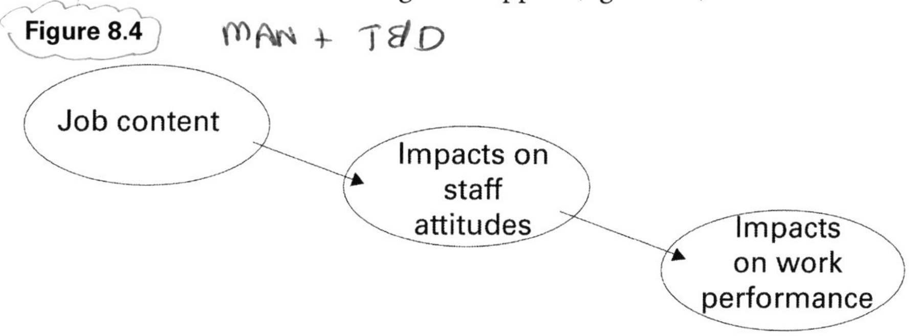

Learning activity 8.4

Distribute a learning styles questionnaire and a team roles questionnaire (Belbin, Honey and Mumford, or similar) among your colleagues at work. Do the results suggest that you have a 'balanced' team?

Feedback on page 107

Self-assessment question 8.4

Explain what behavioural changes you would make at work to switch your team role for the benefit of team balance. How would you change from team worker to chairperson if need be?

Feedback on page 107

Revision question

Now try the revision question for this session on page 298.

Summary

This session has explored the relationship between individual learning and how this relates to teamwork in the workplace. You will be able to assess your own preferred learning style and natural team role, which should enhance self-awareness and enable you to reflect on personal development for the future.

Herzberg and Belbin both provide valuable insights for managers and leaders on what their responsibilities are in developing people and teams.

Suggested further reading

Atherton (2005) Learning and Teaching: *Experiential Learning* (online) UK. http://www.learningandteaching.info/learning/experience.htm.

Belbin (1993) developed many of the ideas on what factors are required in order for teams to be successful.

The work of Herzberg, Mausner and Snyderman (1959) explores individual motivation and the factors which facilitate and hinder motivation.

Mullins (2005), in Chapters 10 and 13, develops content in this study session with regard to successful individual and team learning.

http://www.socionics.com/main/types.htm.

Feedback on learning activities and self-assessment questions

Feedback on learning activity 8.1

Which is your preference? Read the section which follows, from the Honey and Mumford learning styles questionnaire, to see which of the descriptors apply most to how you prefer to learn.

Feedback on self-assessment question 8.1

A basic reflection should conclude that a balance of all these styles is needed in any workplace context. Since it is unlikely that one person can possess an equality of preferences then we need a number of individuals to work together to achieve that effective balance – hence teamwork. Also ask yourself if the preferred style of the leader has a major impact on team dynamics? – clearly it has to.

Feedback on learning activity 8.2

See table 8.1 as a guideline to your thinking.

Feedback on self-assessment question 8.2

Do you fit into one of the nine general types? Is your Belbin team role appropriate with your work role? Belbin certainly suggests you should have a dominant team role, with a preferred secondary role that you could comfortable perform.

Feedback on learning activity 8.3

Try and be as specific as possible. Can you see a relative importance of the factors or will it be contingent on the time and situation?

Feedback on self-assessment question 8.3

You should be able to suggest examples to justify Herzberg's view in a supply chain context:

- Low productivity, work takes a long time to accomplish and is rarely on time.
- Poor production or service quality throughout the supply chain.
- Strikes, industrial disputes or breakdowns in employee communication and relationships.
- Complaints about pay and working conditions.

Feedback on learning activity 8.4

Honey and Mumford results show preferred learning styles. Among your team is there a variety of learning styles?

Belbin suggests that all the team types need to be present in a team in order to get good performance.

Consider the implications of a range of learning styles and a well-balanced team on performance at work.

Feedback on self-assessment question 8.4

Understand the preferred roles of people on the team. Play to people's strengths. Get a good balance of people on a team, not just one type. Awareness and training make it possible for people to change roles if needed. If a natural chairperson is not evident, other people can play that role if they are aware of the skills that are needed to fulfil the chairperson role, and they have been given training.

Study session 9

Teamwork and how to do it successfully

Introduction

What differentiates a successful team from less successful teams? What is it that makes the difference in performance?

This session explores the whole ethos behind teamworking in organisations. How do teams develop and evolve? Who works in a particular team, what do they do and how are they managed? What benefits does diversity bring to the team? Finally, can teams be left alone with less supervision if they are performing well? Clearly if we can understand the dynamics of 'team success' we can be in a position to reproduce it more consistently in the workplace.

Session learning objectives

After completing this session you should be able to:

- 9.1 Evaluate the merits of cross-functional teams and describe the role of sponsorship.
- 9.2 Describe the key stages of team development.
- 9.3 Describe the typical roles/responsibilities of a work-based team in a purchasing project.
- 9.4 Evaluate the merits of diversity within teams.
- 9.5 Evaluate the merits of 'leaderless' teams (for example T-groups or others).

Unit content coverage

This study session covers the following topics from the official CIPS unit content document.

Learning objectives

3.1 Determine the need for people to work effectively, individually and in work-based teams, and justify their development.

- Critical individual and team roles, characteristics, competencies and critique individual roles and behaviour patterns expected
- The merits of cross-functional teams and describe the role of sponsorship
- The key stages of team development
- The typical roles/responsibilities of a work-based team in a purchasing project
- The classification of team roles
- The merits of diversity within teams
- The merits of 'leaderless' teams (e.g. T-groups or others)

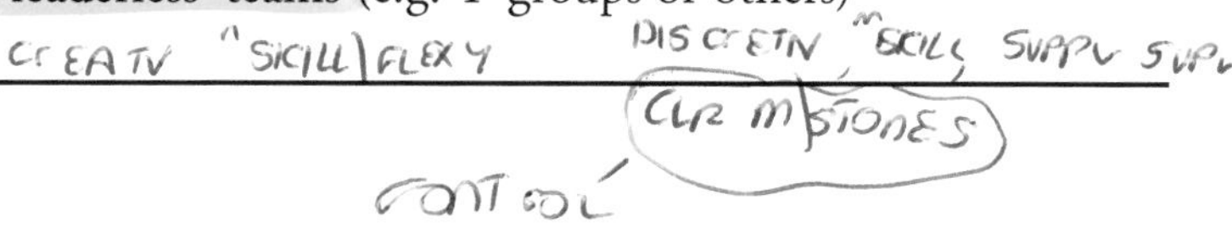

Prior knowledge

Study session 8.

Resources

You will need access to the internet in order to complete this study session.

Timing

You should set aside about 6 hours to read and complete this session, including learning activities, self-assessment questions, the suggested further reading (if any) from the essential textbook for this unit and the revision question.

9.1 Cross-functional teams and team sponsorship

Groups are defined by Schein (1998) cited in Mullins (2005) as 'any number of people who (1) interact with one another, (2) are psychologically aware of one another and (3) perceive themselves to be a group'.

Adair (1986) cited in Mullins (2005) suggests that a group possesses most of the following characteristics:

- a well-defined set of membership criteria
- group consciousness
- a sense of shared purpose
- interdependence on each other
- interaction with each other
- ability to act as one.

Mullins (2005) suggests that 'whereas all teams are by definition, groups, it does not necessarily follow that all groups are teams'.

What do you think are the differences between groups and teams?

Learning activity 9.1

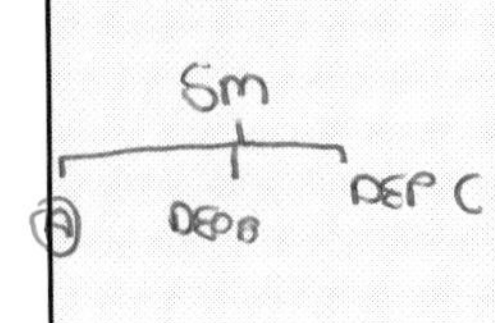

Draw a diagram of the organisational structure of your organisation – what does it look like? Does this have any implications for how the organisation considers teams?

Feedback on page 118

Belbin (2000) suggests that it does not really matter whether you refer to groups or teams as long as you are clear in usage of the terms 'group' in a more general sense and 'team' in a more context-specific sense.

Table 9.1

	Team	Group
Size	Fairly small	Can be quite large
Leadership	Shared or rotating as needed	Solo – for example CEO
Selection	Usually selected	Immaterial
Self-perception	Based on mutual knowledge and understanding	Leader focused
Style	Variety of roles, coordinated and balanced	Conformist
Spirit	Dynamic and interactive	Togetherness, focused on an opponent

Jungalwalla (2000) neatly captures the essence of a team:

> 'Perhaps more than any other factor, common goals and vision mix to form the glue that binds a team together.'

Cross-functional teamworking

Mullins (2005) suggests that effective teamwork is essential in modern organisations, both within a team and between the various teams that compose an organisation. The simple rationale behind teamworking, particularly across the various functions in an organisation, is to harness the diverse skills of people in a cooperative and participative manner, by getting people from different technical functions to work together to achieve common goals.

Clear benefits then become possible such as:

- productivity improvements
- better quality of products and services
- creativity and innovation in products, services and processes
- linking into technological advances to facilitate team operations
- improvements in motivation and commitment through team dynamics
- tangible competitive benefits for the organisation and the team members.

Team sponsorship

Sheard and Kakabadse (2002) expanded and combined previous thinking by Tuckman, Kubler-Ross and Adair into a multifactor model of effective team development (table 9.2).

Table 9.2 Nine key factors in team effectiveness

Key factor	Loose group	Effective team	Focus
Clearly defined goals	Individual opt-out not allowed	Common and understood	Task
Priorities	Split loyalties	Team alignment	Task
Roles and responsibilities	Unclear	Agreed and understood	Individual
Self-awareness	Guarded	Appropriate to team needs	Individual
Leadership	Directive	Catalytic and facilitative	Group
Group dynamics	Guarded	Established and agreed	Group
Communications	Formal	Open	Group

(continued on next page)

Table 9.2 *(continued)*

Key factor	Loose group	Effective team	Focus
Content	Task focus	Influenced but not controlled by the organisation	Environment
Infrastructure	Task focus	Stable support by organisational infrastructure	Environment

In an extensive research study they found that effective performance was strongly influenced in a positive way by clear goals and objectives. But particularly influential was good leadership and a supportive environment created by the organisational infrastructure. This suggests that teams need strong sponsorship by senior management, and a supportive environment in which to operate.

Self-assessment question 9.1

How do 'teams' work in your organisation? What problems does this create? Explore the possible team dynamics and the way managers encourage teams and teamworking, within the formal structure of your organisation.

Feedback on page 119

9.2 The stages of team development

Teams take some time to develop in the organisational context. It is very rare that teams instantly perform to a high level; usually some time is needed.

Bass and Rytebrand (1979) cited in Mullins (2005) identified four discernible stages in development:

- mutual acceptance and membership
- communication and decision making
- motivation and productivity
- control and organisation.

Tuckman (1965) has developed the most widely referred to model of team development, the Tuckman wheel (figure 9.3).

Figure 9.3: Tuckman's stages of teamwork model

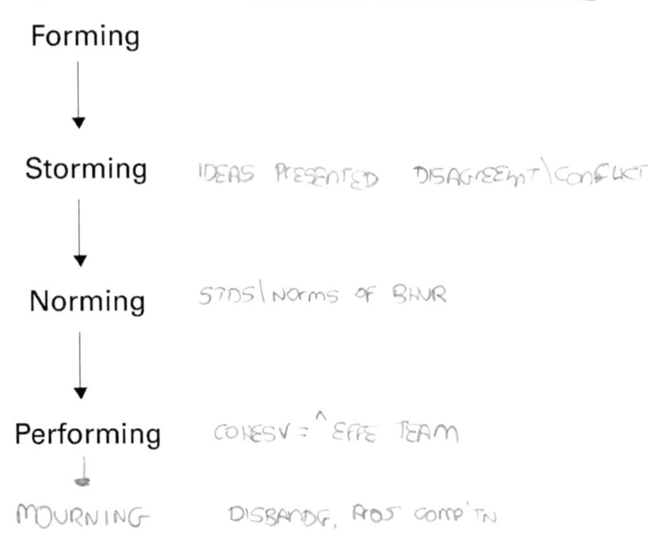

Stage 1 – Forming: The initial stage of group formation.

Stage 2 – Storming: As members get to know each other their ideas are presented more forcefully. Disagreements and conflict may result.

Stage 3 – Norming: Guidelines and standards are developed into norms of behaviour.

Stage 4 – Performing: Structure and cohesiveness are created so that the team can now work effectively.

He later added Stage 5 – Mourning: to signify the end of team activities and possible disbanding as a task is completed.

Learning activity 9.2

Read more extensively on Tuckman's ideas on team formation and reflect on the relevance of the model proposed to your own experience of working in teams in a social or workplace context.

Feedback on page 119

Now that you have critically evaluated team formation, relate this to your own organisation. Reflect on how teams are chosen in your organisation. Is sufficient time allowed for teams to develop and reach the 'performing' stage?

Self-assessment question 9.2

Is 'team development' considered in your organisation? In the public sector, team development involves working with team members who may well belong to other organisations or other departments in your own organisation. What additional problems does 'partnership working' create?

Feedback on page 119

9.3 The typical roles/responsibilities of a work-based team in a purchasing project

Saunders (1997) suggests that people can operate in a variety of structures in purchasing and supply chain projects:

- task forces – problem-solving focus
- teams
- matrix structures.

Task forces consist of people from a variety of different functions, to tackle particular issues of relevance to all the functions in the organisation. The main focus of a task force will be essentially short term; define the problem, identify the causes, develop solutions and fix the problem.

Teams require and enable a longer-term focus of strategic relevance to the organisation. Saunders (1997) cites value analysis and value engineering teams as a good example. More recently buyer/supplier teams working in partnership to drive out costs and focus on mutual value-added activities are increasingly popular.

Matrix structures (figure 9.4) are also a way of allowing project teams from different functions to come together for a common purpose. This enables a combination of multifunctional skills to carry out a project. The focus will be achievements of project goals rather than narrow functional goals.

Figure 9.4: A matrix structure for a purchasing project

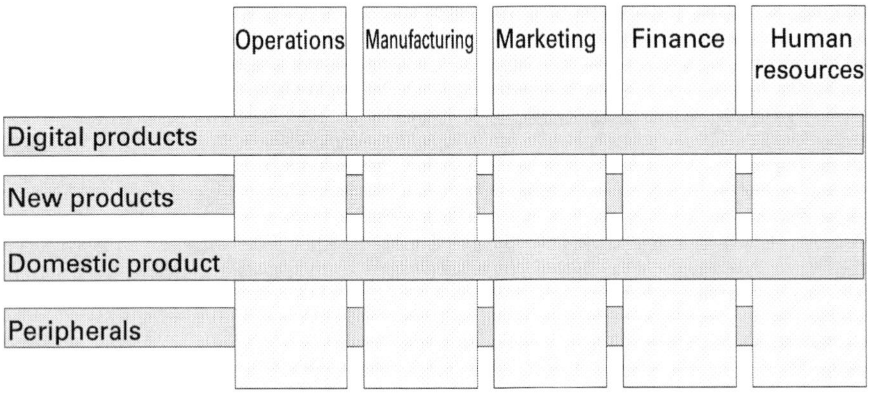

Operations
Manufacturing
Marketing
Finance
Human resources
Digital products
New products
Domestic product
Peripherals

9

Learning activity 9.3

What is a project? How does project working differ from 'normal' (steady state) working?

Feedback on page 119

Now consider project arrangements in your own organisation.

Self-assessment question 9.3

Create a 'matrix' for a work-based team in a purchasing project related to your own organisation.

Feedback on page 119

9.4 Achieving diversity within teams

Learning activity 9.4

Suggest a definition of 'diversity' which best expresses your understanding of the term.

Feedback on page 120

It is clearly of benefit that teams are composed of people who have diverse personalities, skills and interests. One of the skills of managers is to assemble teams that have a range of diversity which enhances performance. You may not get along with every team member, but it is important that you can work together to achieve the same goal. Consider some of the skills needed by managers to blend together different personality styles, attitudes and behaviours.

SKILLS\INTS, ^PERF, BLEND PERS STYLES

If opposites do not attract

- Recognise the importance of getting along with team members who are different from you.
- Match each divergent thinking method to its correct description.
- Choose the positive item, given a negative statement.
- Match the interpersonal problem with an effective solution.

Contrasting personality types

Belbin (1981) noted positive characteristics and allowable weaknesses of each of the team roles in his model.

- Recognise the value of contrasting personality types.
- Specify the characteristics of a goal-oriented person.
- Specify the characteristics of a diligent person.
- Specify the characteristics of an agreeable person.
- Specify the characteristics of an open person.

Gut reactions that get in the way

- Recognise the importance of controlling your gut reactions when dealing with difficult people.
- Identify the behaviours people traditionally exhibit when clashing with others in the workplace.
- Select the alternatives to assigning negative motivations in a given situation.
- Match ways to conquer your gut reactions with the example of each.

Dealing with difficult people

- Recognise the benefits of finding a way to deal with difficult people.
- Identify ways to deal with a 'too good to be true' person in a given scenario.
- Identify the ways to deal with an 'un-team' member.
- Identify how to eliminate destructive 'social bee' behaviours.
- Identify how to deal with the 'backstabber' in a given situation.

Diversity

Diversity is emphasised strongly in current management thinking, and this is reflected in legal and regulatory frameworks as well. Organisations are required to positively promote diversity within their human resource management (HRM) practices and procedures. There is a clear assumption that diversity in the workplace is a reflection of an increasingly diverse social mix in western developed economies, and as such must a good thing, morally and commercially.

At the same time diversity does not just happen naturally; positive actions may well be required to achieve diversity, which can create problems for organisations. The focus on a diverse workforce may mean that individual ability and potential of certain staff could be overlooked in favour of gender balance or racial diversity. There is a careful balance which is not easy for organisations to achieve in a shifting social environment.

Self-assessment question 9.4

Consider the example below of a diversity policy of a typical organisation. Why do they have a diversity policy, and what benefits are they trying to achieve by having one?

Team diversity

Our organisation is absolutely committed to recruit, train and provide career advancement to all associates without regard to gender, race, religion, age, disability, sexual orientation, nationality, or social or ethnic origin.

Diversity in our workplace will always be encouraged, in fact demanded. Bigotry, racism and sexual harassment will not be tolerated. We will never violate the legal and moral rights of employees in any way, and we will not do business with any company that does.

We also believe that a diverse workforce is better able to respond to our consumers' needs and to the competitive demands of the global marketplace in which we do business. Our organisation has a growing international presence, and we strive to maintain a global perspective and an appreciation of world cultures.

Feedback on page 120

9.5 Leaderless teams

Modern approaches to management suggest that when an organisation is composed of highly skilled and competent 'knowledge workers' then self-managed work groups and teamworking are appropriate ways of organising work.

Mullins (2005) suggests that the key features of a self-managed team are:

- Goals are set for the group, but the members determine processes.
- Members have discretion about planning, implementation and controlling tasks.
- Members have the variety of skills and technical knowledge to undertake the tasks.
- External supervision is mostly facilitative and supportive.
- Feedback and evaluation is holistic.

While it is argued that self-managed teams increase motivation and satisfaction among members, there is little evidence to suggest that improved performance is achieved through this way of working.

T-groups

In 1947, the National Training Laboratories Institute started up in the USA. It pioneered the use of T-groups (sensitivity or laboratory training) in which learners use feedback, problem solving and role-play to gain insights into themselves, others and groups. The goal is to change the standards, attitudes and behaviour of individuals.

This type of training is controversial as the behaviours it encourages are often self-disclosure and openness, which many people believe an organisation ultimately punishes. Also, a lot of the sensitivity training taking place uses excessive activities. The feedback used in this type of training can be highly personal, hence it must be given by highly trained observers (trainers).

You can find out more about T-groups at http://en.wikipedia.org/wiki/T-groups.

Learning activity 9.5

When would a self-managed team be appropriate?

Feedback on page 120

Now that you have completed this learning activity, attempt the following self-assessment question.

Self-assessment question 9.5

How do you 'control' a self-managed team?

Feedback on page 120

Revision question

Now try the revision question for this session on page 298.

Summary

Key learning points from this session:

- characteristics of a cross-functional team
- appropriate structures to enable cross-functional working
- task, team and matrix structures in purchasing
- Tuckman's model of team development

- the benefits of diversity in terms
- an evaluation of when self-managed teams can work effectively.

Suggested further reading

The factors which contribute to successful team working are explored from a variety of perspectives by Adair (1986), Belbin (2000) and Jungalwalla (2000).

Saunders (1997) explores team working in the supply context, and Schein (1998) and Tuckman (1965) are worth reading as they originated many of the ideas on which later writers have built.

Feedback on learning activities and self-assessment questions

Feedback on learning activity 9.1

You could have presented the typical and traditional organisational chart, which shows the functional arrangements of the organisation by department (see figure 9.1).

Figure 9.1: Departmental structure

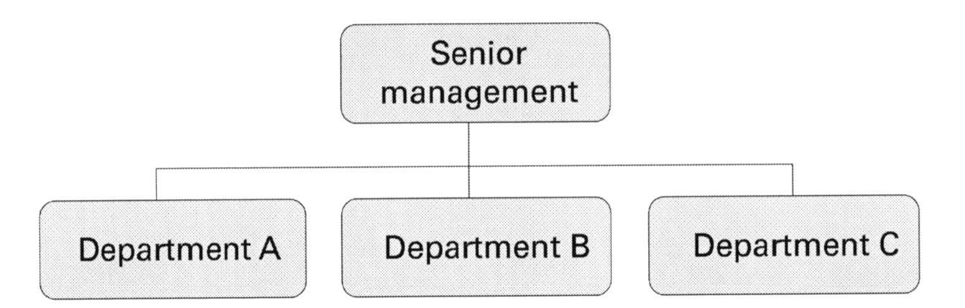

Or maybe the chart is more fluidly presented into process activities and teams rather than functions (figure 9.2).

Figure 9.2: Product group structure

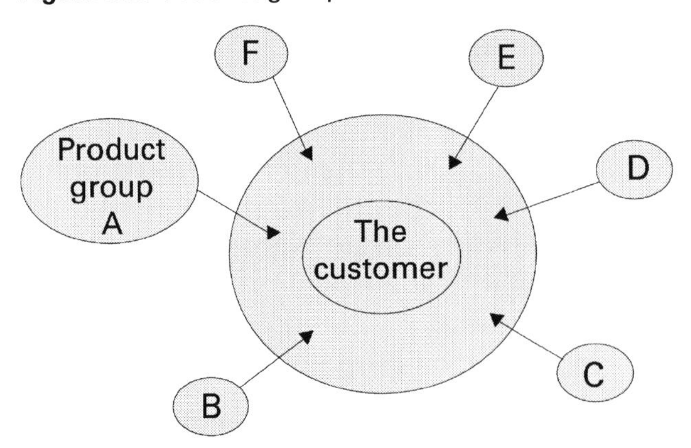

There are no right answers to this activity. But maybe movement away from the traditional way of looking at organisations can lead to a better understanding of what is involved in teams and teamworking.

Feedback on self-assessment question 9.1

You should note distinctions between a formal functional hierarchy or bureaucracy, which often make cross-functional teams slow and unwieldy in operation, and a systems or process view which facilitates cross-functional working, but maybe with some loss of control for senior management.

Real problems can be created when the organisational structure and the team philosophy are not well aligned.

Feedback on learning activity 9.2

Key learning points:

- The model is not linear. Team formation does not necessarily pass smoothly from one stage to the next. Often the team never progresses beyond a certain stage for a variety of reasons.
- Progress can be iterative; teams can go backwards as well as forwards.
- Teams pass through the stages at different speeds, depending on team dynamics and external factors.
- Good team cohesion and dynamics does not of itself guarantee good performance.

Feedback on self-assessment question 9.2

The teams chosen in your organisation may be elected, selected or self-appointed.

Partnership working is an evolving way of working, particularly in the public sector. Distinct organisations come together in formal or informal partnerships to undertake cooperative teams to achieve specific objectives. It is akin to cross-functional working, without the organisation's formal boundaries. Hence planning, control, and roles and responsibilities can be unclear, which places additional difficulties on leaders and managers.

Feedback on learning activity 9.3

A project has:

- A defined beginning and end. Normal work is ongoing.
- A specific goal or objective. Normal working has multiple goals and objectives which cover a wider range of activities than project work.
- Specified resources in terms of quality, cost, time. Normal work is similar, but flexibility and reliability are required to be emphasised.
- Uncertainty and risk are usually greater in project working because of the 'uniqueness' (high variety/low volume) involved. Normal working has more routine, repetitive tasks which we have experience of from previous iterations.

Feedback on self-assessment question 9.3

Reflect on a project which your purchasing department has undertaken recently. How would this project be organised from a 'matrix perspective'?

Consider particularly the different functions which should be involved to fit with the nature of the specific project. Look for a balance of skills and integration of the various functions.

Feedback on learning activity 9.4

Mullins (2005) defines **diversity** as 'visible and non-visible differences which will include sex, age, background, race, disability, personality and work-style'. Compare this with your definition.

Feedback on self-assessment question 9.4

- The first paragraph states an absolute commitment to provide equality to all the staff that they recruit. They emphasise equality of treatment but do not have anything to say about diversity specifically. Will equality of treatment naturally result in diversity? There are disparate views about this.
- The second paragraph has a strong statement about diversity: *Diversity in our workplace will always be encouraged, in fact demanded.* There is no real indication of how that diversity will be actually encouraged, other than by reference to legal and moral rights. For organisations with international dimensions, it will be very difficult to smoothly integrate across a variety of legal, cultural and business frameworks.
- The third paragraph gives a hint of the benefits sought through diversity facilitating customer responsiveness, and global awareness. But is there any clear indication of how this will be achieved?

Feedback on learning activity 9.5

A high degree of creativity and innovation is required. Very flexible responses are needed. Experienced and self-disciplined members compose the majority of team members. Stage 4 of situational leadership model. A high-performance group who have a proven track record.

Feedback on self-assessment question 9.5

- Clear report and communication links.
- Clear milestones and phases identified and agreed.
- Clear objectives agreed in advance.
- Clear roles and responsibilities identified.
- MBWA (management by wandering about) – see Peters (1982), who suggests that the key role of leadership in creating excellence in organisation is the ability to freely engage with staff by being active and visible in their workplaces, rather than in the ivory tower of corporate headquarters.

Study session 10

Teamwork and dealing with conflicts

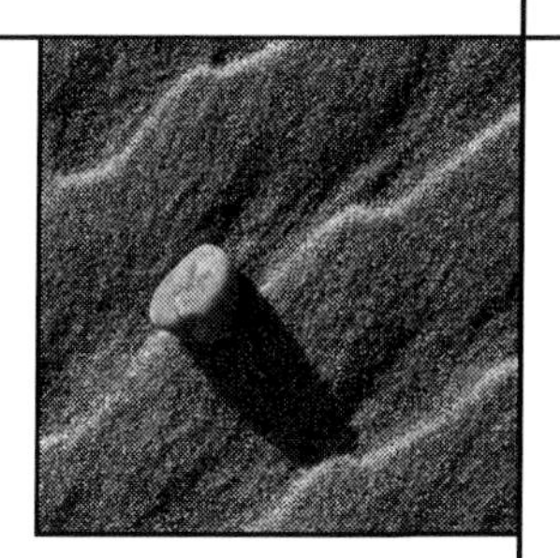

Introduction

This session considers conflicts within and between teams in organisations. How do conflicts arise and are they always bad? How can managers and team members organise things to minimise the harmful effects of conflict and disagreement?

Please spend time revisiting previous sessions which explore areas of good management practice such as communication, team roles, leadership and management styles and managing stakeholders.

'Conflict is a state of opposition, disagreement or incompatibility between people or groups of people, which is sometimes characterised by argument, disagreement or even physical violence.'
Wikipedia

Session learning objectives

After completing this session you should be able to:

10.1 Identify potentials for pitfalls and conflicts within a team.
10.2 Assess the attitudes, behaviours and dynamics which can lead to conflicts within the team.
10.3 Develop a consensus on how to work together within the team.

Unit content coverage

This study session covers the following topics from the official CIPS unit content document.

Learning objectives

3.2 Develop a consensus on how to work together, identifying potentials for pitfalls and conflicts within the team.

- Power
- Politics
- Position
- Lack of resource
- Poor communications
- Poor leadership

Prior knowledge

Study sessions 8 and 9.

Resources

You will need access to the internet in order to complete this study session.

Timing

You should set aside about 6 hours to read and complete this session, including learning activities, self-assessment questions, the suggested further reading (if any) from the essential textbook for this unit and the revision question.

10.1 Conflicts in teams

A variety of perspectives

The *unitary perspective* seeks to develop an organisation that is integrated and harmonious throughout. Conflict is dysfunctional and harmful and caused by:

- poor communication
- personality differences
- resistance and non-cooperation by certain members.

The *pluralist perspective* sees conflict between competing groups within an organisation as inevitable, and inherent in the functional and hierarchical structure of most organisations. Management in this context has to be adept at handling conflict and balancing competing interest groups.

The *radical perspective* sees organisations in terms of a conflict of power and control. Conflict reflects the inequalities within an organisation and is the means whereby change is effected. Conflict is the natural outcome of the struggle between workers and owners and the managers who represent the interests of owners.

Learning activity 10.1

Consider the unitary, pluralist and radical perspective presented briefly in section 10.1 above. Which approach best explains conflict in your organisation?

Feedback on page 125

Mullins (2005) suggests that 'conflict is not necessarily a bad thing. Properly managed it can have potentially positive outcomes.'

Townsend (1985) cited in Mullins (2005) has a similar, largely positive, view: 'A good manager does not try to eliminate conflict, he tries to keep it from wasting the energies of his people.'

Self-assessment question 10.1

Explore possible positive and negative outcomes of conflict in an organisation.

Feedback on page 125

10.2 Why do conflicts arise?

The sources of conflict

There are many potential sources of conflict in an organisational and teamwork context. Some of the main ones are identified by Mullins (2005) as follows:

- Differences in perception. People are individuals and as such see reality in their own terms. This can lead to clashes between people.
- Limited resources mean people and teams have to compete for finite resources in an organisation. Fewer resources usually means more competition and hence more conflict.
- Departmentalisation and specialisation encourages managers and staff to focus on the needs of their own departments and departmental goals, at the expense of other departments. Insular or silo thinking is almost inevitable in functional structures.
- Work activities are dependent and linked and therefore conflict is inherent in increased interdependence.
- Role conflict, role compatibility and ambiguity arise from poor role definition on the part of managers.
- Inequitable treatment, real or perceived, leads to tension and conflict, and people will seek to restore equity in their favour.
- Violation of territory, which is 'owned' and familiar to people.
- External environmental change can affect the organisation and threaten people in the organisation. For example: loss of customers, new technology, increased competition all threaten security and jobs.

10

Learning activity 10.2

Provide examples of positive and negative conflict from your own experience within your own organisation.

Feedback on page 126

Now that you have completed learning activity 10.2 above, please attempt self-assessment question 10.2 below.

Self-assessment question 10.2

Consider ways that conflict can be used in a positive way in the wider supply chain situation within which your organisation operates.

Feedback on page 126

10.3 Working together within the team

Before you commence your reading of this section of the session, please take a little time to reflect on how you approach and manage conflict in your working activities.

Learning activity 10.3

In general, how do you manage conflict within a team in the workplace? How well does it work, in general?

Feedback on page 126

Mullins (2005) suggests that managers can focus on a number of strategies for managing conflict within the organisation and within teams:

- Clarification of goals and objectives avoids misunderstandings and provides a clear common focus for all.
- Resource distribution to be clearly justified so that people understand why and how resources have been allocated throughout the organisation.
- HRM policies and procedures which are fair and equitable. Clear job analysis, recruitment, selection, rewards and punishments, help to create a level playing field for all staff.
- Non-monetary rewards can be emphasised through challenges, delegation and empowerment, and so on.
- Development and training in group process skills, such as communication, problem solving, and so on.
- Group activities and careful team selection reduces role/style conflicts.
- Leadership and management to be more participative and supportive. Demonstration of respect, trust, developing people, and so on.
- Creating appropriate infrastructure processes to reduce unnecessary bureaucracy.
- A system approach which encompasses the social and psychological aspects of work as well as the structural aspects.

Self-assessment question 10.3

Distinguish between conflict resolution and conflict management.

Feedback on page 126

Revision question

Now try the revision question for this session on page 298.

Summary

This session has briefly brought together some of the areas we have explored in previous sessions on good leadership and management.

Conflict often arises from poor management practice and self-evidently can be managed and solved through good management practice.

Suggested further reading

Conflict and how to manage it successfully is dealt with in Mullins (2005) in the section on Improving Organisational Performance.

Feedback on learning activities and self-assessment questions

Feedback on learning activity 10.1

A variety of answers are possible depending on situation and cultural context of the organisation. Some examples are suggested below for you to consider and reflect upon.

The unitary perspective is very prevalent in public sector organisations, where a common concept of stable public service underpins the culture of the organisation. Thus communication and consultation are emphasised, and effort is made to minimise conflict. It is interesting that when radical change is required, unitary organisations find it very difficult to implement because of the desire to minimise conflicts and maintain harmony.

The pluralist perspective is more prevalent in private sector commercial organisations, which have diverse functions and are organised departmentally or have a wide geographical spread. Diversity will always lead to conflict because there are a range of interests which are competing with each other. For example, marketing and sales departments are often violently in conflict with the operational departments, or research and development is at odds with the finance department. Private sector organisations can live with this conflict as long as leadership is clear and decisive, and does not permit conflicts and disagreements to become dysfunctional.

The radical perspective often occurs in fast-moving business environments, where change is rapid, constant and driven by a range of external environmental dynamics. The radical organisation encourages debate, divergence and constructive conflict as the only way to develop creativity and innovation, which is the key to success and survival.

Feedback on self-assessment question 10.1

Positives:

- Better ideas from conflict (debates, disputes)
- Seeking new approaches to resolve the conflict
- Resolution of long-standing issues
- Clarification of individual views through arguments
- A stimulus to creativity and innovation
- Testing capacity of people through the pressures and dynamics that are created.

Negatives:

- People can be defeated and demeaned
- Differences can be polarised between members
- Mistrust and suspicion can develop
- Focus on narrow self-interest to the detriment of the organisation
- Resistance rather than teamwork
- High staff turnover, absenteeism and reduced productivity.

Feedback on learning activity 10.2

A contextualised list of specific examples based on the lists in the feedback to self-assessment question 10.1. Ask yourself if positive and negative conflict means different things depending on whether your organisation has a unitary, pluralist or radical view on conflict.

Feedback on self-assessment question 10.2

Positives through challenging suppliers:

- Using power, leverage and negotiation to get creative responses from the supply chain.
- Build dispute resolution methods into contracts.
- Resolution of long-standing issues through dispute resolution.
- Clarification of individual views through negotiation.
- A stimulus to creativity and innovation.
- Testing capacity of people through the pressures and dynamics that are created, by cost driving, waste elimination and so on.

Feedback on learning activity 10.3

No correct answer, but honest reflection is needed.

Do you have a clear and consistent style of dealing with conflict? Do you reflect on how well your style works?

Feedback on self-assessment question 10.3

Conflict resolution is the process of resolving a dispute or a conflict. Successful conflict resolution occurs by providing each side's needs, and adequately addressing their interests so that they are each satisfied with the outcome. Conflict resolution aims to end conflicts before they start or lead to physical fighting.

Conflict resolution usually involves two or more groups with opposing views regarding specific issues, and another group or individual who is considered to be neutral in their opinion on the subject. This last bit though is quite often not entirely demanded if the 'outside' group is well respected by all opposing parties. Resolution methods can include conciliation, mediation, arbitration or litigation.

These methods all require third-party intervention. A resolution method which is direct between the parties with opposing views is negotiation.

Negotiation can be the 'traditional' model of hard bargaining where the interests of a group far outweigh the working relationships concerned. The 'principled' negotiation model is where both the interests and the working relationships concerned are viewed as important.

It may be possible to avoid conflict without actually resolving the underlying dispute, by getting the parties to recognise that they disagree but that no further action needs to be taken at that time. In a few cases, such as in a democracy, it may even be desirable that they disagree, thus exposing the issues to others who need to consider it for themselves: in this case the parties might agree to disagree.

It is also possible to manage a conflict without resolution, in forms other than avoidance.

Conflict management refers to the long-term management of intractable conflicts, addressing the variety of ways by which people handle grievances – clashes of right and wrong. If left unchecked conflicts can become so intractable that a variety of phenomena can manifest themselves. Some of these can develop into situations which can soon get out of control. Which of these diverse forms of conflict management will be used in any given case is predicted and explained by the social structure – or social geometry – of the case. Refer to the guidelines set out by Mullins in section 10.3 as a way to set some systematic strategies in place which provide a system which managers can adopt to manage conflicts.

Conflict management is not the same as 'conflict resolution', since the latter refers to resolving the dispute to the approval of one or both parties, whereas conflict management concerns an ongoing process that may never have a resolution. For example, gossip and feuds are methods of conflict management, but neither entails resolution.

Study session 11

People and diversity: virtue out of necessity

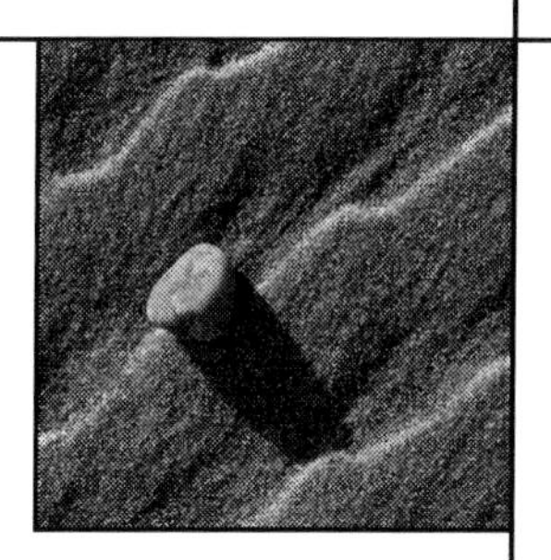

Organisations exist primarily to serve people's needs, so can we organise our arrangements to capture the diversity of people and our customer needs?

Introduction

Diversity was considered briefly in study session 9. This session looks in more detail at diversity issues in the working environment. Diversity is considered important in western workplaces, and is bounded by a legal framework which places duties and obligations on managers to promote and sustain a diversified working environment.

Session learning objectives

After completing this session you should be able to:

11.1 Define what is meant by the term 'equality and diversity'.
11.2 Assess the benefits of diversity to a high-performance culture and evaluate the advantages and disadvantages.
11.3 Explain what is meant by the term 'equal opportunities' and describe the issues associated with discrimination.
11.4 Identify potential areas of discrimination in the workplace and the regulatory framework to protect against it (including gender, race, religion, disability and age).
11.5 Describe proactive measures required to promote equality and diversity in the workplace.
11.6 Outline the potential consequences of failing to pursue a proactive approach to equality and diversity (eg cultural impact, disaffected staff, reputational damage, potential lawsuits and ethical issues).

Unit content coverage

This study session covers the following topics from the official CIPS unit content document.

Learning objectives

3.3 Critically assess diversity issues relating to the success of people and propose approaches to managing them.

- What is meant by the term 'equality and diversity' DIFF'S
- The benefits of diversity to a high-performance culture looking at the advantages and disadvantages
- What is meant by the term equal opportunities, and the issues associated with discrimination
- Potential areas of discrimination in the workplace and the regulatory framework to protect against it (including gender, race, religion, disability and age)

11

- Proactive measures required to promote equality and diversity in the workplace
- Potential consequences of failing to pursue a proactive approach to equality and diversity (for example cultural impact, disaffected staff, reputational damage, potential lawsuits, and ethical issues)

Prior knowledge

Study sessions 8 to 10.

Resources

You will need access to the internet in order to complete this study session.

Timing

You should set aside about 6 hours to read and complete this session, including learning activities, self-assessment questions, the suggested further reading (if any) from the essential textbook for this unit and the revision question.

11.1 Definitions of 'equality and diversity'

Mullins (2005) defines **diversity** as 'visible and non-visible differences which will include sex, age, background, race, disability, personality and work-style'.

To quote from http://en.wikipedia.org (2006),

> 'Amongst humans, particularly in a social context, the term diversity refers to the presence in one population of a (wide) variety of
>
> - *cultures*
> - *ethnic groups*
> - *physical features*, especially if they are recognised by members of that population to constitute characteristics of a *race*
> - *socio-economic backgrounds*
> - *opinions*
> - *religious beliefs*
> - *sexuality*
> - *gender identity*.'

Learning activity 11.1

Organisations by law have to have an 'equality and diversity' policy. Find a copy of your organisation's policy and compare to another organisation

(continued on next page)

Learning activity 11.1 *(continued)*

in your industry sector. Look for similarities and differences between the policies that you find in your research.

Feedback on page 138

Now you have considered your own organisation, seek out information from the government websites.

Self-assessment question 11.1

Visit http://www.dti.gov.uk/er/equality/ and research the legal considerations which cover equality and diversity issues in the UK and Europe. For non-European students, please seek out comparable information from your own country.

Feedback on page 139

11.2 Benefits of diversity: advantages and disadvantages

Learning activity 11.2

What do you feel are the general advantages of having 'diversity and equality' as prominent objectives for organisations?

Feedback on page 139

Wikipedia: http://www.wikipedia.com (2006) presents the case for business benefits for diversity. Their website explains that, in a business context, diversity is approached as a strategy for improving employee retention and increasing consumer confidence. The business case for diversity is that, in a global and diverse marketplace, a company whose makeup reflects the makeup of the marketplace it serves is better equipped to succeed in that marketplace than a company whose makeup is homogenous. Another part of the business case is how well a company makes use of its diversity. This is often referred to as inclusion. If a company is diverse in makeup, but all the decision makers are of one primary group, diversity does not add much value. Consultants and trainers in this field often regard the social consequences of diversity as secondary; their primary focus is to enable the company to function in a heterogeneous or global economy. Companies with diversity initiatives are usually national or international, or comprise large groups of workers from different backgrounds.

Mullins (2005) suggests that, in the changing modern business environment, 'Managers require skills that facilitate achievements through working with colleagues rather than dictating to subordinates.'

The demographic environment is also changing:

- an ageing workforce
- devolution and regionalisation

- multicultural groups
- religious, cultural and ethnic diversity.

According to Mullins (2005) 'It is not only morally and socially acceptable to treat all people fairly in the workplace, legislation insists that managers do so.'

Self-assessment question 11.2

What are the advantages and disadvantages of equality and diversity, in the specific context of your own organisation?

Feedback on page 139

11.3 Equal opportunities and discrimination

Visit the website of the Equal Opportunities Commission to find out more about the work of the Commission in the UK (Equal Opportunities Commission: http://www.eoc.org.uk).

The EOC's vision is for a fair society for every woman and man, whatever their age, race, religion, disability or sexual orientation. Among its aims are:

- equal pay and pensions for men and women and a fair benefits system
- fair treatment at work for men and women, and advice when required
- men and women sharing responsibility in the home, with support for those in caring roles
- no stereotypes in jobs, subjects studied, and leisure activities
- equal access to services for men and women
- women and men in positions of power
- an end to domestic violence.

Specialist legal information can be found at Equal Opportunities Commission: http://www.eoc-law.org.uk.

The Equal Opportunities Commission is an independent, public body, funded mainly by the government and responsible to the Equality Minister.

Learning activity 11.3

Here is a case study scenario for discussion or reflection. Specifically consider whether progress for women into management is improving or is still progressing far too slowly. Justify your views.

Since the mid 1990s, women's representation among executives has doubled and among company directors it has tripled. At the same time there has been an overall increase in women working in management jobs. However, women still comprise less than a quarter of executives and only one in ten

(continued on next page)

Learning activity 11.3 *(continued)*

company directors. The 'glass ceiling', the situation where women can see but not reach higher-level jobs and so are prevented from progressing in their careers, appears still to exist in many organisations.

Why is there still a 'glass ceiling' despite legislation?

Feedback on page 140

You should now tackle self-assessment question 11.3 below.

Self-assessment question 11.3

What is the relevance, if any, of 'equal opportunities' in an international supply chain context?

Feedback on page 140

11.4 Discrimination in the workplace and legal protection

Visit
http://www.direct.gov.uk/Employment/Employees/DiscriminationAtWork
to find out more about discrimination.

What is discrimination?

Discrimination happens when an employer treats one employee less favourably than others. It could mean a female employee being paid less than a male colleague for doing the same job, or a minority ethnic employee being refused the training opportunities offered to white colleagues.

There are some reasons for discrimination that are covered by specific laws ('unlawful discrimination'). If your employer treats you less favourably for one of these reasons, you may be able to take action under these laws. If your employer treats you unfairly for any other reason, this is not unlawful discrimination (to find out what you can do in these situations, see below).

Learning activity 11.4

Research a topical issue in this area, and identify where there are areas of dispute and how this relates to the relevant legal considerations.

Feedback on page 140

There are laws against discrimination in the following areas:

- gender
- marital status

- gender reassignment
- pregnancy
- sexual orientation
- disability
- race
- colour
- ethnic background
- nationality
- religion or belief.

Apart from the discrimination laws mentioned above there are laws which forbid workers from being dismissed or treated less favourably than other workers because of:

- working part time
- working on a fixed-term contract.

You are encouraged to keep abreast of the latest development in employment relations legislation. Visit http://www.dti.gov.uk/er/index.htm which quotes examples of the laws which are relevant in the UK and EU context.

The Employment Relations Directorate (ERD) is working to develop a framework for employers and employees which promotes a skilled and flexible labour market founded on principles of partnership. It deals with relationships between workers and their employers, including individual rights as well as collective arrangements.

The ERD's activities include:

- developing legislation on hours of work, pay entitlement, public holidays, employment, agency standards, individual employment rights, redundancy arrangements, employee consultation, trade unions and collective rights
- negotiating and implementing European employment directives
- research into employment relations and labour markets (EMAR)
- promoting workplace partnership and effective employment relations to improve the quality of working life and the competitiveness of UK organisations
- publishing consultation documents and regulatory guidance.

The website has a hot topics page featuring legislation under consideration and the latest employment issues and developments.

Self-assessment question 11.4

Where would you seek help if you felt you were being discriminated against at work?

Feedback on page 141

11.5 Promoting equality and diversity in the workplace

Visit http://www.oneworkplace.co.uk for more information.

Employers can promote equality of opportunity in the following ways:

- Develop an equal opportunity policy.
- Set an action plan, with targets.
- Provide equality training for all people, including managers, to ensure that they understand the importance of equal opportunities. Provide additional training for staff who recruit, select and train your employees.
- Monitor workforce composition to identify areas for positive action.
- Review recruitment, selection, promotion and training procedures to ensure that you are delivering on your policy.
- Draw up clear and justifiable job criteria, which are demonstrably objective and job related.
- Offer pre-employment training, where appropriate, to prepare potential job applicants. Consider positive action training to help ethnic minority employees apply for jobs in areas where they are under-represented.
- Improve the organisation's image: by encouraging, in recruitment literature, applications from under-represented groups and feature women, ethnic minority staff and people with disabilities, or could you be seen as an employer who is indifferent to these groups?
- Consider flexible working and family-friendly policies, career breaks, providing childcare facilities to help women meet domestic responsibilities and pursue their occupations; and consider making reasonable adjustments for people with disabilities by providing special equipment and assistance. Consider time off for religious holidays and observance.
- Develop links with local community groups, organisations and schools, in order to reach a wider pool of potential applicants.
- Learn from best practice examples and benchmark what you are doing.

Learning activity 11.5

Compare your organisation's approach to some of the initiatives presented above.

Feedback on page 141

You should now tackle self-assessment question 11.5 below.

Self-assessment question 11.5

It is suggested that being proactive is far better than being reactive. Look at the list of policies in section 11.5 above and identify which of the policies mentioned falls into each category.

(continued on next page)

Self-assessment question 11.5 *(continued)*

Compare active ways of promoting equality and diversity in the workplace with more reactive policies.

Feedback on page 141

11.6 Recognising discrimination

How to recognise discrimination

The workplace brings together lots of people who may have nothing in common other than their jobs. Most employees usually seem to get along with one another and put aside any personal and cultural differences. Occasionally, however, employees do not get along as colleagues at work and this spills over into incidents of unacceptable behaviour such as discriminatory treatment or harassment.

Sometimes offensive behaviour is not intentional, or the recipient of the behaviour is seen to be 'over-sensitive'. Occasionally a company may have rules or systems that may lead to discrimination.

Discrimination can be overt, but sometimes it can be hidden and subtle. It can be seen when one group of people is given a particular job or access to training, better terms and conditions of employment, workplace facilities and promotion.

The four main types of discrimination areas within employment are as follows.

Direct discrimination

Treating people less favourably than others on grounds of sexual orientation, religion or belief; for example, a job advertisement that openly says 'no disabled people need apply'. However, in reality discrimination often takes more subtle or indirect forms. Some examples are:

- People with disabilities are automatically rejected without considering how adjustments could easily be arranged to meet their particular need.
- Anyone who does not seem to 'fit in' (for example due to their religion or sexual orientation) is denied his or her rights or the opportunity of employment in the first place.

Indirect discrimination

Applying a provision, criterion or practice which disadvantages people due to race or ethnic origin, age, disability, gender, sexual orientation, religion or belief. An example of indirect discrimination is requiring all people who apply for a certain job to sit a test in a particular language, even though that language is not necessary for the job. Some examples are:

- Particular ethnic groups are given certain tasks and not others.
- Women are only allocated certain jobs, while men take others.
- Stereotyping particular groups and creating an expectation of low performance, which, though unspoken, can permeate an organisation,

creating an atmosphere that can negatively affect someone's work abilities.

Harassment

Unwanted conduct that violates people's dignity or creates an intimidating, hostile, degrading, humiliating or offensive environment on grounds of race or ethnic origin, age, disability, gender, sexual orientation, religion or belief. Some examples are:

- Making derogatory or false remarks about work colleagues.
- Making sexual innuendos about a colleague in his or her presence.
- Making jokes about particular groups of people; for example, religious groups; gays and lesbians or an ethnic group. Everyone is meant to join in the 'joke' including the person who belongs to the particular group being joked about – not joining in will lead to you being isolated and seen to be 'not part of the team'.
- Engaging in physical abuse – slapping, hitting and so on – or threatening violence.

Victimisation

- Treating people less favourably because of something they have done under or in connection with the legislation; for example, made a formal complaint of discrimination or given evidence in a tribunal case.
- Making life difficult for someone who complains about the way they are being treated or discriminating against someone who supports the victim by, for example, not speaking to them or even making them unemployed.

Learning activity 11.6

Find examples from the literature of cases of discrimination which were considered newsworthy. What were the consequences for the company and individuals concerned? How could these consequences have been avoided?

Feedback on page 142

The impact of such discriminatory behaviour, apart from possibly leading to legal action, can sour working relations and may lead to the departure of valued employees or to the loss of business. The victims can suffer personal stress and economic hardship.

All organisations need to look at how they can prevent discrimination from taking place across any of these different grounds.

The responsibility to treat everyone in the workplace fairly extends to both employers and employees. It is possible that individuals acting in a discriminatory way could also be subject to legal action by a victim.

For more information, visit http://www.stop-discrimination.info.

Self-assessment question 11.6

What are the potential consequences of failing to pursue a proactive approach to equality and diversity in the supply chain?

Feedback on page 142

Revision question

Now try the revision question for this session on page 298.

Summary

Diversity and the related areas of equal opportunities and discrimination are highly regulated in most countries in order to protect individual rights. At the same time modern HRM approaches suggest that a positive approach to diversity can bring potential positive business benefits as well.

The legislation on equality and diversity issues is evolving at a very fast pace in most countries. You are encouraged to try and remain up to date by seeking out current sources of information rather than reference to textbooks, which quickly become out of date.

Suggested further reading

Mullins (2005) particularly the chapter on individual differences.

Several websites provide examples of the current legislation on equality, diversity and discrimination, Direct Government: http://www.direct.gov.uk, For Diversity, Against Discrimination: http://www.stop-discrimination.info, One Workplace, Equal Rights: http://www.oneworkplace.co.uk.

Wikipedia: http://en.wikipedia.org/wiki/diversity (2006), diversity in a human context.

Feedback on learning activities and self-assessment questions

Feedback on learning activity 11.1

Ask yourself how detailed the policy is. Does it actively promote and encourage equality and diversity with specific policies and procedures or is it fairly broad-brush, with little detail of how the policy can be implemented?

How diverse is your company workforce?

For an example of a broad-brush approach see http://www.rolls-royce.com/careers/uk/experienced/diversity.jsp.

For a much more detailed policy see
http://www.derby.ac.uk/equalopps/Policy.htm.

Feedback on self-assessment question 11.1

You should have found the section on 'equality and diversity' on the DTI website and looked at the text on 'discrimination at work'.

The website explains that unfair discrimination in employment is wrong, being bad for individuals who are denied jobs and access to vocational training, who suffer victimisation or harassment because of prejudice, and bad for businesses which deny themselves access to the widest pool of talent and do not share in the benefits (such as increased motivation, lower turnover of staff and access to wider markets) that a diverse workforce and effective equality policies can bring.

Relevant legislation includes the Employment Equality (Sexual Orientation) Regulations 2003 and the Employment Equality (Religion or Belief) Regulations 2003. The Regulations implement strands of the European Employment Directive (Council Directive 2000/78/EC).

The section on the Employment Equality Regulations 2003 offers answers to some frequently asked questions about the legislation and where to go for more information and advice.

The Employment Equality (Sexual Orientation) Regulations 2003 have been amended to take account of the introduction of the Civil Partnership Act 2004.

Feedback on learning activity 11.2

Compare your answer to the ideas set out in section 11.2.

Feedback on self-assessment question 11.2

Answers will depend on the specific context of your own organisation, but should include some reference to the following issues.

Advantages:

- Broad base of culture, attitudes and behaviours
- Different talents and experiences
- Opportunity for synergy, creativity and innovation
- Inclusive and widespread range of skills.

Disadvantages:

- Needs a broader range of management skills
- Cultures, attitudes and behaviour can clash, leading to overt conflict, or isolation and polarisation
- Loss of focus of organisational goals in favour of specialist interests

- Divisive and energy sapping with disagreements and misunderstandings.

Feedback on learning activity 11.3

Several key factors account for the continuing low representation of women in management. First, like most other occupations, there is a tendency for some types of management jobs to be associated with either women or men. For example, while women are comparatively well represented in personnel and the public sector, men still predominate in production management and in ICT.

Second, opportunities to work part time are limited, with only 6% of managers and senior officials employed part time. Although it may be difficult to carry out some management functions on a part-time basis, there are still far too few opportunities for flexible working at senior levels in organisations.

Given the increasing levels of stress experienced in the workplace, the EOC believes that flexible working arrangements such as part-time work, job sharing or working from home should be considered more frequently by employers as a way of sharing heavy management responsibilities. Flexible working arrangements can also be used by employers to respond to the increasing demand from parents for more family-friendly work patterns, and to help staff to combine work and personal responsibilities.

Third, the EOC is calling on employers to discourage the long hours culture, which pervades many organisations and means that time spent at work can be valued more highly than what is actually achieved. Those whose family responsibilities restrict the number of hours they can spend in the office are at a particular disadvantage. In fact women in management positions are less likely than men, and women in most other jobs, to have dependent children. Even where women have broken through the glass ceiling into management positions, their pay is often lower than that of men. The gender pay gap for managers and senior officials overall is wider than average and is even wider in some managerial subgroups.

Feedback on self-assessment question 11.3

This would appear to be a non-issue at first sight, but think again:

- The single market in the EU requires equal opportunities for all organisations to compete.
- The single market in the EU requires equal opportunities and free movement of individuals between member states.
- Possible benefits to the organisation of a supply chain that positively assists equal opportunities.

Feedback on learning activity 11.4

Seek information in the quality press about a current issue which is relevant to discrimination.

Feedback on self-assessment question 11.4

The Advisory, Conciliation and Arbitration Service (ACAS) offers free, confidential and impartial advice on all employment rights issues.

Your local Citizens Advice Bureau (CAB) can provide free and impartial advice. You can find your local CAB office in the phone book or online.

If you are a member of a trade union, you can get help, advice and support from them.

Feedback on learning activity 11.5

A broad range of policies shows evidence of a commitment to equality and diversity, and an anti-discrimination attitude in the organisation.

Feedback on self-assessment question 11.5

This feedback is set out in table 11.1.

Table 11.1

Employers can promote equality of opportunity in the following ways:	Active or reactive policy (A/R)
Develop an equal opportunity policy.	A
Set an action plan, with targets.	A
Provide equality training for all people, including managers, to ensure that they understand the importance of equal opportunities. Provide additional training for staff who recruit, select and train their employees.	R
Monitor workforce composition to identify areas for positive action.	R
Review recruitment, selection, promotion and training procedures to ensure that they are delivering on their policy.	R
Draw up clear and justifiable job criteria, which are demonstrably objective and job related.	A
Offer pre-employment training, where appropriate, to prepare potential job applicants. Consider positive action training to help ethnic minority employees apply for jobs in areas where they are under-represented.	R
Improve the organisation's image: by encouraging, in recruitment literature, applications from under-represented groups and feature women, ethnic minority staff and people with disabilities, or could they be seen as an employer who is indifferent to these groups?	R
Consider flexible working and family-friendly policies, career breaks, providing childcare facilities to help women meet domestic responsibilities and pursue their occupations; and consider making reasonable adjustments for people with disabilities by providing special equipment and assistance. Consider time off for religious holidays and observance.	R

(continued on next page)

Table 11.1 *(continued)*

Employers can promote equality of opportunity in the following ways:	Active or reactive policy (A/R)
Develop links with local community groups, organisations and schools, in order to reach a wider pool of potential applicants.	A
Learn from best practice examples and benchmark what you are doing.	R

Feedback on learning activity 11.6

Try and analyse the case in terms of some of the ideas introduced in section 11.6.

Visit http://breakingnews.iol.ie/news/story.asp?j=180074478&p=y8xx75y84 for a good example of the scale of the discrimination issues involved.

Feedback on self-assessment question 11.6

- Legal
- Ethical
- Damage to reputation
- Can create a consumer backlash
- Can create a backlash from the supply market.

There are a number of interesting articles on discrimination issues in *Supply Management* journal. For a good example visit http://www.supplymanagement.com/edit/archiveitem.asp?id=14506.

Study session 12
Developing people

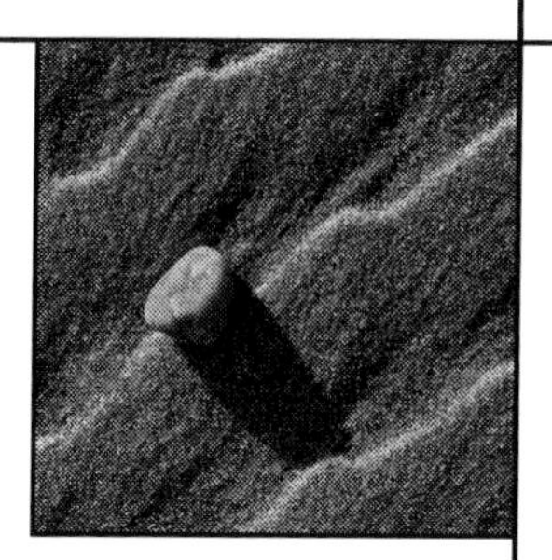

'If you think training is expensive, try ignorance.'
(attributed to both Andy McIntyre and Derek Bok)

Introduction

Lysons and Brewer (2003) argue that training and development are how organisations attempt to maintain the competence and flexibility of their people. This session considers a variety of ways that this can be done in the modern work environment.

Session learning objectives

After completing this session you should be able to:

12.1 Explain why it is important to develop people in the workplace.
12.2 Assess the aims and describe the basic process of training needs analysis (TNA) and express the need for independent assessment.
12.3 Identify a range of skills and competencies for purchasing and supply that can be reliably assessed and measured.
12.4 Contrast 'training' and 'development' and identify a range of training and development initiatives.
12.5 Describe what is meant by 'blended learning' and 'action learning'.

Unit content coverage

This study session covers the following topics from the official CIPS unit content document.

Learning objectives

3.4 Determine and justify ways of developing people and increasing their productivity and effectiveness.
- Why it is important to develop people in the workplace
- The purpose of training needs analysis
- The basic process of TNA and the need for independent assessment
- A range of skills and competencies for purchasing and supply that can be reliably assessed and measured
- Contrast between training and development
- A range of training and development initiatives
- What is meant by blended-learning and action-learning

Prior knowledge

Study sessions 8 to 11.

Resources

In order to complete this study session you will need internet access.

Timing

You should set aside about 6 hours to read and complete this session, including learning activities, self-assessment questions, the suggested further reading (if any) from the essential textbook for this unit and the revision question.

12.1 The importance of people development

Learning activity 12.1

Evaluate and compare the following statements:

> 'People are a cost to the organisation and this cost should be kept as low as possible.'

> 'People are an asset of the organisation which can be enhanced through spending money on training and development.'

Justify which of these statements you would support.

Feedback on page 157

Mullins (2005) suggests that 'Learning means change, but of a relatively permanent kind. Learning involves not only knowledge and skills but also attitudes and behaviour.'

A positive view suggests that it is important to invest in people because they are the most effective way of differentiating one organisation from another (see figure 12.1 for a brief example).

Figure 12.1: People = Assets

> The main concept behind 'People = Assets' is:
>
> Without people, we could not deliver service.
>
> Without people we could not delight our customers.
>
> Without people, we could not figure out how to turn 'technology' into 'solutions'.
>
> So we must treat them and develop them accordingly like the important asset that they are.

Source: http://www.vita.virginia.gov/

Mullins (2005) cites a declaration on learning from eight distinguished scholars in the UK, which highlighted learning as a key process for individuals, organisations and society as a whole for the twenty-first century.

Learning – the central issues:

- Learning as a 'powerful, engaging and rewarding aspect' of experience
- How to capitalise on the learning and abilities of people
- Leadership is needed to harness the knowledge and experience of people, so that they learn more effectively.

Table 12.2 lists the benefits of learning.

Table 12.2 The benefits of learning

Individuals	Organisations	Society
Developing potential Learning *how* to learn Ability to change	Developing capacity Achieving goals effectively Clear purpose, vision, and so on	Survival and growth Cohesion and consensus Underpinning of democratic choices
Learning for life Learning is formal and informal	Learning produces solutions Balances short- and long-term perspectives	Creation of a fulfilled society

Source: Burgoyne et al (1999)

Self-assessment question 12.1

Visit the website http://www.pfizer.co.uk and find and read the section 'Pfizer – a great place to work'.

What aspects of the working environment of its organisation does Pfizer emphasise, and how does this relate to the development of people?

Feedback on page 158

12.2 Training needs analysis

As a manager or team leader you will have to consider and assess the training needs of your team and the contribution that training will have on the performance of the organisation.

People within your team will also have their own thoughts about their own future goals and how they would like to develop as individuals.

Training needs analysis provides the opportunity of getting the best for both parties and can have an immediate impact on the services you offer your customers.

Training needs analysis helps you take a step back and look at the needs of you, your team and your organisation and helps you plan training and development in all areas. No matter what size your organisation, such an analysis is relevant and important.

If you are unsure about the exact nature of your training needs, a training needs analysis (TNA) will help identify the precise areas where training is needed. As well as identifying your training requirements, a TNA has the added benefit of ensuring that training and development initiatives are aligned with your organisational goals and culture, thus creating a training solution that is specific to your organisation.

Many needs assessments are available for use in different employment contexts. A systematic approach should be followed to ensure the analysis is robust and thorough.

- *Context analysis*. An analysis of the business needs and organisational context within which training will take place. The important questions being answered by this analysis are who decides that training should be conducted, why a training programme is seen as the recommended solution to a business problem, what the history of the organisation has been with regard to employee training and other management interventions.
- *User analysis*. Considers the potential participants and instructors involved in the process. The important questions being answered by this analysis are who will receive the training and their level of existing knowledge on the subject, what is their preferred learning style, and who will conduct the training.
- *Work analysis*. This is an analysis of the job and the requirements for performing the work. Also known as a task analysis or job analysis, this analysis seeks to specify the main duties and skill level required. This helps ensure that the training will include relevant links to the content of the job.
- *Content analysis*. This analysis answers questions about what knowledge or information is used on this job. This information comes from manuals, documents or regulations. It is important that the content of the training does not conflict or contradict job requirements. An experienced worker can assist in determining the appropriate content.
- *Training suitability analysis*. Analysis of whether training is the desired solution. Training is one of several solutions to employment problems. However, it may not always be the best solution. It is important to determine if training will be effective in its usage.
- *Cost–benefit analysis*. Analysis of the payback of training. Effective training results in a return of value to the organisation that is greater than the initial investment to produce or administer the training.

Visit http://www.businessballs.com for an MS Excel example of a training needs analysis template, which shows how a training needs analysis can be completed for people in the organisation.

Learning activity 12.2

Visit the website http://www.knowledgepool.com and search for 'training needs analysis. You can read a number of interesting case studies on the effectiveness of training in a variety of well-known UK organisations.

(continued on next page)

Learning activity 12.2 *(continued)*

Relate the examples from the case studies to a structured model of how to conduct and implement a training needs analysis. The list in section 12.2 above should provide some guidance.

Feedback on page 158

Now that you have read the case studies you should attempt the following question.

Self-assessment question 12.2

Research the formal training policy of your own organisation. Does it appear to follow a clearly structured approach? How could the policy be improved?

Feedback on page 159

12.3 Skills and competencies for purchasing and supply

Competencies

Competencies describe the knowledge and skills that people at various roles and levels require. They can thus provide a starting point for determining development needs and for designing programmes. Qualifications such as National Vocational Qualifications (NVQs) have been developed using this framework, which requires evidence of competence at work.

Although competencies have value in pinning down what is required for particular jobs, they have been criticised for being overly rigid and prescriptive. Although things are improving, some are still written in bureaucratic language, which gets in the way of their comprehension and acceptance.

During 2005 CIPS has been involved in a programme of developing best practice within supply chain management, of which purchasing and supply is an inherent part. These standards are innovative, creative and reflect 'good practice' within purchasing and supply. The standards were developed with input from a variety of key stakeholders, including a number of senior practitioners, employers, educationalists and other professional bodies. These standards are government funded and part of an initiative by the Department for Education and Skills (DfES) to improve professional standards of practice within the workplace. CIPS is keen to align with these standards and to promote 'good practice' alongside the standards in the future. A copy of these standards can be downloaded from http://www.cips.org/Page.asp?CatID=33&PageID=912.

In a Guidance Note to the supply chain management standards, CIPS has identified the broad areas of skills and competencies for purchasing and supply as follows:

- Strategic level: units coded with an 'S', for example, Unit S1 Develop a supply chain strategy for the organisation. These units are designed for supply chain practitioners who are senior managers or senior specialists, providing strategic leadership roles within the supply chain.

- Management level: units coded with an 'M', for example, Unit M1 Develop operational relationships within the supply chain. These units are designed for supply chain practitioners who are managers or specialists, providing management roles within the supply chain.
- Technical level: units coded with a 'T', for example, Unit T1 Maintain operational relationships within the supply chain. These units are designed for supply chain practitioners who provide mainly technical or support roles within the supply chain.
- Key skills and core skills, coded 'K': the key skills and core skills that are relevant to the supply chain management units have been identified, and this information is available in a separate document.

Broad areas of skills and competencies are listed in table 12.3.

Table 12.3 National occupational standards for supply chain management, July 2005

Strategic skills	Management skills	Technical skills
• Develop a supply chain strategy for the organisation	• Develop operational relationships within the supply chain	• Maintain operational relationships within the supply chain
• Establish strategic relationships within the supply chain	• Evaluate information on the supply chain	• Analyse information on the supply chain
• Improve the performance of the supply chain	• Propose improvements to the supply chain	• Apply improvements to the supply chain
• Commission projects to develop the supply chain	• Introduce improvements to the supply chain	• Monitor the achievement of project tasks
• Plan the flow of supplies through the supply chain	• Plan projects to develop the supply chain	• Control supplies at storage locations and facilities
• Plan the procurement of supplies	• Manage projects to develop the supply chain	• Complete export procedures and requirements
• Plan the storage of supplies in the supply chain	• Negotiate for supplies	• Complete import procedures and requirements
• Plan the distribution of supplies	• Contract with other organisations	• Administer contracts
• Plan the transportation of supplies	• Review the outcomes of contracts	• Analyse information on the procurement of supplies in the supply chain
• Plan the export and import of supplies	• Evaluate information on the procurement of supplies in the supply chain	• Verify the capability of suppliers to meet supply specifications
	• Select suppliers for the supply chain	• Analyse the performance of suppliers
	• Produce specifications for supplies	• Identify potential suppliers for the supply chain
	• Evaluate the capability of suppliers to meet supply specifications	• Place orders with suppliers
	• Schedule and approve the placing of orders	• Monitor and progress the delivery of orders
	• Evaluate the performance of suppliers	
	• Schedule the flow of supplies in the supply chain	
	• Specify the requirements for the storage of supplies	

(continued on next page)

Table 12.3 *(continued)*

Strategic skills	Management skills	Technical skills
	• Select locations and facilities for storing supplies • Evaluate information on the storage of supplies • Specify the requirements for the distribution of supplies • Select distribution methods for supplies • Schedule the distribution of supplies • Select methods to receive returned supplies • Select transportation methods for supplies • Schedule the transportation of supplies • Select methods for exporting supplies • Select methods for importing supplies	• Monitor the flow of supplies in the supply chain • Obtain information on storage locations and facilities • Obtain information on distribution requirements • Monitor the distribution of supplies • Monitor the flow of returned supplies • Monitor the transportation of supplies • Contribute to operational relationships within the supply chain • Obtain information on the supply chain

Learning activity 12.3

Consider table 12.4, the specification for Unit S1 Develop a supply chain strategy for the organisation, as part of the *National occupational standards for supply chain management, July 2005*. This module concentrates on strategic skills required.

Table 12.4 Specification for Unit S1

Performance requirements		
Outcomes		**Achievement criteria**
1	Identify the organisation's objectives and its strategies for achieving them	a) colleagues are consulted on the organisation's objectives and strategies
2	Review the current supply chain strategy and how it helps to deliver other organisational strategies	b) relevant evaluations are undertaken
		c) results of the evaluations are considered
		d) views of all relevant colleagues and stakeholders are obtained
3	Review all factors that are relevant to the development of the supply chain strategy	e) market, economic, social and political environments are taken into account
		f) realistic forecasts of conditions and trends are produced
4	Explore opportunities that will add value to the organisation	g) opportunities are identified and fully investigated
		h) benefits and risks are fully evaluated

(continued on next page)

12

Learning activity 12.3 *(continued)*

Performance requirements

Outcomes	**Achievement criteria**
5 Establish a supply chain strategy that will make the organisation more effective in achieving its objectives	i) improvements to the supply chain are clearly identified
	j) supply chain strategy is feasible and capable of being implemented by the organisation
	k) organisational strategic objectives can be achieved more effectively
6 Identify obstacles to the development of the supply chain strategy and explore methods for overcoming them	l) obstacles are clearly identified as soon as possible
	m) methods for overcoming obstacles are explored with all relevant people
7 Provide a rationale for the supply chain strategy	n) stakeholders are provided with sufficient information to understand the reasoning behind the supply chain strategy
	o) supply chain strategy can be promoted and defended by others
8 Gain the commitment of stakeholders and colleagues to implement the supply chain strategy	p) stakeholders and colleagues are consulted on their views
	q) presentations are made to all relevant stakeholders and colleagues
9 Implement appropriate communication methods to provide the organisation with information on the supply chain strategy	r) communication methods within the organisation are used effectively
	s) all relevant people are kept informed of developments in the supply chain strategy

How would you measure the achievements of these skills?

Feedback on page 160

Now that you have some appreciation of the complexity of analysis, and the degree of detail that is followed in the example in learning activity 12.3 above, attempt self-assessment question 12.3 below.

Self-assessment question 12.3

How are the skills and competencies which are required by purchasing and supply professionals changing in the modern business environment?

Feedback on page 160

12.4 The meaning of 'training' and 'development' and a range of possible initiatives

A useful background and overview on the broad ideas that need to be considered can be found on the website of the Chartered Institute of

Personnel and Development (http://www.cipd.co.uk). Among other useful information the website contains a fact sheet entitled 'Learning and development: an overview'. You may find it useful to look at it now.

The fact sheet gives introductory guidance, examining the development and use of the terms 'learning' and 'development' and providing brief definitions and issues to consider for the various techniques used.

'Learning', 'development' and 'training' are terms that are often used interchangeably, which leads to some confusion, especially as the way the terms are used has changed over the years. The fact sheet focuses on the terms 'learning' and 'development'. Managers in small and medium-sized organisations have to assume responsibility for developing their employees, and in larger organisations managers are increasingly responsible for developing staff. They need to understand the terms and techniques used, not least to help them in discussions with their colleagues who are involved full time in learning and development, and training.

According to the CIPD the fact sheet is aimed mainly at managers who are not specialists in the area of learning, development and training, and who may need help in understanding the various terms and techniques. However, students and professionals who need to refresh themselves quickly may also find it useful. It defines 'learning' and 'training', then provides brief definitions of the various techniques used and issues to consider.

Learning activity 12.4

Which is your preferred definition of:

- learning
- training
- development

and why?

Feedback on page 161

Definitions of learning

Since the mid 1990s, there has been a gradual shift in the techniques and language used to describe the steps taken by employers to help employees perform their jobs more effectively. Until the closing years of the last century, 'training' would have been the word most frequently employed, whether to describe a job ('training manager') or a development technique (which would probably have been a classroom-based event). Now 'learning', often linked with 'development', is the key term.

In many respects there is little distinction to be made between the terms 'training' and 'development'. CIPD's definition of learning is 'a self-directed, work-based process leading to increased adaptive capacity'. In this respect the process is 'training', the effect – 'increased adaptive capacity' – is 'development' (Sloman 2005). In other words, an environment exists where individuals 'learn to learn' and possess the capabilities that enable them to do so to help their employers to build and retain competitive advantage. Various authors have somewhat different definitions, but what they all have in common is that they link the enhancement of the performance of individuals with that of organisations.

Reynolds (2004) has demonstrated that, in our rapidly changing and increasingly knowledge-based economy, competitive advantage is built where individuals actively seek to acquire the knowledge and skills that promote the organisation's objectives. Organisations are learning environments, and employment in them is (or should be) a continuous learning experience. Of course learning takes place all the time, through experience, though not all such learning is positive. The point about organisational learning and development is that it should be structured to enhance benefits for individuals and their employers.

The shift from training to learning

Training is defined by CIPD as 'an instructor-led and content-based intervention leading to desired changes in behaviour' Sloman (2005), and which, unless it is 'on-the-job' training, involves time away from the workplace in a classroom or equivalent. In some contexts it implies teaching specified skills by practice. Until relatively recently, the implicit assumption was that most, if not all, development of employees would be of this nature.

Clearly, training is one way of making learning happen, but there is no one route to learning. Different people have different learning preferences. For example, some may prefer to read books, others to attend courses. Most learn best from experience. All this has become increasingly recognised, with the result that there is now a much greater variety of what might be called 'learning interventions' than there was in the past. (An 'intervention' can be defined as any event that is deliberately undertaken to assist learning to take place.) CIPD characterises 'the shift from training to learning … as the progressive movement from the delivery of courses to the development of learning capabilities as a people development strategy' Sloman (2005).

This makes the job of the developer more complex and challenging than it was, but it also provides the possibility of better outcomes. CIPD advises that:

> 'because so much learning occurs directly through work, managers should aim to include these responsibilities within their normal repertoire of behaviours, rather than view them as separate learning activities. For that reason they may be viewed as leadership practices that promote learning rather than learning practices that enhance specific knowledge and skills' (Sloman 2005).

Common training terms and initiatives

Classroom training is one of the most used forms of development. It may involve only people from one employer, for example to train them in new equipment or specific procedures, or it might be held externally with people from other organisations. While this form of training may be among the most used forms of development, surveys have shown that it is one of the least popular with learners – on-the-job training is the most popular. This is not to say that there is no place for classroom training, but it may be more effective linked with the other forms of development activities. Managers may be tempted to think that an obvious solution to an individual's development needs is to send him or her on a course, but they also need to consider other options.

If the decision is to go for classroom training, consideration needs to be given as to whether courses should be internal or external. Internal courses will give the opportunity to focus on organisation-specific problems, increasing the possibility of learning transfer, while courses involving people from other organisations may help individuals see things in a different context and learn from others who do things differently.

Training courses are expensive and organisations need to ensure that they have worked. Attempts are therefore made to evaluate them: in other words, to assess their effectiveness. Evaluation is not easy. It is relatively simple, by means of the traditional 'happy sheet' issued at the end of courses, to assess, for example, what learners thought of the trainer, but this does not measure whether the learners returned to do their jobs better, still less the training's impact on the learners' departments or on the organisation as a whole. The further down the line one goes, the more difficult evaluation becomes. Despite the difficulties, it is increasingly accepted that at least a sample of training needs to be evaluated. Setting learning objectives helps, as does involving line managers before and after the training has taken place, but the process can be complex, and is far from an exact science.

Management education and training refers to tutor-led training or education as a part of management development. There are formal training courses of various kinds, from very specific courses on technical aspects of jobs to courses on wider management skills. The term also covers education, which might range from courses for (perhaps prospective) junior managers or supervisors at NVQ level 3 held at further education colleges to Master of Business Administration (MBA) degrees held at universities. Management education and training need to be linked with other means of development to maximise success. Usually management education will involve students in activities based on solving problems at work to maximise learning. However, there is continuing criticism that courses like MBAs are over-academic and not sufficiently based in the real world.

On-the-job training (OJT) is an activity undertaken at the workplace that is designed to improve an individual's skills or knowledge. It has the following characteristics:

- being delivered on a one-to-one basis and taking place at the trainee's place of work;
- requiring time to take place, including potential periods when there is little or no useful output of products or services;
- being a specified, planned and structured activity.

OJT is the most popular method of learning, perhaps because it is seen to be immediately relevant, but on-the-job trainers themselves (who may be work colleagues or line managers) need to be trained as trainers; otherwise, the learning might be less effective than it could be and bad practice may be passed on. Trainees also need to be able to practise what they have learned immediately or the learning may be forgotten. And too much instruction should not be given at once or there may be 'information overload'. Finally, feedback needs to be given by the trainer to encourage the trainee.

Outdoor training offers teambuilding, problem-solving or leadership exercises, usually in the open air and in different or challenging circumstances. Although it is increasingly called 'outdoor development', it is included here because exercises and the reviews which should follow them are very much instructor led, and indeed preparation for and follow-up of the outdoor elements may take place in a classroom. Taking people out of their normal environments and comfort zones can be rewarding, but some may feel uncomfortable. The emphasis should not be too much on physical challenge and exercises should be seen to relate back to the work environment.

Self-assessment question 12.4

What methods are used to provide training and development in your own organisation? What else could be done?

Feedback on page 161

12.5 Different 'learning' approaches

Action learning

Mullins (2005) defines **action learning** as:

> 'an approach to management development which involves a small self-selecting team undertaking a practical, real-life and organisational-based project. The emphasis is on learning by doing with advice and support from tutors and other course members.'

Learning activity 12.5

Reflect on the outcomes of your learning styles questionnaire, completed in study session 8. Consider how different ways of learning can be suitable for different learning styles.

Feedback on page 161

While learning by doing has practical application and is popular with participants, there are some challenges involved. Crainer (1998), cited in Mullins (2005), argues that action learning demands flexibility and fluidity which can be a daunting prospect to participants. It is impossible at the beginning to precisely identify what outcomes will emerge for each of the participants, nor to relate benefits to improved bottom-line results.

CIPD proposes action learning as an approach to learning based on individuals working on real problems that are capable of having action taken on them. The individual needs to be able to identify the problem, own it and identify steps to resolve it. Colleagues work in groups or 'sets', and learn primarily by questioning their own and others' proposed actions, identifying courses of further action and a timescale. It has the substantial benefit of helping to solve real problems and can make a major contribution to freeing up inflexible or traditional thinking. But outcomes can be threatening if radical solutions emerge, so the process needs top-level management support.

Bite-sized learning

It is increasingly recognised that people absorb information better if it is provided in small chunks of perhaps an hour or two and in varying formats, so the traditional lengthy training course (for example) is giving way to shorter sessions, perhaps linked with other techniques such as e-learning. This is a positive and common-sense development, but makes planning and organising learning events more complex.

Career management and development

Most organisations expect employees to take responsibility for their own careers, but recognise that they need support for this which can be provided through a variety of measures, including coaching, counselling and mentoring, and management development.

Coaching, counselling and mentoring

Coaching, counselling and mentoring are one-to-one methods offering personally tailored reflection and discussion in confidence between a manager and another individual about the latter's development. The three terms are often used almost interchangeably, but there are differences.

- **Coaching** is about improving skills and performance, usually for the current job, but also to support career transitions. Usually coaches are hired from outside the organisation, but increasingly some organisations expect all line managers to operate as coaches.
- Coaching's focus on skills distinguishes it from **counselling**, which is about helping people with personal concerns such as motivation and self-confidence.
- **Mentors** usually come from inside the organisation. Typically they will be experienced managers, but for senior managers, outside mentors may sometimes be hired. This blurs the difference between coaching and mentoring, but the differences are usually that mentors have relatively long-term relationships with their junior colleagues and their focus is less on events than is the case in coaching.

Matching the right people as coaches and 'coachees' and mentors and 'mentees' is of key importance, and those managing the programme will need to consider how far gender or age should be a factor; also whether the process should be informal or whether there needs to be a formal agenda with specified learning outcomes.

Continuous professional development

Knowledge changes rapidly and individuals need to keep up to date. Recognising this, professional bodies now require members to show evidence that they are in touch with the latest developments and techniques. Monitoring of members is resource-intensive. For example, some professions require attendance at courses or lectures for continuous professional development (CPD) points but, as every undergraduate knows, being present at a lecture does not imply learning!

Development (or assessment) centres

In development centres, participants take part in a variety of job simulations and tests with observers who assess their performance against predetermined criteria. The data generated is used to diagnose developmental needs. As well as ongoing development, such centres often form part of the selection process. There is a danger that organisations can use such centres to select in their own image and 'clone' candidates. Training of assessors is vital and top management support essential.

Distance learning

The Open University is a very well-known example of a distance learning provider, but there are many others who offer learning materials delivered through the post and (increasingly) in a web-based electronic accessed format. There is thus a growing link with e-learning. One of the main issues with this type of learning is that learner motivation can slip without contact with fellow students and tutors, and tutor support (remote or face to face) is important.

E-learning and blended learning

E-learning is 'learning that is delivered, enabled or mediated using electronic technology for the explicit purpose of training in organisations'. This includes the use of distributed technology products (mainly CD-ROMs – the most popular form of delivery) which do not require the user's computer to be connected to a network, as well as products delivered through the internet or an intranet. E-learning is growing. It provides large populations with the same material, and access is flexible so that people can learn in their own time. Against this, e-learning does not appeal to everyone, and it works better for 'hard' knowledge than for softer skills like communication or leadership. In a 2004 CIPD poll, 81% of respondents agreed that it was more effective when combined with more traditional forms of learning, which emphasises the growing acceptance of what has become known as '**blended learning**'.

Self-assessment question 12.5

Question – contrast the approaches to training in two articles from *Supply Management* magazine which are to be found on the website at http://www.supplymanagement.com/edit/archiveitem.asp?id=5984

(continued on next page)

Self-assessment question 12.5 *(continued)*

(How training built a healthy operation) and
http://www.supplymanagement.com/edit/archiveitem.asp?id=8503f
(Training, the JIT way).

(You will need your CIPS membership number and password to access these web pages.)

Feedback on page 162

Revision question

Now try the revision question for this session on page 298.

Summary

This session has considered the key aspect of developing people in the workplace.

Key learning points are:

- It is important to develop people in the workplace, since the business environment is constantly changing and we need our people to be continually learning.
- Training needs analysis is a useful analytical tool, to determine what the status of our organisation is and what specific training is needed, which can contribute to achievement of organisational goals.
- A rapidly changing range of skills and competencies are required for purchasing and supply, and national standards have made a contribution to setting standards which can be assessed.
- The contrast between 'learning', 'training' and 'development' is evolving and many alternative initiatives are available.
- The growth of 'blended learning' and 'action learning' within the field of management and employee development.

Suggested further reading

A number of texts provide a background to contemporary ideas about learning, training and developing people in the workplace: Burgoyne at al (1999), Sloman (2005) and Reynolds (2004).

A more focused treatment in relation to purchasing and supply can be found in Saunders (1997 and 1988), Cousins (1992), Van Wheele (2005) and Lysons and Brewer (2003).

Feedback on learning activities and self-assessment questions

Feedback on learning activity 12.1

Table 12.1 lists some of the issues which should emerge.

Table 12.1

Cost	Asset
Training is expensive and adds to costs	People interact with other resources and with customers
Increased costs decrease profits	The more they are trained the better they do the work
Managers know what is needed; people provide the labour	More training means more creativity and innovation
Managers can better control a compliant workforce	More learning leads to better performance, motivation and satisfaction

Feedback on self-assessment question 12.1

A variety of tangible and less tangible factors are emphasised, all of which, to a significant degree, depend on the quality of Pfizer's people:

- Integrity in work
- Integrity in the products
- Benefits for customers, staff and the organisation
- Researchers are free to pursue cutting-edge science
- Products and knowledge supports sales and marketing staff
- State-of-the-art technology
- Innovation, creativity and diversity – racial and gender diversity, but also diversity of perspective and thought
- Emphasis on communication and teamwork
- Flexible hours, health and fitness centres, and sports and recreational opportunities strive to meet employees' needs for a balanced life through facilities and services.

Feedback on learning activity 12.2

The sort of model that needs to be developed is provided by seeking detailed assessment about each of the main headings:

- context analysis
- user analysis
- work analysis
- content analysis
- training suitability analysis
- cost–benefit analysis.

The training needs analysis template from http://www.businessballs.com/trainingneedsanalysis.pdf is broken down and scored against the following 21 main competencies:

1. Planning, prioritising and organising tasks and activities, time management, self and team
2. Motivation and leadership of team and individual team members
3. Communication skills, questioning and active listening, building trust, empathy and mutual understanding

4 Performance appraisals planning, conducting and follow-up, for team, and self
5 One-to-one counselling, handling grievances, discipline, helping and enabling others with their challenges
6 Training and developing others, coaching and mentoring, assessing training needs
7 Delegation, identifying and agreeing tasks, measuring, follow-up, management by objectives
8 Effective use of IT and equipment, especially communication, planning and reporting systems
9 Financial and commercial understanding (for example budgets, profit and loss, cash flow, and so on)
10 Managing relationships, inter-department, peers, upwards, obtaining approval for projects, changes and so on
11 Planning and running meetings, effective follow-up
12 Business writing, for example, letters, reports, plans, project plans
13 Recruitment interviewing and selection, and effective induction of new people
14 Administration, reporting performance and financials, monitoring, maintaining and developing reporting systems
15 Creating and giving effective presentations to groups
16 Innovation, creativity, taking initiative, problem solving and decision making
17 Quality awareness and managing, according to quality standards and procedures
18 Employment and HR policy awareness and managing, according to policies (equality, disability, harassment, and so on)
19 Environmental and duty of care awareness and managing according to standards and procedures
20 Customer care and customer service management: external and internal
21 Self-development, self-control, compassion and humanity, seeking responsibility and personal growth.

This analysis is designed to show collective training needs and priorities and also the relative training needs of individuals. For organisational analysis you can use this tool to consolidate and show departmental totals instead of individual names. Replace the sample scores with those from your own group's management skill set assessments. Lowest scores are obviously the training priorities, although consideration needs to be given to the relative importance of the skills. The spreadsheet can be extended right by copying the section to create new sections for other departments, and then to create organisational totals and averages.

Feedback on self-assessment question 12.2

Relate your findings to some of the concepts introduced in this section:

- context analysis
- user analysis
- work analysis
- content analysis
- training suitability analysis
- cost–benefit analysis.

Feedback on learning activity 12.3

See the application guidelines (Key Skills and Core Skills, coded 'K'), listed below. The key skills and core skills that are relevant to the supply chain management units have been identified as follows.

Application of knowledge:

K2) Change management theories, models and practices

K3) Communication methods and procedures

K6) Cost and benefit analysis methods and procedures

K11) Financial analysis methods and procedures

K16) Legal and regulatory requirements

K23) Organisational strategic aims and objectives

K24) Performance measurement and benchmarking theories, models and practices

K26) Presentation theories, models and practices

K29) Quality management theories, models and practices

K30) Risk analysis methods and procedures

K31) Stakeholder management methods and procedures

K33) Supply chain management theories, models and practices

The essential measure of achievement is that people are able to produce evidence that they are able to apply these skills in a practical way in the workplace. Typically, portfolios are assembled by people to show that they actually undertake these tasks and activities competently, and can provide evidence of a sufficient degree of practical application.

Feedback on self-assessment question 12.3

Saunders and Cousins both argue that the changing modern business environment requires new and changing skills from purchasing and supply chain professionals.

Saunders et al (1988) argue that more 'strategic stances of partnerships with suppliers and long-term positioning' by organisations requires changing skills.

Cousins (1992) suggests this has led to 'a higher degree of professionalism in the function'.

Saunders (1997) identifies the following as new strategic general skills which are now needed to a greater degree than ever before:

- communication
- working in groups

- numeracy
- information processing
- information gathering
- problem solving.

Van Wheele (2005) identified four different dimensions to purchasing and supply activities, all of which need competence and skills:

- Technical dimension – functionality, specifications and quality of purchased products
- Commercial dimension – managing relationships with suppliers and the contractual conditions which must be negotiated and maintained
- Logistics dimension – all activities relating to the optimisation of incoming materials from the supplier to when and where they are consumed
- Administrative dimension – relating to efficient order handling, expediting and follow-up and handling of invoices.

Feedback on learning activity 12.4

There are no right answers to this – reflect on the distinctions made by CIPD in the text that follows this learning activity, and see which definition most closely matches your own views.

Feedback on self-assessment question 12.4

You should have considered the broad variety of training and development initiatives which are possible. Try and capture the pros and cons of each approach against the specific context of your own organisation.

Feedback on learning activity 12.5

Activists learn best when involved in action learning:

- involved in new experiences, problems and opportunities
- working with others in business games, team tasks, role-playing
- being thrown in at the deep end with a difficult task
- chairing meetings, leading discussions.

Reflectors learn best when they observe activities and have the time to think about it:

- observing individuals or groups at work
- they have the opportunity to review what has happened and think about what they have learned
- producing analyses and reports, doing tasks without tight deadlines.

Theorists learn best when they start with ideas and are given problems to consider:

- they are put in complex situations where they have to use their skills and knowledge
- they are in structured situations with clear purpose

- they are offered interesting ideas or concepts even though they are not immediately relevant
- they have the chance to question and probe ideas behind things.

Pragmatists learn best when they can see the relevance of learning to their own situation:

- there is an obvious link between the topic and job
- they have the chance to try out techniques with feedback, eg role-playing
- they are shown techniques with obvious advantage, for example saving time
- they are shown a model they can copy, for example a film or a respected boss.

Feedback on self-assessment question 12.5

The first article seems to suggest that training is very much focused on developing individuals, who will contribute to the business because of the improvements that training has enabled.

The second article focuses on the needs of the business and then using training as a means of satisfying that need. This suggests that the benefits for the people are almost incidental.

See table 12.5 which provides evidence from the articles for each case, and judge for yourselves which approach you feel would be most effective for both staff and the organisation.

Table 12.5

GSK article	JIT training
Invest in people	Invest in the business need
Challenging and rewarding work for people	A training environment that changes to meet the needs of individuals or small groups when those needs arise
Opportunities for personal development and career growth	Opportunities to contribute to the success of the business
Focus on developing: • skills • knowledge • attitudes.	Focus on developing: • skills directly linked to organisational needs • key skills for the specific business need.
Development by: • training courses • a resources centre • blended learning • links to external bodies and programmes (MCIPS).	Development by: • gap analysis of skills versus needs • closing the specific gaps when needed • bite-sized training that is ongoing.

Study session 13

Time management: so much to do…

Introduction

This is the final session in Section 3 of the syllabus – 'Develop a culture of productivity through people' – and in this session you will explore how some of the themes covered in study sessions 9 to 12 are developed and translated into detailed implementation plans through project-based working.

You know all the theory about teams and teamwork, and about learning and training as an essential enabler for productivity – what practical steps will bring all this theory to life in the workplace?

Session learning objectives

After completing this session you should be able to:

13.1 Describe what is meant by project planning and resource scheduling, and how they break down into key components.
13.2 Explain how a resource plan is developed and monitored for a given purchasing project.
13.3 Identify the different capabilities required that comprise a purchasing project (for example leadership, planning, research, analysis, strategy, negotiation, implementation, management, communication, and so on).
13.4 Describe how you would develop a case to justify additional resource for a purchasing project.

Unit content coverage

This study session covers the following topics from the official CIPS unit content document.

Learning objectives

3.5 Effectively plan team time, including scheduling, justifying resource, deadlines and delivery dates.

- What is meant by project planning and resource scheduling
- The key components of a project plan and a resource plan
- How a resource plan is developed and monitored for a given purchasing project
- The different capabilities required that comprise a purchasing project (e.g. leadership, planning, research, analysis, strategy, negotiation, implementation, management, communication)
- Development of a case to justify additional resource for a purchasing project

Prior knowledge

Study sessions 8 to 12, particularly projects in section 9.3.

Resources

In order to complete this study session you will need internet access.

Timing

You should set aside about 6 hours to read and complete this session, including learning activities, self-assessment questions, the suggested further reading (if any) from the essential textbook for this unit and the revision question.

13.1 Project planning and resource scheduling: definitions and components

What is a project?

Turner (1992) defines **a project** as:

> 'an endeavour in which human (or machine) material and financial resources are organised in a novel way, to undertake a unique scope of work, of given specification, within constraints of cost and time, so as to deliver beneficial change defined by quantitative and qualitative objectives'.

The Project Management Institute's *Body of Knowledge* (2000) defines **project planning** as:

> 'the application of knowledge, skills, tools and techniques to project activities in order to meet the stakeholder needs and expectations from a project'.

Burke (1999) has a more specific view of the inputs required:

> 'a way of developing structure in a complex project, where the independent variables of time, cost, resources and human behaviour come together'.

Characteristics of a project

Meredith and Mantel (2003) set out the characteristics of projects, which distinguish them from 'normal' workplace activities:

- Purpose – clearly defined outcomes, with an element of complexity, which needs careful coordination
- PLC – project life cycle, with defined start and end point and a range of key activities to be completed (see figure 13.2)
- Interdependencies – links to other projects, and to the routine daily operations all of which need managing
- An element of uniqueness
- An element of potential conflict and risk is inherent, since projects are continually competing for finite resources.

Why work in projects?

- The business environment is characterised by increased complexity and change. In that respect there is hardly anything in the workplace which could be described as 'normal work'.
- The business environment is characterised by increasingly sophisticated and demanding consumers; Richard Sennet referred to these as 'impatient consumers'.
- Global markets and global competition are leading to shorter product life cycles. Organisations have to create products and processes which have to respond in an increasingly speedy and flexible way, and projects are better ways of facilitating this. See figure 13.1.

Figure 13.1: The five-phase project life cycle: detailed stages

Define	Plan	Organise	Control	Close
State the problem	Identify activities	Determine personnel needs	Define management style	Obtain client acceptance
Identify project goals	Estimate time and cost	Recruit project manager	Establish control tools	Install deliverables
List the objectives	Sequence activities	Recruit project team	Prepare status report	Document the project
Determine preliminary resources	Identify critical activities	Organise team	Review project schedule	Issue final report
Identify assumptions and risks	Write project proposal	Assign work packages	Issue change orders	Conduct project audit
Planning phase		Implementation phase		

Learning activity 13.1

What is the project life cycle? Display the main stages of project effort over time in a diagrammatic form.

Feedback on page 173

Resource scheduling can be defined as the process of determining dates on which activities should be performed in order to smooth the demand for resources, or to avoid exceeding stated constraints on these resources.

Essentially project planners need to know:

- When are tasks required to be completed?
- What resources are required to complete those tasks?

- How long does it take to complete the task when we have all the resources in place?
- How long does it take to receive the resources after we have requested them?
- Are there any critical tasks where being on time is essential?
- Are there any tasks where we have some flexibility in terms of scheduling?

With this knowledge, project planners can set out a precise timetable of activities and the linkages and timescales involved. This can be done in a number of ways:

- A simple timetable.
- A Gantt chart (manual or electronic) is a scheduling tool used to display the status of a project's tasks. A Gantt chart shows each task's duration as a horizontal line. The ends of the lines correspond to the task's start and end dates.
- Critical path or network analysis: a type of network analysis planning technique, used to plan complicated projects cheaply. It shows diagrammatically the interrelations in sequence of all the activities in a project in such a way as to highlight those activities which are critical for the due performance of the overall work.
- PERT is a project management technique for determining how much time a project needs before it is completed. Each activity is assigned a best, worst and most probable completion time estimate. These estimates are used to determine the average completion time. The average times are used to figure the critical path and the standard deviation of completion times for the entire project.
- Project software such as MS Project or Primavera.

Self-assessment question 13.1

What are the key stages and key issues to be considered in *planning* a project? Read the article on planning a project which is on the website http://www.see.ed.ac.uk/~gerard/Management/art8.html. The author is a senior lecturer in VLSI Design at the Department of Electrical Engineering, University of Edinburgh.

The article makes it clear that the success of a project will depend critically upon the effort, care and skill you apply in its initial planning, and it looks at the creative aspects of this planning, under the headings:

The Specification, which must be agreed by all involved.

Providing structure deciding what you and your team actually need to do, and how to do it, turning the specification into a complete set of tasks with a linking structure. Here a work breakdown structure (WBS) enables you to describe the project as a set of simpler separate *activities*. In task allocation you will allocate the tasks to different people in the team and, at the same time, order these tasks so that they are performed in a sensible sequence. Obtain a *realistic* estimate of the time involved in the project, avoiding the danger of over-optimism and possible pressure from senior management to deliver quickly.

(continued on next page)

Self-assessment question 13.1 *(continued)*

Establishing controls: The two key elements in controlling the 'doing' phase are milestones (clear, unambiguous targets of what, by when) and established means of communication – to monitor progress, to receive early warning of danger, to promote cooperation and to motivate the team.

The artistry in planning: Involve your team members in planning; use their available experience and creative ideas.

Project review, including testing and quality, and fitness for purpose, planning for error, end-of-project post-mortem.

Planning for the future.

Feedback on page 173

13.2 Development and monitoring of a resource plan

A resource plan is produced at the beginning of the project: http://www.maxwideman.com/pmglossary/PMG_P09.htm#Project. This enables the management and the project team to fully appreciate the range of resources that are needed. It covers all resources which will be required to successfully complete the project.

A purchasing project is usually developed within the general boundaries of the purchasing cycle (figure 13.3), which will be familiar to you from previous units on the CIPS programmes.

Figure 13.3: The purchasing cycle

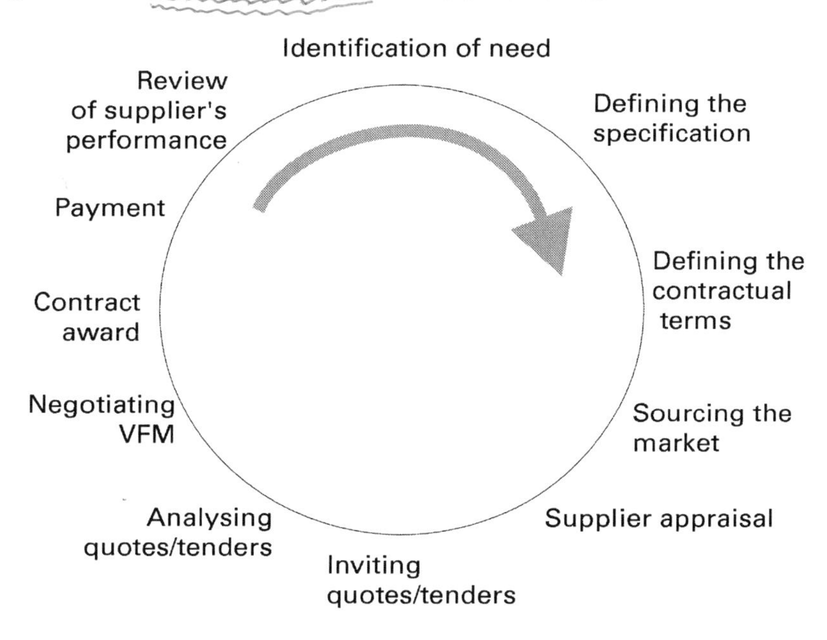

Learning activity 13.2

How would you distinguish between *planning* and *control*?

Feedback on page 173

13

What is a resource plan?

A resource plan identifies the physical resources required to complete the project. A typical resource plan includes:

- a list of the types of resources (labour, equipment and materials) required
- a schedule outlining when each of the resources is required to be utilised
- an assignment of each resource to a set of activities to be completed.

To create a resource plan, the following steps are undertaken:

- List the general types of resources to be utilised on the project.
- Identify the number of resources and purpose of each type of resource.
- Identify when the resources are required by completing a 'resource schedule' table.
- Allocate the resources to project activities by completing a 'resource usage' table.

When to use a resource plan

A resource plan is typically developed towards the end of the project planning phase, after the work breakdown structure (WBS) has been identified. Although summarised resource information may be described within the business case, feasibility study, terms of reference or project plan, a detailed resource plan cannot be created until every activity and task within the project plan has been identified. For simple projects, it may be necessary to enter only the resource name against the project activity (on the project plan), especially if using a planning tool such as MS Project. For larger, more complex projects, a full resource plan should be completed to ensure that the resource allocation is both accurate and appropriate. Following the completion of the resource plan, it will be possible to finalise the financial plan as the fixed cost portion of the project will have been identified.

Monitoring the resource plan

Purchasing projects are generally defined with the 'iron triangle' of quality, cost and time (QCT) (figure 13.4).

Figure 13.4: The project objectives triangle

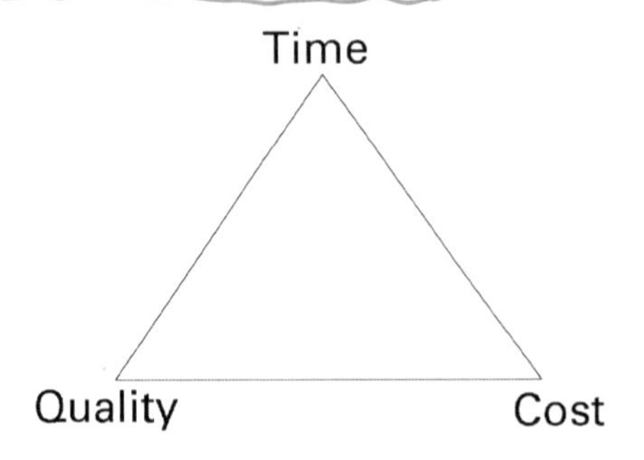

The project deliverables will be defined in terms of quality, cost and time. Measurement and monitoring will therefore be set against QCT specifics, and essentially managed by variance.

Self-assessment question 13.2

How can you measure, monitor and review plans?

Feedback on page 174

13.3 Capabilities for a purchasing project

This section considers the specific capabilities which are required in undertaking a purchasing project. What knowledge, skills and behaviours are critical when undertaking project work in the purchasing function?

Learning activity 13.3

Explore the skills and capabilities which are needed in the purchasing and supply chain functions in your own organisation. Relate these skills to the situation of your industry sector and to the way that the organisation approaches purchasing and supply chain management.

Feedback on page 174

If you refer back to skills and competencies required by the purchasing and supply functions, which were covered in section 12.3, you will recall that CIPS *National Standards* categorise competencies and skills into three generic types:

- strategic
- management
- technical.

Specific skills and capabilities include:

- Shaping goals: setting or receiving overall objectives and directions, interpreting them, reacting to changes in them, clarifying the problem and setting boundaries to it.
- Obtaining resources: identifying them, negotiating for their release, retaining them, managing their effective use.
- Building roles and structures: clarifying and modifying their own and those of other functions.
- Establishing good communications: linking the diverse groups or individuals contributing to the project, to obtain their support and commitment.

- Seeing the whole picture: taking a helicopter view, managing time and other resources, anticipating reactions from stakeholders, spotting links and unexpected events.
- Moving things forward: taking action and risks to keep the project going, especially through difficult phases.

Additional interpersonal skills include:

- Communicating – sensitivity; structures; links; written, oral and face-to-face presentations and listening.
- Negotiating – resolving conflicts, informal and formal.
- Team-building – energy and enthusiasm; role clarity; selection of the team and group development.
- Involving users and staff – ownership and commitment; education and training; reassurance (support and back-up); consultation, listening and awareness.

And for the project manager, do not forget the vital ability of being able to manage in four directions. Refer back to the detailed discussion in section 5.1, where this was fully explored in some detail.

Self-assessment question 13.3

What components are required to make a balanced project team in a purchasing project?

Feedback on page 174

13.4 Develop a case to justify resources for a purchasing project

Learning activity 13.4

Read up in the literature to find out about the key components of a project initiation document (PID). A PID is also referred to as a project charter.

Visit http://www.ogc.gov.uk/sdtoolkit/reference/documentation/p05_pid.html for some generic guidelines from the Office of Government Commerce. Any generic textbook on project management such as Meredith and Mantell (2003) or the Project Management Institute's *Body of Knowledge* will provide useful guidance.

Feedback on page 175

Figure 13.6 is an overview of a purchasing project.

Figure 13.6: A purchasing project overview

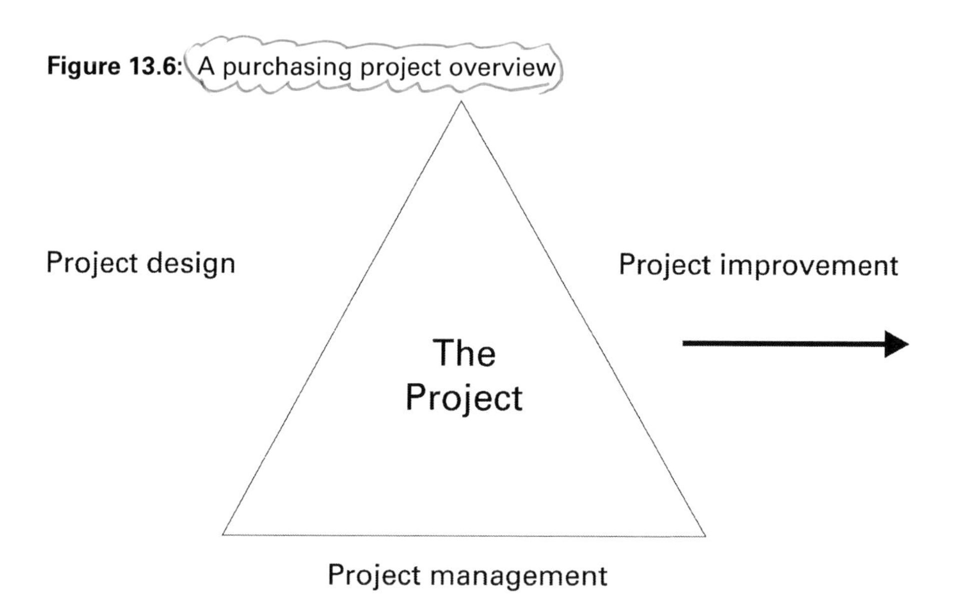

A project charter is the first step in the Six Sigma methodology: http://www.isixsigma.com/me/six_sigma/default.asp. It takes place in the 'define' step of DMAIC, and the charter can make or break a successful project. It can make it by specifying necessary resources and boundaries that will in turn ensure success; it can break it by reducing team focus, effectiveness and motivation.

DMAIC is a useful mnemonic for identifying the various stages required to be undertaken in an improvement process.

DMAIC stands for:

- define
- measure
- analyse
- improve
- control.

For useful guidance on business cases, project charters and project plans and templates to assist analysis visit http://www.projectperfect.com.au/info_project_documentation.php or other similar sites.

When defining a project you should consider the interplay of the interests which are involved in the project (table 13.1).

Table 13.1

Interest involved	Technique
The organisation's overall business goals and objectives	Strategic and business planning
The power and interest of the various stakeholders	Stakeholder mapping
	Stakeholder action plan
The key issues and priorities of your customers	Voice of the customer

(continued on next page)

Table 13.1 *(continued)*

Interest involved	Technique
	Technical requirements
The existing state of the processes which are currently in place, and which may require significant improvement or redesign	Voice of the process Process mapping SIPOC (suppliers, inputs, process, output, customer)

From this detailed analysis will emerge the creation of a business case. This is often described as a project initiation document (PID), a project charter or project scoping document or some similar term.

Self-assessment question 13.4

Identify a purchasing project which could produce significant benefits for your organisation. Produce a brief PID, with sufficient detail in it to enable managers to make a go/no-go decision about the project.

Feedback on page 175

Revision question

Now try the revision question for this session on page 298.

Summary

This study session has briefly explored the way projects can be managed to achieve productive objectives for an organisation.

Key learning points in this session:

- characteristics of project working
- the skills and capabilities needed for working in purchasing projects
- the project life cycle
- various techniques that are available to plan, monitor and control projects
- key steps in developing a business case, a PID and resource plans.

Suggested further reading

There are many good texts on project management and the general principles which appertain. Amongst the better treatments are Maylor (2003), Meredith and Mantell (2003), Burke (2003), Gardiner (2005), Lock (2003). The Project Management Institute is the professional body which produces much useful information and research, PMI (2001), http://www.apm.org.uk, http://www.projectmanagement.com.

Feedback on learning activities and self-assessment questions

Feedback on learning activity 13.1

See figure 13.2.

Figure 13.2: The project life cycle (PLC): the time distribution of project effort

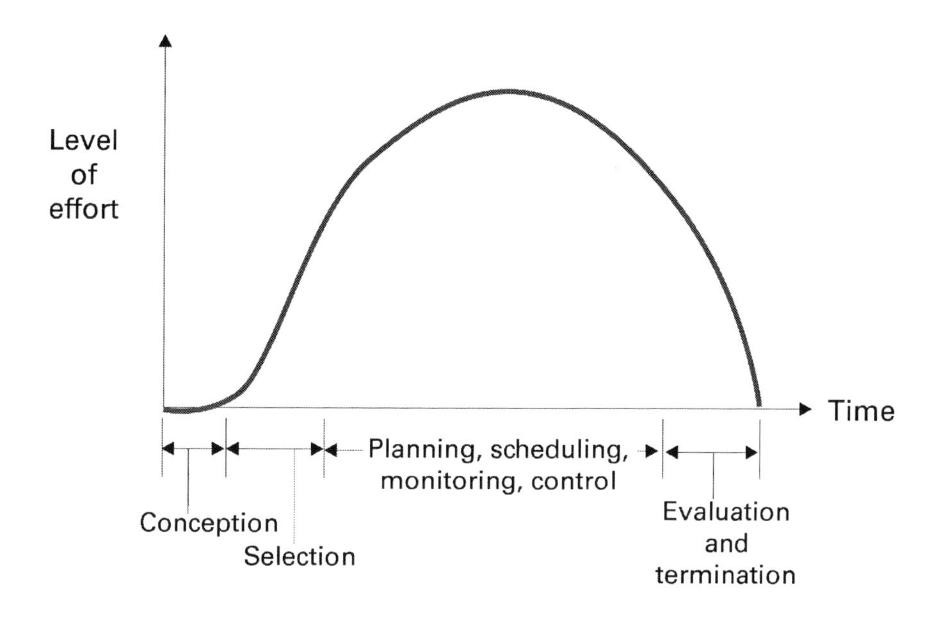

Feedback on self-assessment question 13.1

Key stages and issues can include:

- specification
- clear structure
- work breakdown structure (WBS)
- task allocation
- guesstimates
- establish controls
- creativity in planning:
  (a) team consultation
  (b) timing
  (c) tests and quality
  (d) fitness for purpose
  (e) timing
  (f) planning for errors
  (g) post-mortem
  (h) planning for the future.

Feedback on learning activity 13.2

Planning – a set of intentions, activities and a timetable which are set out in project, resource and financial plans.

Control – checking that the intentions/activities are happening as set out in the plans. If they are then the project is under control. If there are variations, then we need to investigate:

- Why are we not proceeding to plan?
- What do we have to do to get back on track?
- If we cannot get back on track, then what effect will that have on the project, or do we have to modify the project objectives and goals?

Feedback on self-assessment question 13.2

Essentially against:

- quality objectives
- cost objectives
- time objectives.

Feedback on learning activity 13.3

Responses will clearly be contingent on the sector and the approach of the organisation. Try and compare your responses with fellow students from different organisations. Compare you answers in terms of the generic capabilities identified by CIPS (generic skills where knowledge can be applied by purchasing and supply professionals):

- Change management theories, models and practices
- Communication methods and procedures
- Cost and benefit analysis methods and procedures
- Financial analysis methods and procedures
- Legal and regulatory requirements
- Organisational strategic aims and objectives
- Performance measurement and benchmarking theories, models and practices
- Presentation theories, models and practices
- Quality management theories, models and practices
- Risk analysis methods and procedures
- Stakeholder management methods and procedures
- Supply chain management theories, models and practices.

Feedback on self-assessment question 13.3

A balanced project team would probably display one or more of these characteristics:

- Opposing viewpoints are constructively represented with openness and honesty.
- An air of professional respect exists.
- Varying levels of skill and expertise are represented.
- Open challenge to group thinking is permitted.
- Some team members tend to be in a teaching mode while others are in a learning mode – there is a range of learning styles.

Feedback on learning activity 13.4

See an example of a PID in figure 13.5.

Figure 13.5: Project initiation document (PID)

Problem statement (15 words max.):................................
....
SMART goals:...
Business opportunity:..
Scope: ....
Cost/benefit projection:..

Milestones for completion:
....
....
Roles and responsibilities:
....
....
....
....

Feedback on self-assessment question 13.4

Your PID should be brief (three or four pages maximum) and yet provide a good overview of the various details identified in learning activity 13.4.

Study session 14

Leading change: this vision thing...

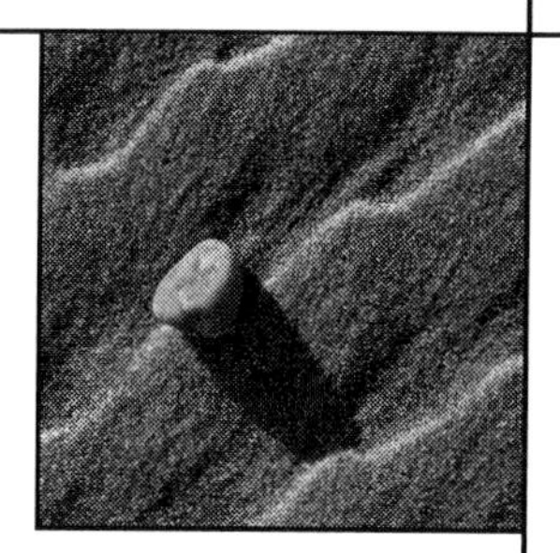

'Vision without action is a daydream. Action without vision is a nightmare.'

Japanese proverb

Introduction

This session is the first of seven sessions which consider the last section of the unit syllabus – 'Leading change in the supply chain'.

Among the topics to be considered in study sessions 14 to 20 are how to:

- Develop a vision, values and culture for the future
- Evaluate a range of different models of change management.
- Develop an appropriate style for leading and managing the strategic change process.
- Set and prioritise justifiable objectives for change and identify strategies for achieving them.
- Determine the resource requirements for the implementation of change within the purchasing function.
- Delegate responsibility for the effective implementation of change.
- Use force-field analysis to identify forces and barriers to change and determine what needs to be done to develop and assist change.
- Negotiate effectively in difficult leadership and management situations, including involvement in negotiating within industrial relations situations.
- Monitor and control the impact of the change process on the supply chain performance.
- Manage continuity of performance while implementing change.

Session learning objectives

After completing this session you should be able to:

14.1 Define what is meant by the term vision and describe the need for strategic alignment between mission, objectives, strategy and tactics.
14.2 Outline how a vision can be created and the actions required to gain 'buy-in' (education and communication, participation and involvement, facilitation and support, negotiation and agreement, manipulation and cooperation and explicit/implicit coercion). Explain the need for vision to be 'compelling'.
14.3 Describe how a vision should be communicated and reinforced.
14.4 Outline what is meant by the term 'culture' in the context of the purchasing function.
14.5 Identify an appropriate range of values for the purchasing function and explain the benefits of having explicit value statements.
14.6 Explain the importance of CSR and ethics in building sustainable values within the purchasing function.

Unit content coverage

This study session covers the following topics from the official CIPS unit content document.

Learning objectives

4.1 Develop a compelling and innovative vision, values and culture for the future, justifying reasons and benefits associated with change, taking into account the relationship between transformational and transactional change.

- The meaning of the term vision
- The need for strategic alignment between mission, objectives, strategy and tactics
- How a vision can be created and the actions required to gain buy-in: education and communication, participation and involvement, facilitation and support, negotiation and agreement, manipulation and cooperation (plus explicit/implicit coercion)
- The need for vision to be compelling
- How a vision should be communicated and reinforced
- The meaning of the term culture in the context of the purchasing function
- An appropriate range of values for the purchasing function and the benefits of having explicit value statements
- The importance of CSR and ethics in building sustainable values within the purchasing function

Prior knowledge

Study sessions 1 to 13 as background.

Resources

You will need internet access in order to complete this study session.

Timing

You should set aside about 6 hours to read and complete this session, including learning activities, self-assessment questions, the suggested further reading (if any) from the essential textbook for this unit and the revision question.

14.1 Vision and strategic alignment

Preliminary ideas about strategy and the strategy hierarchy, that is business operating at the strategic (corporate) level, the tactical (business level) and at the operational level, have already been explored in a number of sessions in this unit. This session develops those preliminary ideas in more detail.

Figure 14.1: Levels of strategy

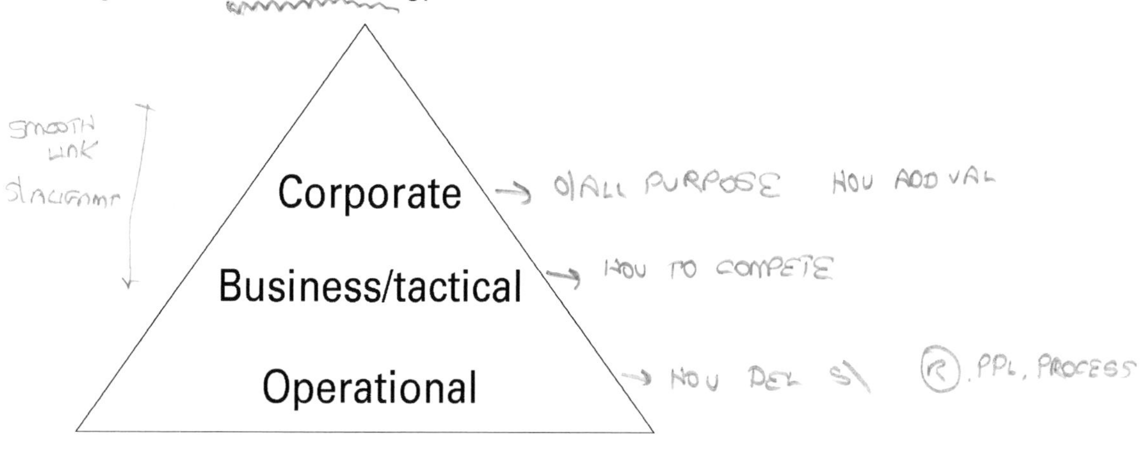

Basic definitions

> '**Strategy** is the direction and scope of an organisation over the long-term, which achieves advantage for the organisation through its configuration of resources within a changing environment and to fulfil stakeholder expectations.'
>
> Johnson et al (2004)

According to Johnson et al (2004) this leads to a number of consequences for organisations:

- Strategic decisions are likely to be complex.
- Strategic decisions are made under conditions of uncertainty.
- Strategic decisions require a holistic and integrated view of the organisation.
- Strategic decisions affect relationships and networks outside the organisation.
- Strategic decisions often involve change in organisations.

Johnson et al (2004) set out the following definitions of the different **strategy levels**:

> 'Corporate level strategy is concerned with the overall purpose and scope of an organisation and how value will be added to the different parts of the organisation.
>
> Business (tactical) unit strategy is about how to compete successfully in particular markets.
>
> Operational strategies are concerned with how the component parts of an organisation deliver effectively the corporate and business level strategies in terms of resources, processes and people.'

The key point is that all levels of strategy are important to the organisation, and that there should be a smooth link and transition between one level of strategy and another. This in essence is what is referred to as strategic alignment. It is no good for an organisation to have a clear corporate strategy and then no idea of how to translate that into operational plans.

Johnson et al (2004) define vision or strategic intent as:

> 'the desired future state of the organisation. It is an aspiration around which the strategist, perhaps a CEO, might seek to focus the attention and energies of members of the organisation'.

Learning activity 14.1

Find out the vision and mission statement of CIPS.

Feedback on page 192

Johnson et al (2004) have recently developed this view of vision into what they now term envisioning:

> 'Envisioning is the overall role and expectations of the organisation, sometimes called strategic intent. This is important for three main reasons.
>
> - Focus: Because in the absence of such clarity it is likely that the corporate parent will undertake activities and bear costs that have nothing to do with adding value to the business units, and are therefore just costs which diminish value.
> - Clarity to external stakeholders: Because corporate managers need to make clear to stakeholders what the corporation as a whole is about.
> - Clarity to business units: Internally, if business unit managers are not able to make sense of what their corporate parent is there for, they inevitably feel as though the corporate centre is either little more than a cost burden, or that corporate executives lack clarity of direction.'

Another succinct but essentially similar definition of vision comes from Nanus (1992) who defines a vision as 'a realistic, credible, attractive future for an organisation.'

Johnson et al (2004) do not really make a significant distinction between mission and vision:

> 'A **mission statement** is a statement of the overriding direction and purpose of an organisation. It can be thought of as an expression of its raison d'être. Some organisations use the term vision statement – some even have both vision and mission statements. If there is substantial disagreement within the organisation or with stakeholders as to its mission (or vision), it may well give rise to real problems in resolving the strategic direction of the organisation. Although mission statements

had become much more widely adopted by the early 2000s, many critics regard them as bland and wide-ranging. However, this may be necessary given the political nature of strategic management, since it is essential at that level to have statements to which most, if not all, stakeholders can subscribe. They need to emphasise the common ground amongst stakeholders and not the differences.'

Table 14.1 The vocabulary of strategy

Term	Definition
Mission	Overriding purpose as supported by stakeholder values and expectations
Vision	Desired future state of the organisation
Goal	General statement of aims or purpose
Objective	Quantification of a more precise statement of goals
Resources and core competencies	Resources, processes or skills which provide a sustainable competitive advantage
Strategies	Long-term direction of the organisation

Source: adapted from Johnson et al (2004)

Self-assessment question 14.1

Compare the vision and values of two leading aero-engine manufacturers, using published information or by visiting websites http://www.rolls-royce.com/careers/usa/who/vision.jsp and http://ge.com/en/company/companyinfo/at_a_glance/ge_values.htm. Are there any significant differences between the visions and values of Rolls Royce Plc (UK) and GE (USA)?

Feedback on page 193

14.2 Creating a compelling vision and gaining 'buy-in'

Creating a compelling vision

Henry Ford dreamed of a car for every family and Steven Jobs of Apple Computers dreamed of a computer in every classroom. At the time, sceptics thought their dreams were impossible. In the face of adversity, their persistence changed the world.

Learning activity 14.2

Give examples of a vision statement.

Feedback on page 194

http://leadinginsight.com/compelling_vision.htm (2006) suggests that managers will be much more effective if they communicate a clear

compelling vision that sets the direction for the organisation. A compelling vision keeps the organisation focused and motivated and also enables other organisations to fully engage with and support you. A compelling vision is a mixture of clear assessment, analysis and communication, within a framework of consultation and discussion within the organisation and its main stakeholders.

Essentially a vision is compelling if it turns people on and makes them want to be an active participant.

Ten steps to build a compelling vision:

- *Assess what is happening around you*. Determine who your stakeholders are and assess their needs and expectations of your organisation. Then review how your competition is responding to changes in the market. Can you learn from them?
- *Look for trends*. Can you identify any trends that need to be addressed? What will be the potential impact of these on your organisation?
- *Think big*. Think about the opportunities that are available. What is the principal organisational objective?
- *Think long term.*
- *Dream your vision*. Imagine yourself in the future – one year or more from now. Write down what will be different in clear simple terms. Your organisation has been successful. Describe what you have achieved and the key people who have contributed to your success. Describe the benefits that this brings to the company, your customers, partners and employees.
- *Have passion*. Does this vision get you excited and motivated to act? Does it have meaning? If not, what would it take for you to have real passion for your vision? Be prepared to revise your vision and face up to any obstacles that are in your way.
- *Access the available resources*. Review the capabilities of your existing resources. Are there any gaps? When you start to implement your vision you will need to address these gaps.
- *Invite others in*. Involve other people in your planning process. People like to collaborate and help. Be open to others' ideas and share your vision with them. Build a joint plan for how to implement the vision.
- *Balance conviction and openness*. As you communicate your vision, you need to believe that your vision is right while still being open to new ideas and suggestions from others. Without the support and commitment of others you cannot succeed.
- *Keep objective*. If people reject your ideas they are not rejecting you. Always be objective so you can be open to suggestions that will improve your vision.

Gaining buy-in to the vision requires a variety of strategies to be developed by managers and leaders:

- Education – what skills are needed?
- Communication – who needs to know and how do we tell them?
- Participation and involvement – who do we wish to involve in the consultation and how do we obtain that involvement?
- Facilitation – how do we organise consultation and open debate?

- Support – what are the tangible and intangible resources that will be needed?
- Negotiation – how do we negotiate with a variety of stakeholders?
- Agreement – consensus, majority rule, collaboration, how do we decide to agree and how can we be sure that we are agreed?
- Manipulation, cooperation, explicit/implicit coercion – what is the balance between the 'tender and the tough' approaches that are required? Refer back to the sessions on influencing and power.

Benefits of a vision

Nanus (1992) goes on to say that the right vision for an organisation can accomplish a number of things for that organisation:

- *It attracts commitment and energizes people.* This is one of the primary reasons for having a vision for an organisation: its motivational effect. When people can see that the organisation is committed to a vision it generates enthusiasm about the course the organisation intends to follow and increases the commitment of people to work towards achieving that vision.
- *It creates meaning in workers' lives.* A vision allows people to feel like they are part of a greater whole and hence provides meaning for their work. The right vision will mean something to everyone in the organisation if they can see how what they do contributes to that vision.
- *It establishes a standard of excellence.* A vision serves a very important function in establishing a standard of excellence. In fact, a good vision is all about excellence. The standard of excellence also can serve as a continuing goal and stimulate quality improvement programmes, as well as providing a measure of the worth of the organisation.
- *It bridges the present and the future.* The right vision takes the organisation out of the present and focuses it on the future. It is easy to get caught up in the crises of the day and to lose sight of where you were heading. A good vision can orient you on the future and provide positive direction. The vision alone is not enough to move you from the present to the future however. A vision is the desired future state for the organisation; the strategic plan is how to get from where you are now to where you want to be in the future.

Self-assessment question 14.2

Take 'vision' from learning activity 14.2 above and make it 'compelling'.

Feedback on page 194

14.3 Communicating and reinforcing the vision

Communicating an exciting vision can:

- inspire, challenge and motivate the workforce
- arouse a strong sense of organisational purpose, build pride and enable employee buy-in

- bring the workforce together, galvanise people to act and cause people to bring the organisation to life.

The best mission statements:

- are simple and concise
- speak loudly and clearly
- generate enthusiasm for the organisation's future
- ensure effort and dedication from all the staff.

Learning activity 14.3

How is the vision communicated in your organisation?

Feedback on page 195

The major difference between a company with a vision statement and a company with a clear sense of vision is that a company with a clear sense of vision will have employees who have very strong alignment with the organisation's core values. That strong sense of vision is achieved through a clearly articulated and communicated vision statement.

Goldberg (1997) argues that once a vision is created, it must be communicated and articulated effectively so that it becomes the *shared* vision of everyone in the organisation. The key part of creating shared vision is in articulating it and communicating it in an enduring fashion. Once this shared vision is created, it will become a driving force.

Gadiesh and Gilbert (2001) describe an excellent way to articulate a vision. They suggest creating a simple statement that they call a 'strategic principle' defined as 'a pithy, memorable distillation of strategy that guides employees as it empowers them'. A well-crafted and communicated strategic principle, or vision, enables employees and managers at all levels to work toward the same strategic objective without being overly rigid about how they do so.

14

Examples of well-articulated visions which are clear, concise and easy to remember are:

- AOL – Consumer connectivity first – anytime, anywhere

- Ford – Quality is Job #1
- Wal-Mart – Low prices, every day.

Collins (1996) suggests that communicating the vision is achieved when the vision is driven deep into the organisation and when it is communicated to all the far reaches of the organisation. Clear alignment to a vision can be seen when a visitor to your business sees your vision without having to read it on paper, based solely on the actions and behaviours of the people that they observe.

Effectively communicating the vision means the business lives the vision that is aspired and articulated. The business means what it says and it practises what it preaches – in other words 'walking the talk'. It is through such action that all members of the business will believe in and live a meaningful manifestation of the vision.

Another way to communicate the vision is to repeat it at every opportunity. Repetition breeds awareness, acceptance and understanding of your vision. The repetition and consistency in the communication of the vision can be a critical component in organisational awareness and thence good performance.

Vision, therefore, should be worked into as many conversations at the workplace as possible. The vision should also be integrated into as many communication channels as possible; in personal presentations, written communications, emails, company newsletters, meetings, advertising, marketing campaigns, and by placing plaques and engravings stating the vision in corporate hallways, offices and lobbies.

Most importantly, top business executives should use every opportunity available to them to share the vision and always act in a manner consistent with the vision. People both inside and outside the organisation will notice when the vision is truly being lived by watching the actions of the business leaders. Truly great business leaders act in accordance with their vision and serve as living examples of behaviours they wish others in their company to model.

Once the vision is understood, it is likely to be accepted by everyone in the business and there will be a strong desire to live it. Once all participants in the business share and live the vision, they will create an environment of true alignment with the vision and collectively drive the business towards its goals. The sense of shared vision will guide behaviour and also be self-reinforcing and self-motivating. Once the leader establishes a sense of shared vision within his or her business, not only will the business benefit but all the members of the organisation will benefit also.

Lengel and Daft (1988) suggest that reinforcement of message can be communicated by a variety of media depending on the complexity of the message:

> 'Communication media have varying capacities for resolving ambiguity, negotiating varying interpretations, and facilitating understanding.'

This assumes that people want to overcome equivocality and uncertainty in organisations, and a variety of media commonly used in organisations work better for certain tasks than others. Using four criteria, Daft and Lengel present a media richness hierarchy (figure 14.2), arranged from high to low degrees of richness, to illustrate the capacity of media types to process ambiguous communication in organisations. The criteria are (1) the availability of instant feedback; (2) the capacity of the medium to transmit multiple cues such as body language, voice tone and inflection; (3) the use of natural language; and (4) the personal focus of the medium. Face-to-face communication is the richest communication medium in the hierarchy followed by telephone, electronic mail, letter, note, memo, special report, and finally, flier and bulletin. From a strategic management perspective, the media richness theory suggests that effective managers make rational choices, matching a particular communication medium to a specific task or objective and to the degree of richness required by that task

Figure 14.2: Media richness model

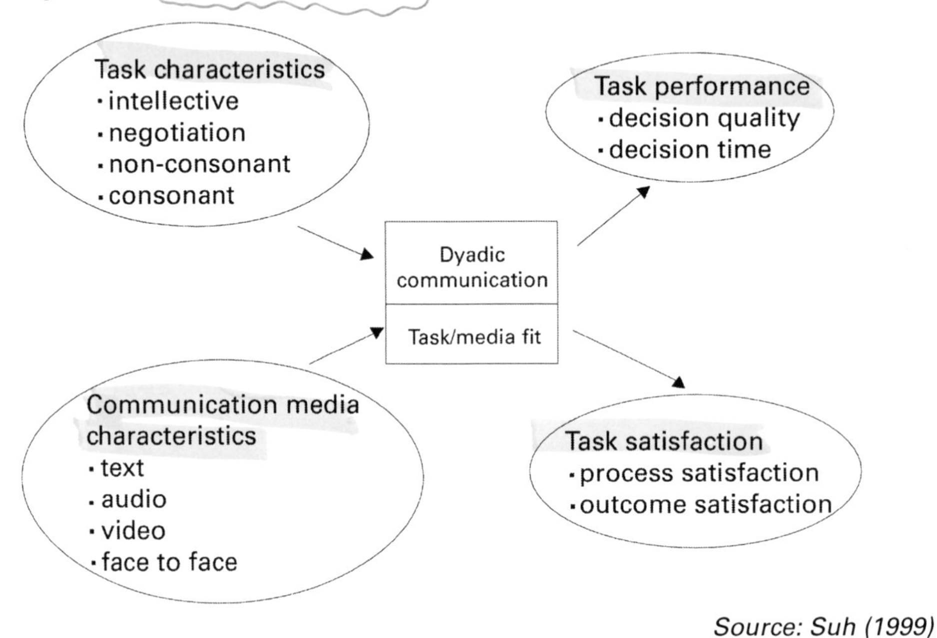

Source: Suh (1999)

Self-assessment question 14.3

You have considered methods of communication of the vision in learning activity 14.3 above. Now assess how well and with what benefits your organisation communicates and reinforces the vision in the way that it:

- is shared
- becomes a driving force
- is widespread
- is meaningful
- is repeated at every opportunity.

Feedback on page 195

14.4 Culture in the purchasing function

Organisational culture is defined by Mullins (2005) as:

> 'the collection of traditional values, policies, beliefs and attitudes that constitute a pervasive context for everything we do and think in an organisation'.

Culture has been considered at a variety of levels:

- national cultures (Hofstede 1981)
- leadership style (Kreitner 2001)

- as the shared perceptions and daily practices in organisations (Mullins 2005)
- as a component part of organisation development (Mullins 2005).

An often quoted description of culture is 'the way we do things around here' which suggests that within an organisation it should be possible to describe succinctly how things are done, which would be readily recognised by people in the organisation.

Learning activity 14.4

Using no more than one sentence, describe the 'purchasing culture' in your organisation.

Feedback on page 195

Mullins (2005) suggests that culture generally is developed and reinforced through the system of:

- rites and rituals
- patterns of communication
- informal organisation
- expected patterns of behaviour
- perceptions of the psychological contract.

Schein (1985), cited in Mullins (2005), suggests three different levels of culture.

Artefacts – the actual physical and social environment, including physical space and layout, the technology used, the written and unwritten language and behaviour of people. These are mostly the tangible elements. In the purchasing function it would be demonstrated by:

- the actual location of the function, centralised or decentralised, open or cellular layout
- the degree of sophistication of technology and automation and integration of information systems and databases
- language highly formal and documented, or informal and relaxed
- behaviour can be highly structured and according to written or unwritten rules, or very flexible, laid back and evolving.

Values and beliefs which develop as part of the conceptual process by which people justify actions and behaviours. In the purchasing function it would be conscious decisions to take certain strategic positions, such as a focus on competitive processes or trade-offs as a way of negotiation.

Basic underlying assumptions – are the taken-for-granted ways that issues are tackled, based on previous experience of past situations. In purchasing this would be an implicit faith in a particular approach – for example, that we have to start a negotiation from an extreme position, or that we have to play suppliers off one against the other, since these are the only ways to get the best outcomes.

Deal and Kennedy (1982) cited in Mullins (2005) described four generic types of culture in organisations, which could well be identified in the purchasing function:

- *Tough-guy/macho culture* – individuals who take high risks and get quick feedback about the outcomes. In purchasing this can be seen in commodity departments, futures buying and in the increasing use of e-auctions and e-procurement.
- *Work hard, play hard culture* – fun and action with lesser risks and quick feedback. The organisation is very dynamic, mostly team based and customer focused. In purchasing it can be sales-led organisations where volume or output is emphasised, sometimes at the expense of quality.
- *Bet-your-company culture* – high-risk decisions which may well take some time to come to fruition before feedback comes in. The focus is in investing in the future and on the rituals and routines of planning, analysis and control through hierarchy and bureaucracy. In purchasing this is mostly reflected in capital expenditure decisions or investment in new products, technologies and processes.
- *Process culture* – a low-risk, slow feedback approach, where it is hard to measure success in tangible ways. Banks, insurance companies and the public sector often are dominated by the uncertainty of the external environment, and in response people focus on process, how things are done, rather than what is done. This often results in a protective mentality, reflected by high dependence on contracts and legalistic approaches to purchasing and supply, which create safe but slow and costly processes.

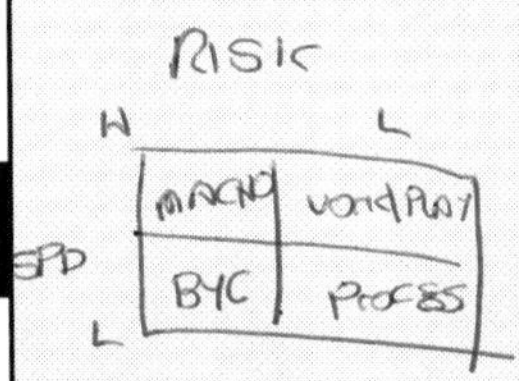

Self-assessment question 14.4

Create a continuum of 'purchasing cultures' for different sorts of organisations. Try and place your organisation's purchasing culture in the relevant place on the matrix.

Feedback on page 196

14.5 Values and value statements for the purchasing function

Developing a values statement

- Values represent the core priorities in the organisation's culture, including what drives people's priorities and how they truly act in the organisation. Values are increasingly important in strategic planning. They often drive the intent and direction for strategic planners.
- Developing a values statement is a quick way of making the broad goal and objective of the organisation culture-specific. Therefore people may create value statements that are from highly analytical and rational to highly creative and divergent.

- Establish four to six core values from which the organisation would like to operate. Consider values of customers, shareholders, employees and the community.
- Notice any differences between the organisation's preferred values and its true values (the values actually reflected by members' behaviours in the organisation).
- Incorporate, into the strategic plan, actions to align actual behaviour with preferred behaviours.

Learning activity 14.5

Where do 'values' fit in to the vision, mission and strategy of an organisation? Compare your answer to the feedback found on the website of a town council in Australia.

Feedback on page 196

The 'pyramid of goals' (figure 14.4) and how they evolve one from another gives a framework which the whole organisation and constituent departments such as purchasing can use to develop a clear set of aligned statements.

Figure 14.4: The pyramid of goals

Self-assessment question 14.5

Try and provide a pyramid of goals and value statement for your purchasing department.

Feedback on page 196

14.6 CSR and business ethics

CIPS has highlighted the importance of the role of corporate social responsibility on its website (http://www.cips.org).

Learning activity 14.6

Visit http://www.cips.org and access and make notes on the document *Principles of CSR.*

Feedback on page 196

To quote from the CIPS website:

> 'Corporate Social Responsibility is an ever-increasing subject which must be borne in mind when dealing with suppliers, although the extent of the breadth and depth of its impact will vary across sectors.
>
> CSR embraces a number of distinct but interrelated topics as follows:
>
> - environmental responsibility
> - human rights
> - community involvement
> - impact on society
> - equal opportunities
> - ethics and ethical trading
> - sustainability
> - bio-diversity
> - corporate governance.'

It is clear that the purchasing function in any organisation has a major impact on the efficient operation of procurement in all of the areas of the bulleted list set out above. All inputs from whatever source are mostly channelled via the purchasing function, so CSR involvement is increasingly relevant.

CIPS has gone so far as to set out a challenge to its members:

> 'Ian Taylor, CIPS president in 2005, asks you to consider making a commitment to do something positive for corporate social responsibility in purchasing and supply management in 2005. Just imagine what 36,000 CIPS members could achieve for the public good if we all set out to make a difference and create value for our organisations.
>
> Your actions do not have to be on a grand scale; even a small practical step with 35,999 others will make a considerable difference.
>
> Examples of the kinds of commitment you could make might be:
>
> - Changing the specification of a product you buy to be more environmentally friendly

- Encouraging a supplier to introduce an environmental management system or become more energy efficient
- Changing your distribution network to reduce vehicle journey distances and fuel consumption
- Finding out what labour practices are used by a supplier in a developing country and helping them to improve
- Offering support/information on CSR in the supply chain to your suppliers including local SMEs/ethnic community businesses/community organisations
- As a purchasing and supply team supporting a local initiative to offer help to voluntary organisations (business or labour).'

A simple definition of corporate social responsibility is that it is about how an organisation manages its business processes to produce an overall positive impact on society.

Other definitions

The World Business Council for Sustainable Development defines corporate social responsibility as:

> 'the continuing commitment by business to behave ethically and contribute to economic development while improving the quality of life of the workforce and their families as well as of the local community and society at large'.

Other definitions are as different as 'CSR is about capacity building for sustainable livelihoods. It respects cultural differences and finds the business opportunities in building the skills of employees, the community and the government' from Ghana, through to 'CSR is about business giving back to society' from the Philippines.

Traditionally in the United States, CSR has been defined much more in terms of a philanthropic model. Companies make profits, unhindered except by fulfilling their duty to pay taxes. Then they donate a certain share of the profits to charitable causes. It is seen as tainting the act for the company to receive any benefit from the giving.

The European model is much more focused on operating the core business in a socially responsible way, complemented by investment in communities for solid business case reasons.

You may wish to consider which approach to CSR appeals most to you.

Self-assessment question 14.6

Can ethics and CSR create sustainable value? If so, how?

Feedback on page 196

Revision question

Now try the revision question for this session on page 298.

Summary

This session has covered a number of significant topics of relevance to leading change in organisations.

Key learning points are:

- Understanding the pyramid of the organisation's goals and how they align together.
- How to develop compelling and innovative vision, values and culture for the future.
- How to communicate and reinforce the vision and how to derive business benefits.
- How to relate these concepts to the purchasing function and develop purchasing objectives, vision and goals which contribute to the whole organisation.
- CSR and business ethics are relevant in building sustainable values within the purchasing function.

Suggested further reading

A leading text on strategy and visions, missions and so on can be consulted in the relevant sections of Johnson, Scholes and Whittington (2004). Any current strategy textbook should provide the basic information in this area.

Feedback on learning activities and self-assessment questions

Feedback on learning activity 14.1

The following information is from CIPS's website http://www.cips.org.

The Chartered Institute of Purchasing and Supply (CIPS) is an international education and qualification body representing purchasing and supply chain professionals. It gained a Royal Charter in September 1992, the year of its Diamond Jubilee. It is the largest organisation of its kind in Europe and a central reference point worldwide on matters relating to purchasing and supply chain management. Its Professional Code of Ethics is the model for the international code and the domestic codes of many countries.

The Institute acts as a centre of excellence for the whole profession of purchasing and supply chain management. In particular, it works:

- continuously to improve the professional standards of practitioners;
- to raise awareness of their contribution to corporate, national and international prosperity; and

- to represent the interests of individuals within the profession.

The Institute's Mission Statement is to:

- promote and represent the profession of purchasing and supply management, demonstrating the contribution it makes to national and international prosperity;
- develop improved methods of purchasing and supply, promoting their use in all organisations;
- promote and maintain high standards of skill, ability and integrity within the profession;
- educate and develop the skills of individuals, ensuring relevant testing to demonstrate competence at appropriate grades within the profession;
- promote the value of membership of the Institute.

The profession itself is increasingly recognised for the enormous contribution it can make to public and private sector organisations, in terms of value extracted for money spent, and CIPS is pre-eminently well equipped to represent and serve the interests of all those involved in this rapidly developing field. Besides the recognition of professional status that membership bestows, involvement in the work of CIPS allows its members to keep up to date with latest developments through a comprehensive range of courses, conferences and publications. Advice, both from the Institute's staff and through membership contact, is widely available.

CIPS exists to promote and develop high standards of professional skill, ability and integrity among all those engaged in purchasing and supply chain management.

Feedback on self-assessment question 14.1

There are many similarities and differences between the two organisations: table 14.2 highlights some key points. Note how RR focuses on its products, whereas GE focuses on providing solutions for customers. This reflects the broader range of business areas within which GE operates. At the same time core values and how their objectives are to be achieved are very similar, yet GE appears to use more dynamic words to express them.

Table 14.2

Rolls-Royce seeks to become the first choice for power solutions across the entire spectrum of civil aerospace, defence aerospace, marine, and energy	For GE, the big question has a simple answer: We exist to solve problems – for our customers, our communities and societies, and for ourselves
Teamwork	Imagine
Communication	Build
Commitment	Solve
Always testing ourselves	Lead

(continued on next page)

Table 14.2 *(continued)*

Integrity	Passionate
Reliability	Curious
Innovation	Resourceful
	Accountable
	Teamwork
	Committed
	Open
	Energizing
	Always With Unyielding Integrity

Feedback on learning activity 14.2

Two examples are provided.

For a restaurant

Our restaurant is a place where people come to relax, have a good time, and enjoy a great meal. From the moment our customers walk in the door, they are greeted by a warm atmosphere, subtle music, and friendly and courteous staff.

We cater to large groups that are out to have fun, as well as romantic dinners for people celebrating a special occasion. The restaurant is packed full of customers, and yet we efficiently avoid long delays while they are being seated and while their food is prepared.

The lighting, table arrangements, atmosphere, and decorations all encourage our customers to relax, let go of their concerns, and open up to new taste sensations. We provide exceptional service all night long.

When they are done, we take care of their check quickly and efficiently. They leave happy, satisfied, but not overly bloated or full. They leave with the desire for just one more bite of our wonderful food.

For a secondary school

Wombleborough School is dedicated to providing the highest-quality educational programme based on value learning, self-worth among students and staff, quality performance among students and staff. Our students will make the transition to a productive and responsible participation in society at large.

Feedback on self-assessment question 14.2

For a restaurant

Our restaurant is a place where people come to relax, have a superb time and enjoy an excellent meal. From the moment our customers walk in the door, they are greeted by a stunning atmosphere, subtle music and knowledgeable, friendly, highly competent and courteous staff.

We seek to be the first restaurant of choice in our city for large groups that are out to have fun, as well as romantic dinners for people celebrating a special occasion. The restaurant is busy with contented customers and yet we efficiently avoid long delays while they are being seated and while their food is prepared and served.

The lighting, table arrangements, atmosphere and decorations all combine to guarantee that our customers will relax, let go of their concerns and be amenable to the sensations that are provided to them. We provide exceptional service all night long.

When customers are ready to leave, we take care of their bills quickly and efficiently. They leave happy, satisfied and looking forward eagerly to the next time. They leave with the desire for just one more bite of our wonderful food.

Feedback on learning activity 14.3

Consider the various media used by the organisation:

- face-to-face meetings
- interactive – telephone, video conference
- personal memos, letters, emails
- generic communication, circulars, notice boards and so on.

Feedback on self-assessment question 14.3

Your assessment should consider how well the vision is communicated and reinforced in terms of the way it:

- is shared
- becomes a driving force
- is widespread
- is meaningful
- is repeated at every opportunity.

Is there a clear benefit in terms of attitudes, behaviours and results or not?

Feedback on learning activity 14.4

Contrast the different cultures evoked by phrases such as:

- playing off one supplier against another
- feed the factory
- seek win–win
- develop relationships
- lowest cost
- lowest total cost of acquisition

- adversarial
- strategic.

Feedback on self-assessment question 14.4

See figure 14.3. Is there a clearly identifiable purchasing culture in your organisation?

Figure 14.3

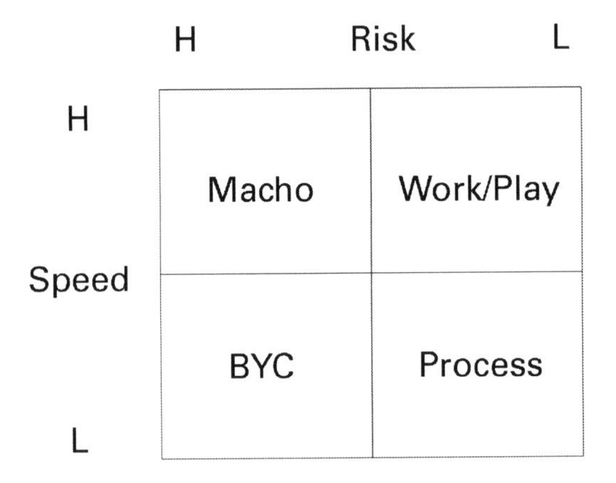

Feedback on learning activity 14.5

Read the mission statement and values statement and how these are reflected in the strategic plan, found at http://www.shoalhaven.nsw.gov.au/council/pubdocs/statements.htm#vision.

Feedback on self-assessment question 14.5

Visit the website of Rolls Royce plc to see the approach being taken by their procurement function at http://www.rolls-royce.com/suppliers/supplier_info/overview.jsp.

Feedback on learning activity 14.6

Focus in particular on the 'handy hints' which suggest practical actions that organisations can take to introduce CSR for positive benefits.

Feedback on self-assessment question 14.6

A company's social responsibility policies can improve its competitiveness, according to a government-sponsored initiative described on http://www.forumforthefuture.org.uk/news/Sustainabilitycanimproveb_page1488.aspx.

The report, *Sustainability and business competitiveness*, arose from a workshop commissioned by the Department of Trade and Industry and organised by Forum for the Future. It was attended by 70 senior business researchers and practitioners, from the chief economists of Shell and BA to the senior corporate responsibility adviser at Vodafone.

The report concluded that past attempts to measure the business case for sustainability, concentrating on eco-efficiency cost savings and green or ethical price premiums, had omitted the major contribution made to business success from stakeholder and environmental management, helping a company's competitive advantage in its main markets. The workshop found that many of the tools to measure business intangibles could also measure the shareholder value of a company's CSR policies and performance.

The workshop's findings are important given that some influential commentators had regarded the cost of CSR and sustainability programmes as an expense rather than a potential investment.

Visit the website for more detail.

Study session 15

Approaches to change: how will it affect us?

'The one unchanging principle of life is the principle of change.'

Introduction

The old saying on the right is certainly true, both for individuals and organisations. The pace of change may vary, but it is all around us. This study session explores some of the main factors which drive change, as well as factors which inhibit change. You will also start to consider how change can be managed successfully from a number of academic and practical perspectives. The emphasis in this session will be on organisational change rather than change at the individual level.

Session learning objectives

After completing this session you should be able to:

15.1 Identify the factors driving change and describe their effect using appropriate tools (for example Lewin's force field analysis).
15.2 Describe what is meant by the organisational development movement.
15.3 Describe Lewin's model for planned change and outline the three key stages of unfreezing, movement and refreezing.
15.4 Describe the action research model and outline what is meant by cyclical change.
15.5 Evaluate the merits of employing external resources to lead organisational change.
15.6 Summarise how change impacts on the organisation and on the supply chain.

Unit content coverage

This study session covers the following topics from the official CIPS unit content document.

Learning objectives

4.2 Critically evaluate a range of different models of change management and consider the implications of implementation of each one for the purchasing function and the wider organisation as a whole

- Factors driving change and their effect using appropriate tools (e.g. Lewin's force field analysis)
- The meaning of the organisational development movement
- Lewin's model for planned change and the three key stages of unfreezing, movement and refreezing
- The action research model and what is meant by cyclical change

- The merits of employing external resources to lead organisational change

Prior knowledge

Study session 14 and selected 'Strategic Supply Chain Management' unit materials.

Resources

In order to complete this study session you will need internet access.

Timing

You should set aside about 6 hours to read and complete this session, including learning activities, self-assessment questions, the suggested further reading (if any) from the essential textbook for this unit and the revision question.

15.1 The drivers of change

Change can be predictable or unpredictable, fast or slow. Change can be planned or unplanned, incremental or transformational. In other words change is uncertain in most respects. This uncertainty has particular implications for managers, and Mullins (2005) suggests that:

> 'The manager needs to understand the nature of organisational culture and climate, employee commitment, conflict and the successful implementation and management of organisational change.'

Drivers of change are those factors, often but not always from the external environment, which encourage organisations to change. The list of change drivers is not definitive or exhaustive, but gives a flavour of the dynamic influences which are likely to impact in terms of change and organisations.

- *Technology*. Technological change is ever accelerating in the modern competitive business environment, and organisations need to keep pace with technology or risk falling behind competitors. Technological advances can often impact upon organisational structures, job design and work processes, and this adds to the complexity of change which has to be managed.
- *Globalisation*. Increased competition is reflected in the global nature of business and markets which enhance the dynamics of the external environment in numerous ways. Organisations are affected by trends such as changing consumer preferences, shorter product life cycles, new products and processes, and the emergence of China, the Indian subcontinent and eastern Europe as likely major players in the future.

- *Knowledge explosion.* Education has enabled much higher levels of learning in the population, and communication technology has enabled that knowledge to be shared more widely. Consumers are better informed and are more demanding of quality and economy than ever before. This requires that organisations need to be increasingly responsive to consumers.
- *Demographics*. The demographic profile of the population and the workforce is changing dramatically in many countries. In western society we see an older population and a younger population, and a shrinking workforce. Trends will vary significantly in many different countries.
- *Privatisation of the public sector* is growing significantly, in the belief that a 'market economy' will be more effective and efficient than a 'public monopoly'.
- *Regulation and deregulation at the same time.* A paradox of modern trends is that within trading blocks such as the EU, trade is being deregulated into a 'single market' in the belief that this will create wealth and ease of trading for all the member states. At the same time external barriers between the EU and other areas are as strongly protectionist as ever.
- *Demanding stakeholders.* Shareholders, staff, customers, financial markets and society in general all demand a say in what organisations do, and have the power to influence organisations.

Learning activity 15.1

Identify and prioritise the main drivers for change affecting your organisation at the current time. How have these factors changed over time?

Feedback on page 213

The challenge for organisations is to be able to respond positively to the dynamics of the external environment, and yet still effect change in a planned and controlled way, so that they are 'masters of their own fate' rather than constantly being reactive to circumstances which they cannot control.

Heller (1997), cited in Mullins (2005), gives a good feeling of how difficult and challenging this is:

> 'The truth about organisational change is that getting the structure and the numbers right is only the first step. Animating the structure to achieve the right actions by right motivated people is vital. The central purpose is to create so thriving and developing an organic activity that the organisation can provide excellent, well-paid employment for all its people.'

Anderson and Anderson (2006) create a very useful systematic model of drivers for change, to assist organisations in identifying drivers of change which could affect them. Each driver affects the next in the chain.

The seven drivers are:

- *Environment*, which considers the dynamics of the larger external environment within which organisations and people operate. These forces are typically referred to as the PESTLE factors.
- *Marketplace requirements for success* encompasses the totality of customer requirements that determine what it takes for a business to succeed in its marketplace. This includes the actual product or service needs, and also requirements such as speed of delivery, ability to customise, level of quality, need for creativity and innovation, level of customer service, and so on. Changes in marketplace requirements are clearly affected by the external environment.
- *Business imperatives* set out what the company must do strategically to be successful, given its customers' changing requirements. This requires systematic rethinking and review and even changes to the company's mission, strategy, goals, products and services, pricing or branding.
- *Organisational imperatives* specify what must change in the organisation's structure, systems, processes, technology, resources, skill base or staffing to successfully realise its strategic business imperatives.
- *Cultural imperatives* show how the norms or collective way of being, working and relating in the company must change to support and drive the organisation's new design, strategy and operations.
- *Leader and employee behaviour*. Collective behaviour creates and expresses an organisation's culture. Behaviour describes the style, tone or character that permeates what people do, and how their way of behaviour must change to create the new culture.
- *Leader and employee mindset* encompasses the world view, assumptions, beliefs or mental models that will cause people to behave in ways that will drive a sustained change in behaviour and culture.

Anderson and Anderson (2006) suggest the model is helpful to assist you in understanding the drivers for change in your organisation. Having identified the drivers you can then 'formulate them into a story that paints a compelling and integrated story about why your change is needed'.

Anderson and Anderson (2006) set out the 'full story, which is incorporating…'

- Building the case for change.
- Defining the rationale and motivation for the change in a compelling way (akin to the compelling vision).
- The full scope of the change effort, how extensive and deep-rooted is the change to be?
- Clarification of the type of change occurring: fine-tuning or corporate transformation?
- Identifying the specific target groups that must make the change happen, those responsible for the implementation of change.
- The degree of urgency and general timescales for the change.
- An overall change strategy, which is broken down into a series of specific change initiatives.
- Clarification of the theme that integrates all the multiple initiatives.
- Communication media to be used.

- Clear training plans for the skills, knowledge and attitudes needed for the change to succeed.

Self-assessment question 15.1

Apply the seven stages of change model to a change situation with which you have been involved.

Feedback on page 213

15.2 The organisational development movement

Organisational development (OD) is defined by French and Bell (1999), cited in Mullins (2005), as:

> 'a long-term effort, led and supported by top management, to improve an organisation's visioning, empowerment, learning and problem-solving processes, through an ongoing, collaborative management of organisational culture – with special emphasis on the culture of intact work teams and other team configurations – utilising the consultant-facilitator role and the theory and technology of applied behavioural science, utilising action research'.

Mullins (2005) simplifies that complex definition of French and Bell:

> 'OD is concerned with attempts to improve the overall performance and effectiveness of an organisation. Essentially it is applied behavioural science approach to planned change and development of an organisation.'

Learning activity 15.2

Identify the main topics associated with OD.

Feedback on page 214

OD is therefore characterised by:

- A practice-based approach that helps people and organisations work toward collective outcomes in a way that considers both organisational and individual interests.
- People and organisations – OD may deal with individual considerations but only in the context of the organisations that they belong to.
- Collective outcomes – OD is concerned with meeting goals and needs as opposed to simply inculcating values or behaviours.
- Organisational and individual interests – OD does not support manipulating people toward an end but rather promotes OD for mutually achieved results.

OD is not:

- Management science, which includes areas such as business strategy, product development and financial planning, whereas OD's core concerns are people oriented.
- Human resource development. These two practices are related but have different outlooks and approach people issues differently.
- Psychological science. Although it may be said to have originated from, and draws from the findings of, applied psychology, industrial psychology, organisational psychology and social psychology, OD is concerned with practice, not with theory or research.
- Organisation science. The latter is an academic discipline, whereas OD is a field of work.
- Action research. OD may be said to include action research as a school of thought or movement, but the field of practice of OD is more comprehensive.

OD is therefore a complex strategy intended to change the beliefs, attitudes, values and structure of the organisation so that they can better adapt to new technologies, markets and challenges of the competitive external environment of the twenty-first century.

Self-assessment question 15.2

What characterises the OD movement?

Feedback on page 214

15.3 Force field analysis

Force field analysis (FFA) is a management technique for diagnosing situations; it was developed by Lewin (1951). FFA can be useful when looking at the variables involved in planning and implementing a change programme and in team-building projects when attempting to overcome resistance to change.

Lewin (1951) argued that in any situation there are both driving and restraining forces that influence any change that may occur.

- *Driving forces* are those forces affecting a situation that are pushing in a particular direction which tends to initiate a change and keep it going. In terms of improving productivity in a work group, pressure from a supervisor, incentive bonuses in terms of earnings, and competition may be examples of driving forces.
- *Restraining forces* (resistance) are forces acting to restrain or decrease the driving forces. Apathy, hostility and poor maintenance of equipment may be examples of restraining forces against increased production. Equilibrium is reached when the sum of the driving forces equals the sum of the restraining forces. In figure 15.1, equilibrium represents the present level of productivity.

Figure 15.1: Force field analysis model

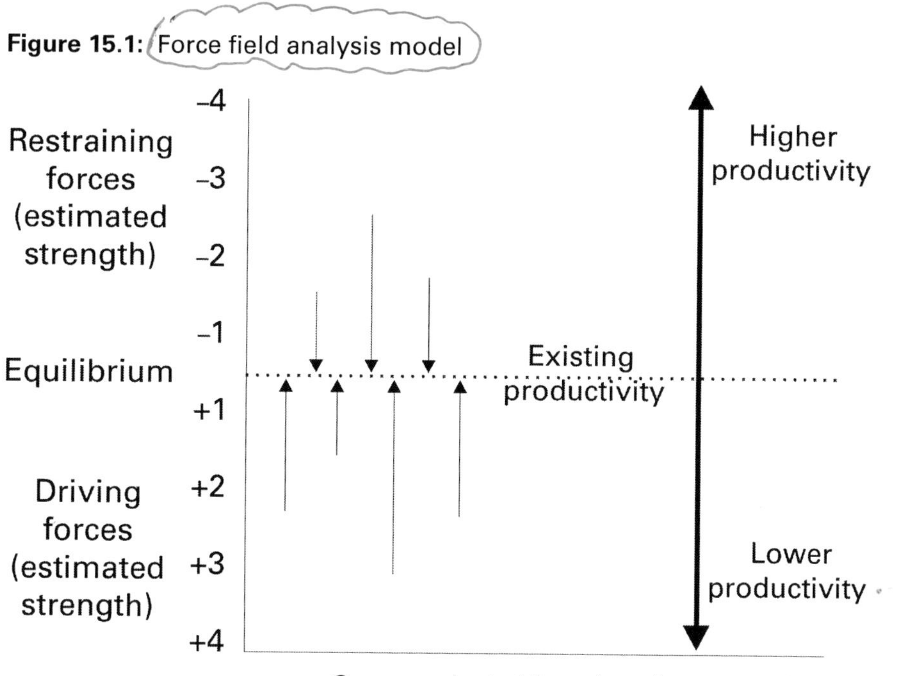

Source: adapted from http://www.accel-team.com/

- The equilibrium, or present level of productivity, can be raised or lowered by changes in the relationship between the driving and the restraining forces.

Force field analysis is widely used in change management and can be used to help understand most change processes in organisations (figure 15.2).

Figure 15.2

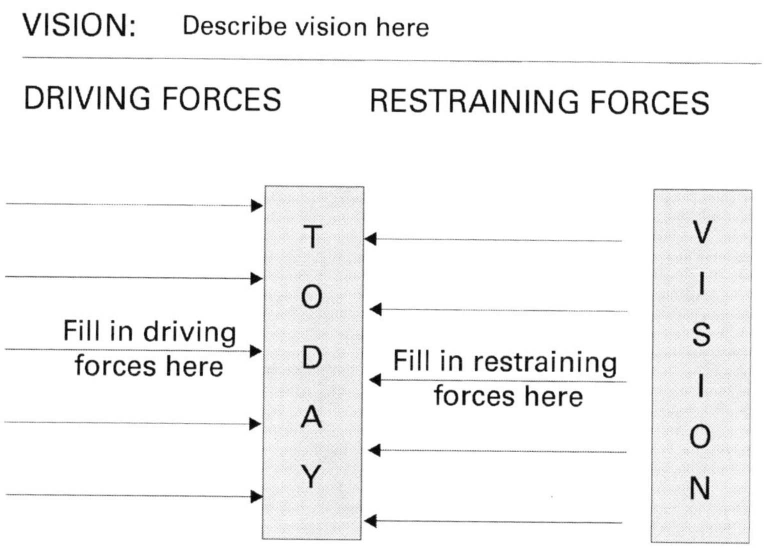

VISION: Describe vision here

DRIVING FORCES RESTRAINING FORCES

Fill in driving forces here

TODAY

Fill in restraining forces here

VISION

In force field analysis, change is characterised as a state of imbalance between driving forces such as new staff, changing markets and new technology and restraining forces such as individuals' fear of failure, or organisational inertia. To achieve change towards a goal or vision three steps are required:

- First, an organisation has to unfreeze the driving and restraining forces that hold it in a state of quasi-equilibrium.

- Second, an imbalance is introduced to the forces to enable the change to take place. This can be achieved by increasing the drivers, reducing the restraints or both.
- Third, once the change is complete the forces are brought back into quasi-equilibrium and refrozen. This refreezing can be accomplished by processes such as developing clear procedures, supported by training and monitoring that the changes have been embedded in an ongoing way. Joseph Juran (http://www.juran.com) refers to this stage as 'holding the gains' and not slipping back to the old ways.

For example, imagine that you are a manager deciding whether to install new manufacturing equipment in your factory. You might draw up a force field analysis like the one in figure 15.3.

Figure 15.3: Force field analysis example

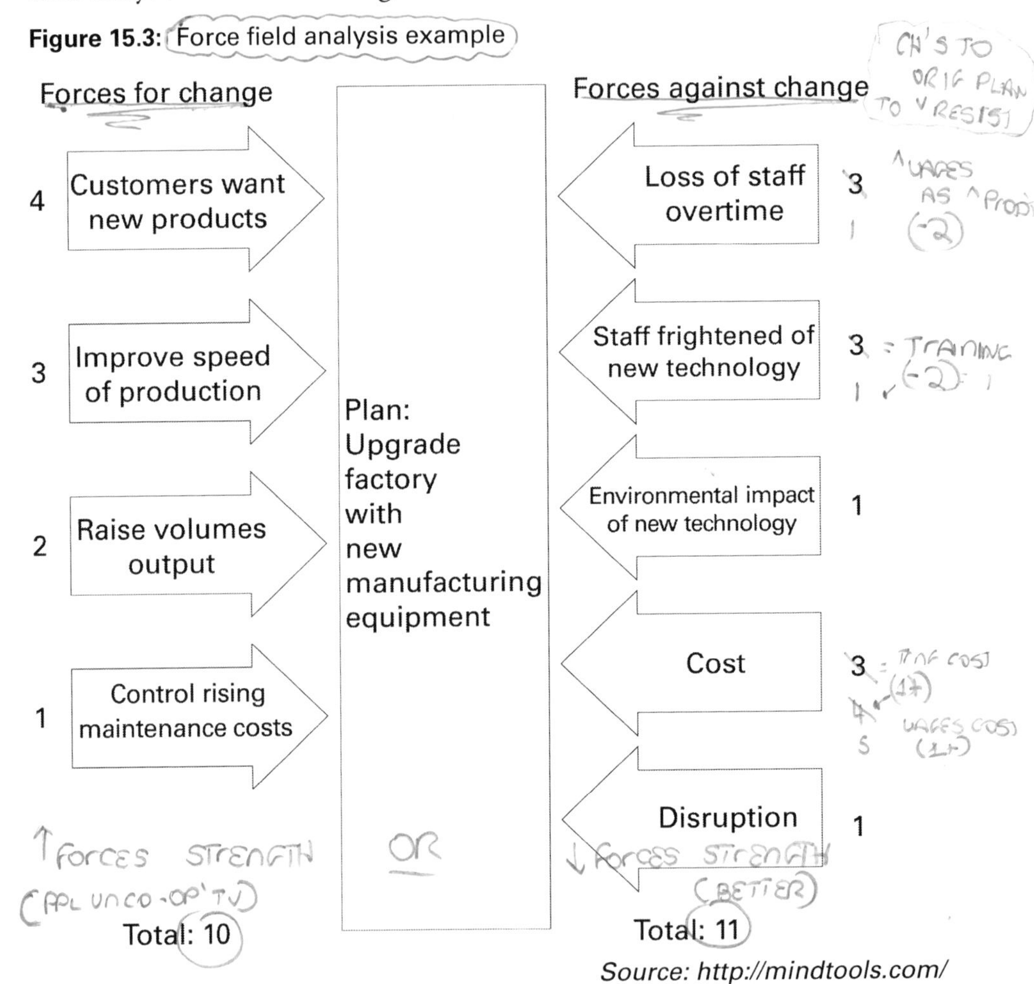

Source: http://mindtools.com/

Once you have carried out an analysis, you can decide whether your project is viable. In the example above, you might initially question whether it is worth going ahead with the plan.

Where you have already decided to carry out a project, force field analysis can help you to work out how to improve its probability of success. Here you have two choices:

- to reduce the strength of the forces opposing a project, or
- to increase the forces pushing a project.

Often the most elegant solution is the first: just trying to force change through may cause its own problems. People can be uncooperative if change is forced on them.

If you had to implement the project in the example above, the analysis might suggest a number of changes to the initial plan:

- By training staff (increase cost by 1) you could eliminate fear of technology (reduce fear by 2).
- It would be useful to show staff that change is necessary for business survival (new force in favour, +2).
- Staff could be shown that new machines would introduce variety and interest to their jobs (new force, +1).
- You could raise wages to reflect new productivity (cost +1, loss of overtime –2).
- Slightly different machines with filters to eliminate pollution could be installed (environmental impact –1).

These changes would swing the balance from 11:10 (against the plan), to 8:13 (in favour of the plan).

Learning activity 15.3

Attempt a brief definition of each of the three stages of force field analysis.

Feedback on page 214

Now that you are clear on your definitions at each stage of FFA, try and apply this knowledge to a practical situation.

Self-assessment question 15.3

Identify a 'change' required by external stakeholders to your own organisation – describe and justify how you would deal with it.

Feedback on page 215

15.4 Action research and cyclical change

Action research can be described as a family of research methodologies which pursue action (or change) and research (or understanding) at the same time. In most of its forms it does this by:

- using a cyclic or spiral process which alternates between action and critical reflection

- in the later cycles, continuously refining methods, data and interpretation in the light of the understanding developed in the earlier cycles.

It is thus an emergent process which takes shape as understanding increases. It is an iterative process which converges towards a better understanding of what happens, through each cycle.

In most of its forms it is also participative, based on the assumption that change is usually easier to achieve when those affected by the change are involved.

Action research is a method for intentional learning from experience, originally formulated by social psychologist Kurt Lewin.

Action research is characterised by intervention in real-world settings, followed by close scrutiny of the effects. Its aim is to improve practice and it is typically conducted by a combined team of practitioners and researchers.

An example of the action research cycle can be found on

http://education.qld.gov.au/students/advocacy/equity/gender-sch/action/action-cycle.html (observe, reflect, plan, act).

There are four basic steps in the action research cycle:

- *Observe*: monitor what is going on and capture data by observations.
- *Reflect* about what was observed so that we can understand what is going on.
- *Plan* what actions can be taken to deal with the issues and problems that have been identified.
- *Act* on your plan through implementation. Did the plan work or does it need to be modified?
- *Observe*: the cycle starts again through an endless cycle or spiral of learning.

Note also the similarities of this approach to similar models that you have studied previously, such as the Kolb experiential learning cycle, or the Deming cycle.

Learning activity 15.4

A more detailed treatment of action research can be found on

http://www.nsdc.org/library/publications/jsd/glanz203.cfm. What are the main themes identified in the article?

Feedback on page 215

You should now tackle self-assessment question 15.4 below.

Self-assessment question 15.4

Describe what is meant by cyclical change. Assess how 'action research' can make a helpful contribution in understanding the nature of change.

Feedback on page 215

15.5 Consultants and organisational change

When a business leader realises that his organisation is in need of significant change, one of the first and most critical actions is to consider who will be appointed as part of the team to spearhead a change initiative. Typically, a change management team's leadership consists of project sponsor (usually a senior manager) with overall responsibility, supported by project managers who focus on specific aspects. These people will be the change agents – the ones on whom the success of the organisation's change effort will depend. Before you consider whether these project managers should be internal or external to the organisation, you should consider what makes a good change agent.

Learning activity 15.5

What generic sets of skills are needed by change managers?

Feedback on page 216

When assessing potential candidates for roles as change agents, three questions need to be asked.

Do they have the right attitude?

Change agents cannot succeed without great persistence. Change is a complex and labour-intensive process that arouses feelings and emotions. Angry people, frustrated team-mates, conflicting priorities, unforeseen problems and behind-the-scene resistance are typical daily challenges. Project leaders or managers cannot lead teams through these difficulties without determination and stamina.

Figure 15.4

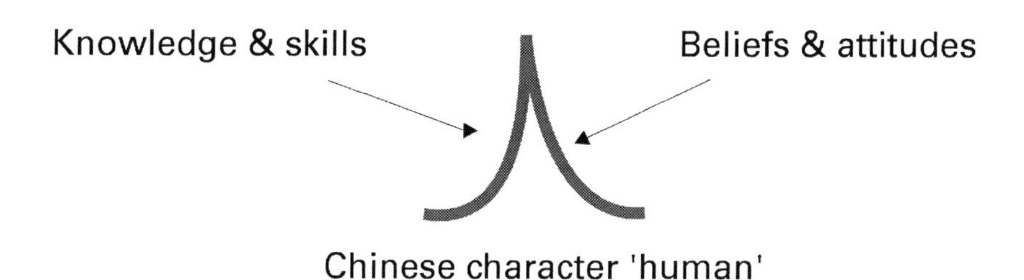

Attitude is one aspect of good change agents that is often overlooked. As depicted by the Chinese word 'ren' in figure 15.4, the two strokes supporting each other signify that 'knowledge and skills' have to be complemented by 'beliefs and attitudes'.

A person with relevant knowledge and skills but inappropriate attitude will not be able to contribute as much to the organisation and the community. Moreover, the higher the skills and knowledge of a person, the greater damage they can do to the organisation if their attitude is flawed. Change agents must be prepared to stand up for their projects, even if it means tactfully challenging powerful executives – including the senior leadership. In many cases, implementation problems are due to the project sponsors or top management underestimating the significance of their own duties. They are reluctant to commit the necessary resources; they sometimes send conflicting messages about the importance of change by failing to apply enough pressure to those who resist; or they alter priorities halfway through the change.

Do they have the appropriate knowledge?

Project sponsors should be seasoned change agents with a general understanding of the business. However, project managers should be subject-matter experts in their respective area of responsibility. Having someone with excellent project management skills is simply not enough. Simply put, change agents better understand how a business works – in particular, the business in which they are involved. This entails understanding money – where it comes from, where it goes, how it goes and how to keep it. The job also requires knowledge of markets and marketing, products and product development, customers, sales, selling, buying, hiring, firing and just about every other aspect of the business.

In addition to the relevant expertise, change agents also should be well connected throughout the organisation. Active relationships in all areas of the organisation are important in communicating effectively with stakeholders, developing coalitions and designing a successful rollout.

Do they have the necessary skills?

The pressure on the project leadership can be tremendous. Change agents have to be able to operate during times of instability and uncertainty. They have to manage conflicting priorities, multiple constituencies and fast-approaching deadlines. They are responsible for guiding the organisation through the numerous challenges of transition. Therefore, in order to survive, change agents must possess the ability to remain highly effective under intense pressure.

In addition change agents need strong analytical skills. Insight is useful and is sometimes mistaken for brilliance, but insight is often difficult to sell and almost impossible to defend. A rational, well-argued analysis can be ignored but not successfully contested. Change agents must learn to take apart and reassemble operations and systems in novel ways, and then determine the financial and political impacts of what they have done. In short, a disciplined and yet flexible approach is needed to tackle the challenges of change.

People skills – team-building, forging strong interpersonal relationships and communicating within groups – are mandatory for good change agents. The challenge is to build the project team, putting the team members' competencies to best use. To succeed, change agents must create a strong sense of identity, purpose and joint ownership, as well as a high-performing mindset. During the change, communication is the glue that keeps the organisation together and moving toward the desired goal. Change agents need to be able to communicate effectively at all levels and across all organisation boundaries.

Choosing a good leader for change – internal and external

Change is never easy and the failure rate can be high. Top management must take a hard look at the candidates for change agent positions. If none of the internal candidates closely match the requirements of the job, then a search outside the company is required. Once an organisation finds the right individual to be its change agent for a project, management has to ensure that the change agent has 100% of their work time available to dedicate to the success of the initiative.

Self-assessment question 15.5

What are the pros and cons of employing external consultants for a change management issue?

Feedback on page 216

15.6 Impact of change on supply chains

A number of modern trends can be identified in supply chains which reflect the dramatic changes which are occurring.

- An increasing focus is required on integrating suppliers into your organisation's supply chain. Organisations need to keep pace with flexible manufacturing systems, new approaches to inventory based on material requirements planning, just-in-time methods and a growing emphasis on quality. Traditional arm's-length approaches are increasingly outdated. At the same time it could be argued that the growth of e-auctions is a continuation of traditional practices.
- An increasing focus on the development of an agile supply chain. This can involve outsourcing certain components of the operation, establishing a global logistics information system and continual strategic review of where the organisation fits in the supply chain.
- The creation of key performance indicators (KPIs) that seek to develop skills, not just measure them. Examples from a recent study included 100% accuracy of EDI data, 100% on-time picking, 100% accuracy, 98% on-time delivery, and zero damages and loss.
- Building relationships with suppliers that should allow for change and negotiation. Ideas can encompass a well thought-out strategy for outsourcing; select providers rigorously; define your expectations clearly; spell out everything in the contract; establish sound policies and

procedures; identify and avoid potential friction points; communicate effectively; and motivate and reward providers.
- Above all, do not forget the golden rule – 'do unto others as you would have them do to you'!

Learning activity 15.6

It has been emphasised throughout this unit that the business environment is changing dramatically in numerous ways. Section 15.6 above identifies some of the modern trends which are influencing the supply chain environment. Try and reflect creatively about what effect these trends would have on your organisation. In what ways will your organisation be different in, say, 2025?

Feedback on page 216

Now consider the following question.

Self-assessment question 15.6

What effect will these changes have on your supply chain?

Feedback on page 216

Revision question

Now try the revision question for this session on page 299.

Summary

Key learning points from this session:

- There are a wide range of different models of change management and each one considers the implications for the purchasing function and the wider organisation as a whole. Change is complex and models attempt to assist in management understanding.
- Force field analysis assists in providing an analytical assessment of the dynamic involved in change.
- The OD approach is a way of managing change in a planned rather than a reactive manner.
- Action research is a practical way of learning through reflection and action in an iterative way.
- There are pros and cons to be considered in employing external consultants to manage or facilitate change.

Suggested further reading

The section by Mullins (2005) on Organisational Development provides an excellent summary on thinking about the management of change.

Feedback on learning activities and self-assessment questions

Feedback on learning activity 15.1

The main drivers which have been identified in the text are listed below. Are these present in the environment of your own organisation? Are there other factors which are important? Which factors are the most important for your organisation at this current time? You should appreciate through this activity that drivers for change are not fixed, but change according to the organisation's circumstances and the interplay with the external environment.

- technology
- globalisation
- knowledge explosion
- demographics
- privatisation
- regulation and deregulation at the same time
- demanding stakeholders.

Feedback on self-assessment question 15.1

Application will clearly vary with the situation that is involved. See below an example of an organisation which is shutting down its manufacturing facility in the UK and switching production to a low-cost overseas country.

Environment, which considers the dynamics of the larger external environment within which organisations and people operate. PESTLE factors would include: economic pressure from customers to reduce manufacturing costs, social pressures resisting change from local staff employed in the UK, technological availability in the low-cost country, the legal trading environment which governs trading from outside the EU, and environment factors such as low-cost country wage rates and working conditions.

Marketplace requirements for success encompasses the totality of customer requirements that determine what it takes for a business to succeed in its existing markets. Can levels of quality be maintained from the new source? Is speed of delivery not compromised with increased distance from the manufacturing base to the marketplace?

Business imperatives set out what the company must do strategically to be successful. Does trading strategy and operational strategy need to be changed? How is the new facility to be managed, locally or from a centralised and remote head office?

Organisational imperatives specify what must change in the organisation's structure, systems, and so on. Processes (centralised or localised?), technology capture and transfer, resource allocation, staff and training and development need to be reassessed in the light of the cultural interactions which are now needed to successfully realise its strategic business imperatives.

Cultural imperatives show how the norms or collective way of being, working and relating in the company must change to support and drive the organisation's new design, strategy and operations. How can the different cultures be linked together? Is the head office culture to be migrated to the low-cost facility, or will local culture be recognised and accommodated?

Leader and employee behaviour: What style will the CEO and senior managers follow for best results? What norms of behaviour will be expected of staff?

Leader and employee mindset encompasses the worldview, assumptions, beliefs or mental models that will cause people to behave in ways that will drive a sustained change in behaviour and culture. Can we make these significant changes, which have a clear economic logic, lead to performance improvements?

Feedback on learning activity 15.2

Mullins (2005) identifies six major topics associated with OD as:

- organisational culture
- organisational climate
- employee commitment
- organisational conflict
- management of change
- management development.

They interlink to the theme of organisational development, that is, how to improve performance in an organisation by careful planning.

Feedback on self-assessment question 15.2

Fundamentally the OD movement is underpinned by a firm belief that change can be planned by organisations and is not always a reaction to external events.

- People and organisation working together with shared mutual interests.
- OD may deal with individual considerations but only in the context of the organisations where they work.
- Collective outcomes – OD is concerned with meeting goals and needs – cooperation for mutual benefit.
- OD does not support manipulating people toward an end but rather promotes OD for mutually achieved results.

Feedback on learning activity 15.3

- First, an organisation has to *unfreeze* the driving and restraining forces that hold it in a state of quasi-equilibrium.
- Second, an imbalance is introduced to the forces to enable the *change to take place.* This can be achieved by increasing the drivers, reducing the restraints or both.
- Third, once the change is complete the forces are brought back into quasi-equilibrium and *refrozen.*

Feedback on self-assessment question 15.3

Can you clearly identify the distinctive phases?

Unfreezing – challenges to the forces that resist change.

Change – developing strategies to change things.

Refreezing – holding the gains, by ensuring that the changes are underpinned so that they become permanent.

Feedback on learning activity 15.4

Action research is a way of using research in an interventionist way, so that the researcher is both a discoverer of problems and solutions, and is involved in decisions about what is to be done and why. It sees organisational change as a cyclical process where theory guides practice and practice in turn informs theory.

Specifically, action research is a process that involves:

- systematically collecting research data about an ongoing system relative to some objective, need, or goal of that system
- feeding this data back into the system
- taking action by altering selected variables within the system based both on the data and on assumptions about how the system functions
- evaluating the results of actions by collecting more data.

In other words, it involves a researcher working as a consultant with a group of participants. The principle is that if participants are engaged in understanding their situation more fully, they design actions that they themselves will take which will move them toward the aim of their change programme.

Feedback on self-assessment question 15.4

Cyclical change is in essence the unending search for knowledge and understanding through the ongoing cycle of:

Observe >> Reflect >> Plan >> Act >> Observe.

Below is a list of some of the potential benefits of action research.

- People who conduct action research are directly responsible for making decisions. They determine the issues or problems to be researched and they develop and implement the inquiry.
- Action research allows for the improvement of learning for the benefit of all participants.
- Collaboration enriches working relationships.
- Through action research, people gain a greater understanding of their own practice and behaviours.
- Action research allows people to integrate and apply theory and practice.

- Action research can increase teamwork, performance, achievement and morale among people.
- Action research allows people to gain knowledge in research methods.

Feedback on learning activity 15.5

See the section which follows learning activity 15.5 and compare with the skills that you identified.

Feedback on self-assessment question 15.5

See table 15.1. Not an exhaustive list!

Table 15.1

Pros	Cons
Expertise and experience of a wide range of organisations	They lack an initial intimate knowledge of the organisation
Knowledge of theory and application	Maybe they have a particular approach which does not suit our organisation
External expertise may provide an unbiased focus on issues because they have no political baggage from the organisation	Possibly expensive
Can provide a strategic perspective	Do they implement solutions or facilitate us? Issues of ownership
Reputation	Customised solution or off the shelf?

Feedback on learning activity 15.6

Identify some of the patterns and trends which may evolve over the next 20 years.

For a provocative insight read the article entitled 'Ahead of his time' in *Supply Management*, 13 April 2006, which CIPS students and members can access via the CIPS website.

Feedback on self-assessment question 15.6

Questions to reflect upon:

- More global or less?
- More strategic alliances and partnership or less?
- More outsourcing or less?
- More international outsourcing or less?
- Changes to supply patterns as a result of technology?
- Changes to supply patterns as a result of fuel and alternative sources of energy?
- More change or less?

Study session 16

Getting support for change: leading and managing

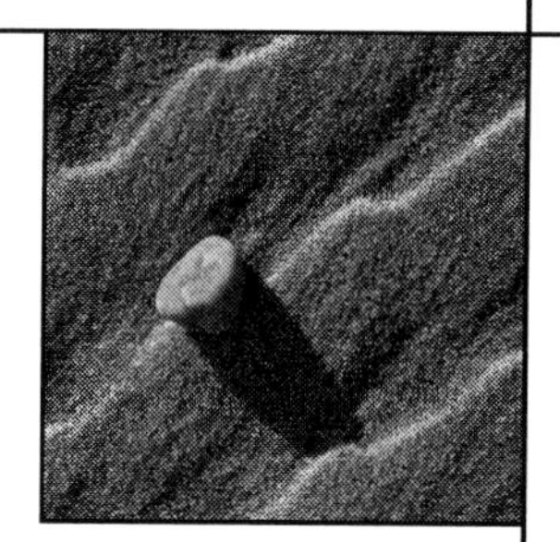

'If you don't like something, change it. If you can't change it, change your attitude. Don't complain.'
Maya Angelou

Introduction

This session develops on the theme of 'planned change' that was explored in study session 15. This session will consider what sort of support is needed from stakeholders in order to make it possible for change to occur, and how that support can be best obtained by effective leadership.

Session learning objectives

After completing this session you should be able to:

16.1 Outline Crainer's seven skills required for managing change.
16.2 Outline the importance of stakeholder consultation and identify key stakeholders who should be consulted when leading change in the purchasing function.
16.3 Identify principal methods of consultation and engagement of stakeholders and explain the need for communication as a vehicle to assist the change process.
16.4 Identify ways and means of resolving conflict with stakeholders using the Thomas–Kilmann conflict model as a framework and describe how this applies to the workplace.
16.5 Determine an appropriate style for leading and managing the strategic change process that will encourage stakeholders to welcome and embrace change within the purchasing function.

Unit content coverage

This study session covers the following topics from the official CIPS unit content document.

Learning objectives

4.3 Develop an appropriate style for leading and managing the strategic change process that will encourage stakeholders to welcome and embrace change within the purchasing function.

- Crainer's seven skills required for managing change: managing conflict, interpersonal skills, project management skills, leadership and flexibility, managing processes, managing strategy and managing personal development
- The importance of stakeholder consultation and the identity of key stakeholders who should be consulted when leading change in the purchasing function
- Principal methods of consultation and engagement of stakeholders, and the need for communication as a vehicle to assist the change process

- Ways and means of resolving conflict with stakeholders using the Thomas–Kilnmann conflict model as a framework. And how this applies to the workplace.

Prior knowledge

Study sessions 14 and 15.

Resources

You will need internet access in order to complete this study session.

Timing

You should set aside about 6 hours to read and complete this session, including learning activities, self-assessment questions, the suggested further reading (if any) from the essential textbook for this unit and the revision question.

16.1 Crainer (1998): skills for managing change

Crainer (1998), cited in Mullins (2005), suggests that managers are often reluctant to change and that change is often viewed as a last resort:

> 'The vast majority of managers are neither trained nor equipped to manage in such an environment [of change].'

Crainer (1998) suggests seven key skills that are involved in managing change:

- *Managing conflict.* The ability to manage conflict in a constructive way so that positive outcomes can emerge. Conflict of itself is not seen as negative. Indeed, constructive openness can unearth disagreements, which can stimulate innovative and creative solutions. Conversely managers also need the skills to diffuse and divert conflict that is potentially destructive and counterproductive.
- *Interpersonal skills.* The effective change manager will have a range of soft interpersonal skills, such as communication, empathy, listening and motivation, such that people are likely to respond positively to him/her.
- *Project management skills.* A blend of the systematic skills of being able to deliver to the required level of quality/cost/time in a complex environment, with the team-building skills to get the best out of the people involved in the project.
- *Leadership and flexibility.* The ability to set clear objectives and to motivate people to achieve them. At the same time understanding that the business environment is capable of rapid change, to which flexible, innovative and creative responses may be required.
- *Managing processes.* Processes are 'how things get done'. Change managers need the ability to manage these carefully so that processes are properly designed, planned and controlled, and improved as necessary.

- *Managing strategy*. Staying mindful of the contribution of the proposed changes to the overall strategic aims and objectives of the organisation, so that the changes smoothly align and make a positive contribution.
- *Managing their own development*. The ability to take responsibility for one's own learning in the context of the organisation and how it is evolving. Particularly important is the acknowledgment that self-development is a lifelong process which never ends.

Crainer argues that managers who possess these seven skills are much less likely to be reactive when it comes to change situations. They will be capable of actively promoting and initiating change in a positive and constructive way.

Learning activity 16.1

Assess Crainer's seven skills required for managing change to determine the completeness of his approach.

Try and link these skills into a structured model which shows the links between the various skills.

Feedback on page 228

Now try to answer the following question.

Self-assessment question 16.1

What particular change management skills are important to external/internal stakeholders – do the needs of external/internal stakeholders differ?

Feedback on page 228

16.2 Stakeholder consultation in the purchasing function

The concept of stakeholders and how to assess them has been considered in some detail in study sessions 4 and 5. The section below is a brief summary, but you should refer back to these sessions for a revision of what has been covered previously.

With reference to Crainer's seven skills, the ability to identify and manage stakeholders is a key management skill. Stakeholders can be inside or outside your organisation. With reference to the purchasing function, stakeholders will exist both inside and external to the organisation at the same time. The manager must build a sense of ownership among other departments and external stakeholders towards change, so that it is not seen as someone else's problem. The manager also expects and needs support from other departments to meet deadlines set, come up with ideas to overcome difficulties and generally to support the change. This will only happen if the staff and stakeholders feel a sense of ownership and responsibility towards the change.

The key management skill in managing stakeholders is to be able to identify ways of influencing the key players and integrating with a range of inside and outside stakeholders, so as to align their interests within the new ideas which you wish to promote:

- Find out whose commitment you need.
- What benefits can be offered to the various stakeholders? In other words, what is in it for them if they support the changes that are proposed?
- Involve others in the work – do not just keep changes within the project team, but also involve the other stakeholders as much as possible.
- Build good relationships with the various stakeholders, since sometimes change projects can take a long time to come to fruition.

Stakeholder mapping

Johnson and Scholes (2004) define stakeholderg mapping as 'identifying stakeholder expectations and power to help understand political priorities'.

What they are suggesting is that when organisations and individuals are thinking about taking actions or developing policies and objectives, they should take careful note of the people who will be affected by those resulting actions, policies and objectives. In taking note they should carefully assess:

- how interested each stakeholder is in the proposed actions, policies and objectives
- how much power and influence they can exert on the proposed actions, policies and objectives.

Learning activity 16.2

Do a stakeholder mapping of a purchasing project in which you are involved.

Feedback on page 228

Using stakeholder mapping as a basis for consultation

Stakeholder mapping (figure 16.2) helps you to address a number of issues in a more structured way.

Figure 16.2

Power \ Level of interest	Low	High
Low	A Minimal effort	B Keep informed
High	C Keep satisfied	D Key players

Who are likely to be the main resistors and supporters of your actions, policies and objectives, and what can you do to influence or persuade them?

Would you wish to reposition any stakeholders, and what strategies can be developed to make those changes happen in the way that you desire?

Remember that stakeholder attitudes may change over time. You therefore need to re-map stakeholders regularly to see if anything has changed, and what actions you then need to take.

- Group A: Low power–low interest. Do not really require much effort in consultation.
- Group B: Low power–high interest. Need to be kept informed, but mostly as a matter of courtesy, since they have little power.
- Group C; Low interest–high power. Need to be kept satisfied because they have high power and they could prove difficult if they were to be upset by your actions.
- Group D; High interest–high power. These are the key players, who must be consulted and considered at every stage of a change because their active support is needed to get things done. They are likely to have direct influence and responsibility for resources which are needed.

Self-assessment question 16.2

Refer back to learning activity 16.2 above, and the stakeholder map that was developed as an example of an IT purchasing project to install a new MRP system across a manufacturing organisation (figure 16.1).

As the installation of the MRP system is proceeding, there have been some major technical problems. You are the project manager for this and find that costs are likely to rise by 20% over budget, and the completion time will be extended by an additional six months.

1. Review your stakeholder map in the light of these changed circumstances.
2. What consultations would you undertake with your key players?

Feedback on page 229

16.3 Consultation and engagementof stakeholders via communication processes

Principles to consider

Consultation and engagement mechanisms need to be effective and adaptable.

Learning activity 16.3

Is there a difference between 'consultation' and 'engagement'?

Feedback on page 230

Consultation and engagement aims to:

- Provide for the views of stakeholders to be considered.
- Inform the process for developing appropriate stakeholder strategies which are likely to be supported.
- Provide for increased accountability and transparency in decision making. If stakeholders are consulted they feel part of the process.
- Enhance stakeholder confidence in the organisation and build closer relationships with those who develop strategies for change in the organisation.

An effective mechanism will be such that it ensures:

- transparency
- accountability
- flexibility
- increased stakeholder awareness of policy issues
- broad stakeholder input and involvement
- efficiency and effectiveness
- promotion of stakeholder confidence
- an understanding of stakeholder perspectives.

Communication and engagement processes should be varied and could encompass some of the following options:

- working through already established jurisdictional advisory, expert or technical committees or groups
- targeted consultation with specific stakeholder groups or in specific geographic areas
- workshops
- meetings
- public forums
- discussions at seminars and conferences
- purpose-specific, time-limited advisory committees
- hard-copy mailouts or web-based mechanisms calling for views
- interactive web-based consultation (for example surveys, response sheets, 'frequently asked questions')
- surveys.

Choice of communication channel will be contingent and will depend upon:

- the amount and type of consultation already undertaken
- the level of broad stakeholder interest
- the degree of complexity of the issue
- the range of stakeholder groups affected
- the level and type of expertise required (expertise may be required on a variety of factors)
- the time and resources available.

Self-assessment question 16.3

You will find a case study at http://www.executiveboard.com/EXBD/Images/PDF/

(continued on next page)

Self-assessment question 16.3 *(continued)*

Crisis%20Management%20Planning%20in%20the%20purchasing%20function.pdf, which consider extreme responses required in a crisis situation. Pay particular note to the sections on stakeholders and communications.

How does good 'communication' assist change, particularly in terms of developing a crisis strategy as referred to in the case study? What immediate steps would you take if the potential disaster actually occurred?

Feedback on page 230

16.4 Thomas–Kilmann conflict model

Thomas and Kilmann developed an instrument and a model for looking at interpersonal conflict, which can be applied to stakeholder situations. They explored possible individual attitudes for handling conflict as well as noting that certain conditions require different approaches.

Using the Thomas–Kilmann instrument, it can be found that individuals may respond according to their predispositions or according to ways they have learned to handle conflict situations. In other words, conflict reactions may be instinctive or based on previous experiences.

The dimensions identified by Thomas and Kilmann – assertive to unassertive and cooperative to uncooperative – are very similar to the social styles dimensions. Four of their conflict styles – competing, avoiding, accommodating, collaborating – map well to the four interaction styles.

Thomas–Kilmann is one of a number of conflict styles type instruments. Among others in common use are DiSC styles, Bolton and Bolton's styles, Alessandra's, and the MBTI Type code. The relationships are based on a match of content and fit of descriptions from the explanations given by the authors, not on instrument results. None of these relationships are perfect matches, yet the essence of each is represented in the interaction styles.

The Thomas–Kilmann conflict mode instrument (TKI) has been the leader in conflict resolution assessment for more than 25 years. This instrument requires no special qualifications for administration, and it is used by human resources (HR) and organisational development (OD) consultants as a catalyst to open discussions and facilitate learning about how conflict handling styles affect personal and group dynamics.

The TKI is designed to assess an individual's behaviour in conflict situations, that is, situations in which the concerns of two people appear to be incompatible. In such situations, we can describe a person's behaviour along two basic dimensions: (1) *assertiveness*, the extent to which the individual attempts to satisfy his or her own concerns, and (2) *cooperativeness*, the extent to which the individual attempts to satisfy the other person's concerns. These two basic dimensions of behaviour can be used to define five specific methods of dealing with conflicts:

- *Competing* is assertive and uncooperative, a power-oriented mode. When competing, an individual pursues his or her own concerns at the other person's expense, using whatever power seems appropriate to win his or her position. Competing might mean standing up for your rights, defending a position you believe is correct, or simply trying to win.

- *Accommodating* is unassertive and cooperative, the opposite of competing. When accommodating, an individual neglects his or her own concerns to satisfy the concerns of the other person; there is an element of self-sacrifice in this mode. Accommodating might take the form of selfless generosity or charity, obeying another person's order when you would prefer not to, or yielding to another's point of view.
- *Avoiding* is unassertive and uncooperative. When avoiding, an individual does not immediately pursue either his or her own concerns or those of the other person. He or she does not address the conflict. Avoiding might take the form of diplomatically sidestepping an issue, postponing an issue until a better time or simply withdrawing from a threatening situation.
- *Collaborating* is both assertive and cooperative, the opposite of avoiding. When collaborating, an individual attempts to work with the other person to find a solution that fully satisfies the concerns of both. It involves digging into an issue to identify the underlying concerns of the two individuals and to find an alternative that meets both sets of concerns. Collaborating between two persons might take the form of exploring a disagreement to learn from each other's insights, with the goal of resolving some condition that would otherwise have them competing for resources, or confronting and trying to find a creative solution to an interpersonal problem.
- *Compromising* is intermediate in both assertiveness and cooperativeness. When compromising, the objective is to find an expedient, mutually acceptable solution that partially satisfies both parties. Compromising falls on a middle ground between competing and accommodating, giving up more than competing but less than accommodating. Likewise, it addresses an issue more directly than avoiding, but does not explore it in as much depth as collaborating. Compromising might mean splitting the difference, exchanging concessions, or seeking a quick middle-ground position.

A best way?

When you look at your results on the TKI, you will probably want to know what are the correct answers. In the case of conflict-handling behaviour, there are no right or wrong answers. All five modes are useful in some situations and each represents a set of useful social skills. Conventional wisdom recognises, for example, that often 'two heads are better than one' (collaborating). But it also says, 'Kill your enemies with kindness' (accommodating), 'Split the difference' (compromising), 'Leave well enough alone' (avoiding), and 'Might is right' (competing).

The effectiveness of a given conflict-handling mode depends upon the requirements of the specific conflict situation and the skill with which you use that mode. People are capable of using all five conflict-handling modes: you should not be thought of as having a single, rigid style of dealing with conflict. However, it may be possible that you use some modes more readily than others and therefore tend to rely upon those modes more heavily. The conflict behaviours you use are the result of both your personal predispositions and the requirements of the situations in which you find yourself. Also, your social skills may lead you to rely upon some conflict behaviours more or less than others.

Learning activity 16.4

Consider topical examples of each generic conflict-handling approach.

Feedback on page 231

Now try self-assessment question 16.4 below to access the TKI instrument and see how you rate.

Self-assessment question 16.4

Visit http://www.teamtrainingsolutions.com/tki.html and go to 'Take the test online, learn your conflict management style'.

Conflict is often seen as negative, yet it can lead to great change and improvement. Learning when your conflict management style is appropriate and adding new styles to your abilities will give you the edge you have been missing up until now. Most of us prefer one style; learning about other styles will increase your effectiveness and ability to work well with others. You could take the test online, but you will have to pay to do so. There is an example of a completed report which may provide useful insights into how the TKI can help you improve your conflict resolution skills.

Feedback on page 231

16.5 Appropriate style for leading and managing change processes

Change is a common occurrence in business today. Because of this, it is important that you possess strong change management skills if you want your business to be a success. Change management skills include:

- leadership development (to get people to believe in you)
- marketing and sales abilities (to promote your case for change)
- communication skills (to help build support for the decision to change).

It will also help if you know a little about the stages people go through psychologically when they are dealing with change so that you are able to tell if you have managed a successful transition or if there are additional problems that you need to address.

The first thing you will want to focus on is your leadership ability. Companies continue to make the mistake of focusing too much on business processes and not enough on good, strong examples of leadership. To be an effective leader in the change management process, it helps if you:

- *Set an example.* As the top person in your business, others look to you for direction, not only in terms of business needs, but also related to behaviour, ethics and standards. If you want others in your business to change, you must set an example for them to follow.
- *Eliminate perks.* Perks suggest division and hierarchical thought processes. By eliminating or reducing your own perks, you show your desire to level the playing field.
- *Walk around and talk to people.* The old school of business management promoted the idea that the top person was off limits, enclosed in his or her own glass tower. Leaders of today interact more with their employees. They manage by walking around and getting to know their employees and learning about the problems they are facing on a day-to-day basis.
- *Be genuine.* As a leader of change, it is important to be as real and honest as possible in your interactions with others. Let others get to know you. Being a leader does not mean hiding your emotions. By interacting with employees on a one-to-one basis, you will build rapport and trust.
- *Have passion.* To be a strong leader, you must have passion around your vision. Without it, you will soon find yourself facing burnout. Leadership is tiring and saps energy at a very high rate so make sure you are passionate about what you do. Without it, you will soon find yourself facing burnout.

It is important to realise that although you can use techniques to smooth the change transition, building your ability as a leader is the first step in the change management process. Once employees believe in you and trust what you are doing, you can then begin your campaign for change. Your campaign for change should target the different 'groups' within your business and outline for each the reasons why a change is necessary. For instance, the board of directors will want to know what the long-term effects of the change will be. Similarly, your employees will want to know how they will be personally affected by the changes you are proposing.

Once a change occurs, it is very important to communicate on a regular basis with all affected. Let your employees know what is happening. If your communication skills are weak or you do not have a formal way of letting your employees know what is happening, set one up before you hit this stage of the change process. By keeping everyone informed, you reduce the chances of low productivity and low morale that often accompany unaccepted change.

To reduce your frustration with this process, it helps to know the six phases people go through whenever they are experiencing any type of change, be it personal or professional.

1 *Anticipation.* People in phase 1 are in the waiting stage. They really do not know what to expect so they wait, anticipating what the future holds.

2. *Confrontation*. At some point, people reach phase 2 and begin to confront reality. At this stage, they are beginning to realise that the change is really going to happen or is happening.
3. *Realisation*. Once the change has happened, people will usually reach phase 3, the stage where they realise that nothing is ever going to be as it once was. Often this realisation will plunge them into phase 4.
4. *Depression*. Phase 4 is a necessary step in the change process. This is the stage where a person mourns the past. Not only have they realised the change intellectually, but now they are beginning to comprehend it emotionally as well.
5. *Acceptance*. Phase 5 marks the point where the person begins to accept the change emotionally. Although they may still have reservations, they are not fighting the change at this stage. Usually, they are beginning to see some of the benefits even if they are not completely convinced.
6. *Enlightenment*. In phase 6, people completely accept the new change. In fact, many wonder how they ever managed the 'old' way. Overall, they feel good about the change and accept it as the status quo from here forward.

Learning activity 16.5

Remember the results of your learning style questionnaire. Reflect on your leading style and its appropriateness – how would you modify it in the light of change situations which you may wish to promote?

Feedback on page 231

Now consider self-assessment question 16.5 below.

Self-assessment question 16.5

What are the impacts of changes in purchasing on other functions in the organisation?

Feedback on page 231

Revision question

Now try the revision question for this session on page 299.

Summary

Key learning points in this session:

- Crainer identified seven key skills required by managers to lead and initiate change in an effective way.
- Stakeholders need to be identified and consulted when change is required in the purchasing function.

- Style and media of communication is vital in any change process.
- Change can lead to conflict and disputes at an individual and group level. The Thomas–Kilmann conflict model is a useful framework for analysis of conflict types and what do with them.
- There is no one best way to lead and manage the strategic change process. Careful stakeholder analysis can assist in successful change initiatives within the purchasing function, which can impact positively on the whole organisation.

Suggested further reading

In addition to Mullins (2005) it is worthwhile trying to read the works of Crainer (1998) and the Thomas–Kilmann conflict mode instrument.

Feedback on learning activities and self-assessment questions

Feedback on learning activity 16.1

You should identify that the seven skills encompass hard and soft skills in equal measure. Reflect on the similarities of Crainer's approach with the Seven-S framework, explored in an earlier session.

Feedback on self-assessment question 16.1

It could be argued that the softer skills are perhaps more relevant to internal stakeholders within the company, who need to be influenced. External stakeholders are likelier to be more influenced by the harder analytical skills of objective facts and figures.

Feedback on learning activity 16.2

Figure 16.1 is an example of stakeholders connected to an IT purchasing project to install a new MRP system across a manufacturing organisation.

Figure 16.1

Power \ Level of interest	Low	High
Low	Trade press The media The local community	Ultimate system used Subcontractors Competitors Other departments in the organisation
High	Shareholders Unions Finance director	Senior managers Software and hardware suppliers Operational staff Customers Suppliers

Feedback on self-assessment question 16.2

1 Changed circumstances mean quite a few more potential 'key players' (figure 16.3).

Figure 16.3

Power \ Level of interest	Low	High
Low		Competitors Other departments in the organisation Trade Press The media The local community
High	Shareholders Unions	Senior managers Software and hardware suppliers Operational staff Customers Suppliers Ultimate system users Subcontractors Finance director

2 More key players require to be consulted (table 16.1).

Table 16.1

Key player	Actions
Senior managers	Explanation of why changes have happened
	Implications of the change for the organisation
	Resources requirements
	A reassessment of the business benefits
Software and hardware suppliers	Review why delays and costs have escalated
	Plans to mitigate further delays and costs
	Resource requirements
	Reassessment of the business benefits
Operational staff	How circumstances affect them
	What they can do to keep on track
Customers	How it affects them
	Interim arrangements for business as usual
	Revision of implementation of the new system

(continued on next page)

Table 16.1 *(continued)*

Key player	Actions
Subcontractors	How it affects them – maybe additional opportunities
	Arrangements for possible catch up
	Revision of implementation of the new system
Finance director	Additional resource requirements
	Revision of the business case
	Revision of project aims and objectives
Suppliers	How it affects them – maybe additional opportunities
	Arrangements for possible catch up
	Revision of implementation of the new system
Ultimate system users	How it affects them – may be additional opportunities
	Arrangements for possible catch up
	Revision of implementation of the new system

Feedback on learning activity 16.3

If done well then they are the same thing. Poor consultation processes can however result in a lack of engagement by stakeholders if they perceive that consultation is not genuinely aimed at eliciting their views.

You will find an example to reflect upon at

http://www.birmingham.gov.uk/Discover?QUERY00=what+we+mean+by+engagement.

Feedback on self-assessment question 16.3

Immediate issues to address in the event of a crisis:

1 *Immediately inform stakeholders.* Decide when to inform each stakeholder and how much each needs to know depending on their personal interest or relevance to the problem. The messages must be similar, but tailored to fit individual needs of information and understanding. Clearly this is a communication and information issue.
2 *Notify media.* Proactively release press statement detailing what is wrong and recovery plan. Appoint a specific spokesperson to represent the company. Only address questions regarding areas of responsibility, such as values, safety precautions and changes in current/future operations. This is the development of an external communication strategy via the media to inform and assure wider stakeholders.

3 *Begin asset recovery process.* Assess the damage and identify what is salvageable. Contact the necessary assistance resources and try to save or replace data, equipment, inventory and other resources.
4 *Address employee needs.* Consider how employees were affected and what assistance they need to continue their duties. Establish childcare, counselling, financial assistance or medical care as needed, or connect employees with community assistance resources. Re-evaluate the flexibility of organisation policies.

Feedback on learning activity 16.4

- *Competing*: A sporting contest.
- *Avoiding*: Many political negotiations when delay indicates opposition to the change. EU budget negotiations in 2005.
- *Compromising*: Negotiation supplier and customers who are long-term partners.
- *Collaborating*: Long-term strategic alliances.
- *Accommodating*: When you are the weaker partner and have little negotiation power.

Feedback on self-assessment question 16.4

What styles do your colleagues use? The TKI gives each person a report on the five conflict styles or modes. Each mode is appropriate in different situations; each is effective at different times. Learn which mode is your primary and when to use it for best results. Discover how to use your less preferred modes for conflict resolution in work, family and social settings. Test each person in your group to learn how you can all get along better.

Conflict is unavoidable. We even have conflict within ourselves without any outside interference. Given that we have to live with conflict, how can we adapt and adjust to make the process go more smoothly and create a positive end result? We can take our results from the TKI to learn new conflict resolution skills. Frequently, our emotions and desires can make communication difficult. Use the TKI to learn what others are doing in those situations and learn to understand your own behaviour during tense moments. You can master these challenges with knowledge and practice.

Feedback on learning activity 16.5

Refer back to the Dunphy and Stace (1993) model which was considered in study session 7. Depending on the degree of change and the style of change required, which of the various quadrants is most appropriate in different situations?

Feedback on self-assessment question 16.5

You should show an awareness of the integrative nature of modern organisations, where each department can affect every other department and function in an iterative way. In this respect the 'drivers of change' and 'resistances to change' can be identified from almost anywhere internal or external to the organisation.

In the highly competitive modern business environment there is generally significant pressure to reduce costs and obtain efficiencies. This means that the purchasing function has a pivotal role to play in implementing such policies, which impact throughout the organisation.

Study session 17

Objectives, strategies and resources

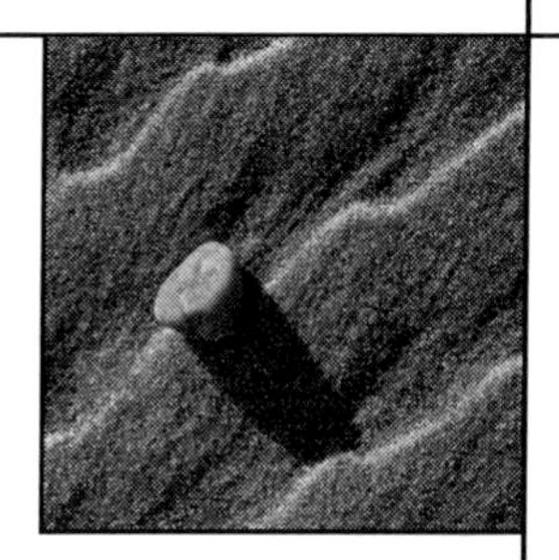

Introduction

Developing a vision for the organisation creates a broad perspective, but this needs to be backed up by objectives, strategies and resources in order to turn the vision into reality. Rudyard Kipling's poem gives us some idea about the various factors that need to be considered when we seek to translate the organisation's vision into tangible plans of action. Refer back to study session 14 for the vocabulary of strategy and the link between vision, objectives, strategies and resources.

'I keep six honest serving-men,
They taught me all I knew,
Their names are What and Why and When and How and Where and Who.'
Rudyard Kipling

Session learning objectives

After completing this session you should be able to:

17.1 Explain why change needs to have objectives and targets.
17.2 Explain how objectives are set for a change programme and describe how objectives should be defined (SMART) and aligned with a broader strategic intent.
17.3 Describe how objectives can be broken down to individual tasks and components and describe the prioritisation process and allocation of resources to achieve targets.
17.4 Evaluate the relative merits of incremental vs. step change and the respective implementation strategies these require.
17.5 Suggest ways in which a change programme can be structured using a steering group, work streams, focus groups, cross-functional teamwork and change agents.
17.6 Determine the resource requirements required for the implementation of change within the purchasing function including human, physical and financial.

Unit content coverage

This study session covers the following topics from the official CIPS unit content document.

Learning objectives

4.4 Set and prioritise justifiable objectives for change and identify strategies for achieving them.

- The need for objectives and targets for change programmes
- How objectives are set for a change programme and how objectives should be defined (SMART) and aligned with a broader strategic intent
- The relative merits of incremental versus step [fundamental] change and the respective implementation strategies these require
- How objectives can be broken down to individual tasks and components

- Contrasts between project and programme management
- Ways in which a change programme can be structured using a steering group, work-streams, focus groups, cross-functional teamwork and change agents
- The prioritisation process and allocation of resources to achieve targets

4.5 Determine the resource requirements for the implementation of change within the purchasing function including:

- Human
- Physical
- Financial

Prior knowledge

Study sessions 14 to 16, particularly study session 14.

Resources

You will need internet access in order to complete this study session.

Timing

You should set aside about 6 hours to read and complete this session, including learning activities, self-assessment questions, the suggested further reading (if any) from the essential textbook for this unit and the revision question.

17.1 Change needs to have objectives and targets

In study session 16 you were asked to consider how to achieve change in an organisational setting. While change can be reactive or proactive, it is very difficult to achieve any sort of change unless there is absolute clarity about what is to be achieved. That clarity comes from having clear objectives and targets.

Johnson and Scholes (2002) define **objectives** as 'statements of specific outcomes that are to be achieved'. In this sense objectives are specific and capable of being measured, so that it is possible to evaluate whether the objective has been achieved, or what else needs to be done to achieve the objective that is desired. Thus objectives and targets are synonymous.

It could be argued however that objectives are broad statements of what is to be achieved and targets are specific measures. For example, the objective for a purchasing department would be to cut costs consistently; the target would be to cut costs by 5% per annum for the next five years.

A neat way of paraphrasing the idea of objectives is provided by Lewis Carroll, in *Alice's Adventures in Wonderland* when the cat is talking to Alice:

> 'If you don't know where you're going, any road will take you there.'

A modern adaptation of the quote above is also useful for our purposes:

> 'If you don't know where you are going, you might wind up someplace else.'

This suggests that without a clearly specified objective it is very easy to drift and not achieve your target. Specific objectives tend to encourage you to stay on course.

Learning activity 17.1

Read up on management by objectives (MBO), and consider whether it is still a relevant concept in today's modern business environment.

Feedback on page 244

Management by objectives (MBO) is a term which was first popularised by Drucker (1954) and has been used by many authors since then.

It is very easy for managers to fail to outline, and agree with their employees, what it is that everyone is trying to achieve. MBO requires precise written description of objectives for the period ahead and timelines for their monitoring and achievement. The process requires that the manager and the employee agree what the employee will attempt to achieve in the period ahead, and that the employee accept and buy into the objectives as a way of developing commitment. Refer to Mullins (2005) Chapter 5 for a detailed discussion of the components which go together to form a cycle of MBO activities.

Self-assessment question 17.1

Explore the link between objectives and targets in the purchasing function of your own organisation.

Feedback on page 245

17.2 Change programmes and SMART objectives

All organisations need to set objectives for themselves, for the products, services or changes that are proposed. Change, if it is to be well organised, needs to be set out as an overarching programme, akin to a project, with detailed goals and objectives, which are to be achieved within the time frame of the change initiative.

Setting objectives is important, since they focus the organisation and staff on specific aims over a period of time and thus can motivate staff to meet the objectives set.

A simple acronym used to set objectives is called SMART, which stands for:

- Specific – objectives should clearly and unambiguously specify what they want to achieve.

- Measurable – you should be able to measure whether you are meeting the objectives or not.
- Achievable – are the objectives you set achievable and attainable?
- Realistic – can you realistically achieve the objectives with the resources you have? Relevant is often substituted for realistic, in that *relevant* asks you to reflect on whether the objective is consistent with the broad purpose of the organisation.
- Time bound – when do you want to achieve the set objectives, and can these objectives be tracked over the life of the change initiative?

Learning activity 17.2

Refer back to your answer to self-assessment question 17.1 above, and show how your operational objectives in the supply chain support a broader strategic intent in your organisation.

Feedback on page 245

Now that you have explored and practised the broad links between strategic goals and operational objectives, try to develop your objectives so that they become SMART.

Self-assessment question 17.2

Visit http://www.ala.org/ala/acrlbucket/is/organizationacrl/planningacrl/smartobjectives/suggestionswriting.htm and follow the instructions on the tutorial. Develop a SMART objective for one of the operational areas that you identified in learning activity 17.2 above.

Feedback on page 246

17.3 Individual tasks and components, prioritisation and resource allocation

Kipling's quote gives a good guide as to the factors which need to be considered in looking at how individual tasks can be developed from a broad set of objectives. Breaking down the whole objective into a set of detailed activities is the essence of a good action plan, and if you can answer the questions in table 17.1, you are well on the way to identifying what needs to be done.

Table 17.1 An implementation plan for individual tasks

What is being done?	**Why** is it being done?	**What else** is being done?
Who is doing it?	**Why** are they doing it?	**Who else** could do it?
When are they doing it?	**Why** then?	**When else** could it be done?
Where is it being done?	**Why** there?	**Where else** could it be done?
How is it being done?	**Why** that way?	**How else** could it be done?

Setting priorities

Setting priorities is invariably a difficult task. Plans for change management initiatives can often seem haphazard and disorganised since there are so many different factors to be considered, and they often interlink with each other, so it is hard to distinguish cause and effect.

There is a real need to rank or prioritise all these important 'high priority or special attention' items in order to minimise implementation confusion which clearly exists if you are unsure about priorities. It is in this area that management and leadership come to the fore.

There is also another real need to resolve from the outset problems related to inconsistent and conflicting objectives and targets of the plan between and among such goals. In one way or another and to different degrees, these objectives need to be made compatible with each other.

Trade-offs and sacrifices between and among the different goals and objectives have to be clearly resolved to arrive at a well-conceived and easy-to-implement plan.

A development plan is a statement which presents and describes:

- The organisation's view on how the change initiative contributes to the overall vision or mission of the organisation.
- What impact the change will have on existing objectives, strategies and targets.
- What resources will be required to enable change to take place, and where those resources will come from.
- Whether the change is to be broken down into a number of contributing subprojects.
- What appropriate incentives (pecuniary and non-pecuniary) are needed to ensure the support of staff and other stakeholders.

The plan needs to brings together in one place a well thought-out and clear *need* and *policy statement*, *objectives* and *targets*, *development strategies*, *available resources* in terms of budgetary allocations, and finally an *implementation* procedure of the change initiative which is proposed.

Prioritisation

An essential part of organising candidates for action into high-level plans is prioritisation. Prioritisation may also be useful at earlier stages of the strategy creation process, for instance when considering which strategic themes have greater importance to the organisation.

Learning activity 17.3

What sort of tools and techniques are available to assist in the prioritisation of the tasks that need to be done in a change initiative?

Feedback on page 246

There are a vast range of tools and techniques available for evaluating priorities which you can explore in your further reading. Among the most useful ones to consider are:

- *Pareto analysis* – what are the vital few tasks which make the biggest contribution to success of the change initiative, and which are the more trivial tasks, which can be addressed later on?
- *Suitability, feasibility, acceptability* as a range of screening questions, which identifies the most important options to consider (Johnson and Scholes, 2002).
- *Importance–performance matrix* (Slack et al, 2004) considers change options from a customer perspective. What change issues are important to the customer? How does your organisation perform according to the customer? From this analysis emerge the urgent actions which need to be done first and the other actions which can take longer to effect.
- *Critical path and network analysis.* Critical path analysis and PERT are powerful tools that help you to schedule and manage complex projects. They were developed in the 1950s to control large defence projects, and have been used routinely since then. As with Gantt charts, the essential concept behind critical path analysis is that you cannot start some activities until others are finished. These activities need to be completed in a sequence, with each stage being more-or-less completed before the next stage can begin. These are 'sequential' activities. Other activities are not dependent on completion of any other tasks. You can do these at any time before or after a particular stage is reached. These are non-dependent or 'parallel' tasks.

Self-assessment question 17.3

A change programme has identified the following as activities which need to be completed in order to complete a project. The programme also identifies dependencies and estimated durations (table 17.2).

Table 17.2

Activity	Depends upon	Duration (days)
A	–	10
B	–	3
C	A	5
D	B	8
E	C, D	6
F	B	8
G	F	12

1 Draw a diagram of the network.
2 How long will the project take, and what is the critical path?

Feedback on page 246

17.4 Relative merits of incremental vs. step change

It is generally accepted that there are two main approaches that organisations can take towards change: incremental change and step change.

Incremental change is literally seeking to achieve small improvements in any element of the organisation's activities, but to do so continuously and consistently over time. This approach is often referred to as the *kaizen* approach. Step change, often referred to as business process re-engineering (BPR) , or transformational change, is altogether more radical, seeking to achieve significant improvement in activities in a relatively restricted timescale. Figure 17.3 expresses these approaches in a simple and graphical way.

Figure 17.3: Kaizen and BPR

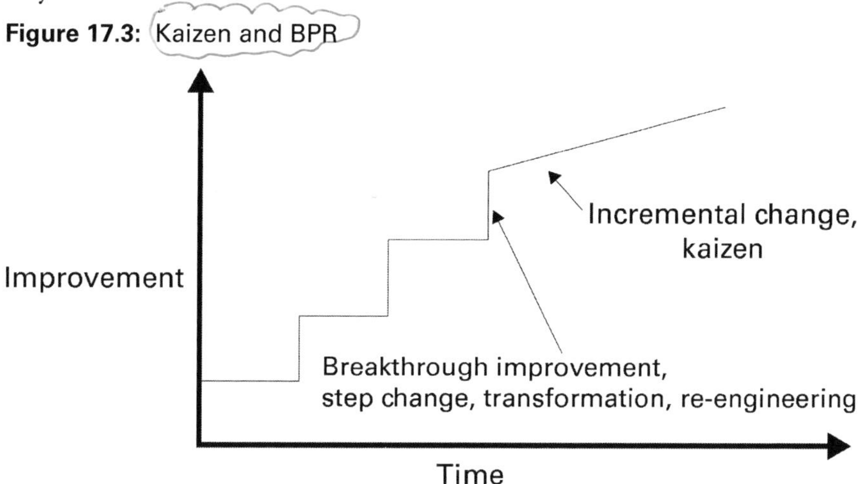

Kaizen literally means 'improvement' which is often interpreted as a gradual process of incremental change. Mullins (2005) defines **kaizen** as:

> 'a Japanese concept of a total quality approach based on continual evolutionary change with considerable responsibility to employees within certain fixed boundaries'.

Mullins (2005) identifies the following main components of a kaizen approach to change:

- Detailed analysis of all the steps in a process, via process mapping.
- The process mapping demonstrates where changes can be made by looking at eliminating any non-value-added activities.
- Improvements can be in equipment (better machinery), materials (the items that are used) or in behaviours of employees.
- Kaizen looks at eliminating non-value-added activities and expressing the savings in terms of time or money.

BPR has been defined by Hammer and Champy (1993) as:

> 'the fundamental rethinking and radical redesign of business processes to achieve dramatic improvements in critical, contemporary measures of performance, such as cost, quality, service and speed'.

Distinctive features of BPR are, among others:

- A zero-based approach which means starting from scratch, and largely ignoring past trends in performance. This approach is often referred to as *greenfield thinking.*
- A focus on process, how we deliver goods and services to the customer across the organisation.

- A focus on radical thinking to achieve significant improvements.

Incremental and step change: together or separate?

While the two approaches are often suggested as alternative philosophies towards change, there are benefits to be derived from both approaches, and there is no real reason why both approaches cannot be used by organisations:

- BPR if properly implemented can lead to dramatic, quantifiable improvements in a short time frame. Hammer and Champy (1993) suggest that BPR initiatives, even if they are extensive, should be capable of producing measurable benefits within a year.
- At the same time BPR is often complex, difficult and risky. This means that clear leadership and management is an absolutely essential component for success.
- Kaizen is often easier than BPR because only small improvements are needed which may require far less complexity and can often be driven and initiated by staff themselves since often relatively small amounts of resources are required.

At the same time, kaizen may not deliver sufficient improvements to catch up or keep pace with competitors who are working and improving at a faster rate than your organisation. There is a risk that you may be falling behind by proceeding too slowly. But if you are ahead of the competition, then kaizen helps you to keep ahead by not getting complacent and over-confident.

Learning activity 17.4

Provide examples of both approaches to change from contemporary issues.

Feedback on page 246

Now that you have explored kaizen and BPR in a topical environment, consider them in a more business-focused way by attempting self-assessment question 17.4 below.

Self-assessment question 17.4

Assess the pros and cons for the kaizen and BPR approaches to change management.

Feedback on page 247

17.5 Change programme structures

The Department for Education and Skills has comprehensive guidance on its website about programme and project management.

Visit http://www.dfes.gov.uk/ppm/index.cfm?ContentID=151&SiteID=1 for a useful discussion.

What is programme management?

Broadly a programme is a collection of projects and other items of work managed coherently together as a portfolio. There are several distinct types of programme which are found in the public sector, that is, change, work or policy. Working definitions of theses are as follows:

- A change programme is a group of projects and other items of work managed coherently together.
- A work programme is a group of initiatives which may or may not be related but which have to be coordinated because they call on the same pool of resources.
- A policy programme is a change programme that is focused on making societal changes.

The working definition of a project is as follows:

> A project is a temporary organisation, either as a freestanding entity or now more commonly as an integrated component of a programme, set up to produce something or manage a particular change.

It is worth noting that programmes as well as projects can be temporary; however, most programmes span over a longer period of time than projects.

Components of a well-structured change initiative

A steering group consists of a number of senior managers from a variety of specialist areas whose purpose is to take a broad overview of the change initiative from a strategic perspective to ensure that the change contributes positively to the overall corporate strategy and satisfies various stakeholder perspectives. At the same time the steering group is there to advise, guide and support the team or teams who are actually responsible for the day-to-day implementation of programmes or projects.

Complex projects and change management initiatives often comprise a wide range of different tasks and activities which need to be implemented. Deconstruction of an initiative into its various components is effectively achieved by breaking the whole project into its individual activities and assigning work streams, which place the responsibility for delivery of the objectives to distinct groups who each have a manageable activity to perform which is SMART defined and thus capable of being measured, monitored and controlled. In this sense the term work stream is synonymous with work teams. Modern approaches combine the idea of work streams with the concept of a value stream. A value stream is an end-to-end collection of activities that create or achieve a result for a customer of the enterprise. The value stream is made up of everything that supports the value stream tasks and activities.

It is clear that the steering group must be aware of what the work streams are doing, to ensure that they are aligned, well resourced and working in a holistic way to achieve the overall objectives. Refer to study session 4 concerning the role of project managers in these activities.

Learning activity 17.5

Research examples of steering groups and their purpose from the literature.

Feedback on page 247

Focus groups constitute a form of scientific social, policy and public opinion research using external stakeholders. Focus groups should be distinguished from 'discussion groups', 'problem-solving groups', 'buzz groups' or 'brainstorming groups'. They are not designed to help a group reach consensus or to make decisions, but rather to elicit the full range of ideas, attitudes, experiences and opinions held by a selected sample of respondents on a defined topic. Through focused interaction on questions of interest to the organisation, respondents from target groups can provide a wealth of qualitative data not available from surveys alone. Participants are chosen because of background characteristics of special interest to the organisation and are given the opportunity in a guided interaction setting to discuss and debate issues surrounding a programme, policy, service, plan or product. Focus groups normally range from one to two hours in duration. The moderator can pursue ideas that are generated during the discussion. Motivations, feelings and values behind reactions to change initiatives can be elicited through probing, restating questions and eliciting opinion from others in the group. Advantages of the focus group are that the organisation is brought closer to the target groups through observation of the session and/or through listening to tapes; participants stimulate each other in an exchange of ideas that may not emerge in individual interviews or surveys; ideas can be linked to areas of particular interest to the organisation for in-depth exploration. Focus groups provide an external stakeholder perspective, which the change initiative should encompass positively if success is to be achieved.

A cross-functional team is a team composed of at least three members from diverse functional entities working together towards a common goal. This team will have members with different functional experiences and abilities, and who will likely come from different departments within the organisation. Organisations are now faced with a dynamic business environment. With this rapidly changing and highly competitive world of business, companies are forced to be timely and error-free. In light of this, traditional corporate structuring must be revised to address the needs of today's marketplace. Bureaucracy is inefficient and time consuming. Cross-functional teams are much more likely to be relevant to the new structures that are now required. Refer to study sessions 8 – 10 on teams and teamworking for the underpinning rationale.

Finally, change agents are the catalysts (managers and leaders) who will actually make change happen. Their involvement can be detailed and hands on, actually implementing the change, with teams, or more strategic and distant, providing the vision and direction, but leaving the implementation more to the team itself. Change agents can also be either internal or external to the organisation. The merits of 'consultants' have already been considered in an earlier session.

Self-assessment question 17.5

Consider a change programme that you have been involved in at your workplace. What was the change programme structure? Did the structure prove appropriate for the change that was required?

Feedback on page 247

17.6 Human, physical and financial resources

A final element of a change plan is how many resources will actually be needed to support the change initiative.

Resource requirements are the things that are needed to achieve the change objectives, expressed in a quantifiable way, so that managers can assess needs against the potential benefits that the change will bring.

Learning activity 17.6

What sorts of resources are going to be needed to run the London Olympics in 2012? Where will they come from?

Feedback on page 247

Categories of resources can be classified in terms of:

- *Human resources*. How many people will be needed to work on the change programme, and for how long will they be required? Will these people be from within the organisation or hired in from outside? If from within, how long can they be available for our change initiative, full time or part time, and who replaces them in their normal jobs? What training and support is required for our change people, whether internal or external? What assistance will be needed from people in other departments who are not directly involved in the change but who may provide some limited but useful support from areas of their technical expertise? This all needs to be calculated in terms of people requirements.
- *Physical resources*. What equipment and materials will be needed? Equipment can be classified in terms of equipment directly required in productive activities, or equipment to provide support services such as databases and information processing. Again, is this available from internal sources or is capital expenditure required? Materials can be classified in similar ways to equipment.
- *Financial resources* are the cash requirements to finance the human and physical resources. Financial requirements can be working capital, which will flow outwards and inwards over the life of the change initiative and thereafter, and capital expenditure which will depreciate over the lifetime of the assets acquired.

It is beyond the scope of this unit to consider these resource plans in more detail, but other modules in the course will provide a thorough grounding in the knowledge and skills required.

Self-assessment question 17.6

What factors need to be considered before making changes to strategic and operational plans?

Feedback on page 247

Revision question

Now try the revision question for this session on page 299.

Summary

Key learning points from this session:

- Change is only meaningful if we have clear objectives and targets. They provide a clear focus and a means of assessment.
- Objectives should SMART and clearly aligned with the broader strategic intent.
- Objectives should be broken down into individual tasks and components. You need to be clear how prioritisation is critical to achieving objectives and targets.
- Kaizen and BPR are different ways of achieving improvement over time, but they can be blended together in appropriate circumstances.
- Change programmes need to be clearly structured to achieve objectives.
- Change needs a variety of human, physical and financial resources, which need regular monitoring and evaluation.

Suggested further reading

Three texts explore, from quite different perspectives, the aspects of how to turn strategic plans into actual operational plans.

Drucker (1954) explores the management aspects. Slack, Chamber and Johnston (2004) explore the operational aspects, and Hammer and Champy (1993) propose BPR as the best way to achieve radical change.

Feedback on learning activities and self-assessment questions

Feedback on learning activity 17.1

You should find a variety of views on MBO from the literature:

- Mullins (2005) suggests that MBO provides an opportunity for staff to accept greater responsibility and to make a higher level of personal contribution to the organisation.

- Crainer (1998) suggests that MBO demands too much data and becomes too complex and time consuming.
- Others suggest that modern human resource management (HRM) has supplanted MBO by being far more integrative in recognising the complexity of the relationship between people, management and performance.

Feedback on self-assessment question 17.1

Refer back to the strategy hierarchy model and consider the broad purpose of the organisation's purchasing function at a corporate level. How do targets and objectives underpin this broad purpose at a tactical and business level? Figure 17.1 is an example of the link between objectives and targets in a local authority context.

Figure 17.1: The strategic scope of purchasing, The Anywhere Council at three levels

Feedback on learning activity 17.2

Is there a clear link between operational specifics such as:

- e-tendering
- speeding things up
- dispatch
- records and system
- maintenance
- invoice/order handling
- enquiries/quotes/complaints
- pricing
- dealing with external failure
- developing partnerships

and the strategic objectives of:

- politics
- partnering
- agenda for change
- Gershon Report
- Long-range planning
- predicting availability
- policy
- sourcing
- reciprocal trading
- ethical stance
- post-tender negotiations.

Feedback on self-assessment question 17.2

Is your objective SMART? Can you make it even more focused by quantifying the measure even more narrowly?

Feedback on learning activity 17.3

To find out about some of the available tools and techniques, read the rest of section 17.3.

Feedback on self-assessment question 17.3

1 The network diagram (figure 17.2) is drawn according to one of the several conventions which can be used.

Figure 17.2

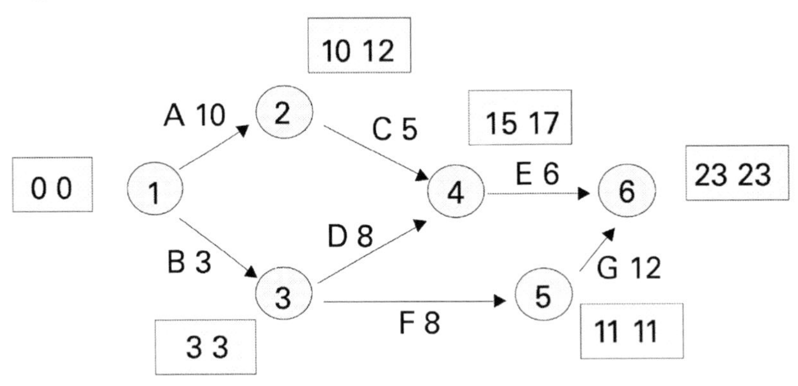

2 Duration of the project is 23 days. The critical path = B–F–G.

Feedback on learning activity 17.4

http://www.timesonline.co.uk/article/0%2C%2C13509-2094724%2C00.html quotes from an article about Belarus and the uncertain political climate there at present. Kaizen would focus on a gradual development of democracy as a way of steadily improving the political and economic conditions in that country. BPR would look at more revolutionary activity to speed up the pace of change dramatically.

The Commonwealth Games were taking place at the time of writing. Consider kaizen and BPR as alternative philosophies of improvement of athletic performance.

Feedback on self-assessment question 17.4

Visit http://www.systems2win.com/LK/kaizen/kaizen_vs_reengineering.htm for an interesting tabulation of the relative merits of each approach. A more advanced debate can be accessed on http://ocw.mit.edu by entering ESD84DocSemSession12Nov20SsytemsChange1 into the search box.

Feedback on learning activity 17.5

You will find information on a Software Engineering Institute steering group's purpose, responsibilities, membership and operation at http://www.sei.cmu.edu/cmmi/background/sg.charter.html.

Visit http://www.greencampus.harvard.edu/about/campuswide.php for an example from higher education.

Feedback on self-assessment question 17.5

Try and distinguish elements in your example of a structure, for example:

- steering groups
- work streams
- focus groups
- cross-functional teams
- change agents.

Were any of these elements missing in the structure and did this impact on achievement of objectives?

Feedback on learning activity 17.6

A balance of human, physical and financial resources should be identified. Sources of resources should include some sort of stakeholder assessment.

Feedback on self-assessment question 17.6

Are goals and objectives being achieved or not? If they are, then acknowledge, reward and communicate the progress. If not, then consider the following questions which look at both the broad strategic objectives (the big picture) and the detailed implementation issues (the physical, human and financial resources):

- Will the goals be achieved according to the timelines specified in the plan? If not, then why?
- Should the deadlines for completion be changed? Be careful about making these changes; you need to know why efforts are behind schedule before times are changed.

- Does staff have adequate resources (money, equipment, facilities, training and so on) to achieve the goals?
- Are the goals and objectives still realistic?
- Should priorities be changed to put more focus on achieving the goals?
- Should the goals be changed? Be careful about making these changes; you need to know why efforts are not achieving the goals before changing the goals.
- What can be learned from our monitoring and evaluation in order to improve future planning activities and also to improve future monitoring and evaluation efforts?

Study session 18

Implementing change at the coal face

Change is needed but how do we implement it in a day-to-day situation? How do we turn the theory into practical day-to-day reality?

Introduction

This session considers in particular how leaders and managers can delegate authority to their staff in order to implement change successfully. Delegation is just one of the ways that leaders and managers can choose to implement policies and strategies. Delegation is increasingly regarded as an effective way of managing staff in today's fast-changing business environment because of the extra responsiveness and flexibility that empowered staff can bring to dynamic situations.

Session learning objectives

After completing this session you should be able to:

18.1 Understand what is meant by delegation and identify the requisite leadership behaviours that enable effective delegation and outline what support is needed for delegated responsibility to work successfully.
18.2 Link to Hersey's model of situational leadership, and explain the roles and responsibilities of the leader.
18.3 Describe how to monitor and review delegated responsibilities and tasks and develop appropriate reward and recognition associated with the successful delivery of them.
18.4 Use force field analysis to identify forces and barriers to change and determine what needs to be done at an individual level to develop and aid change so that it is successful.

Unit content coverage

This study session covers the following topics from the official CIPS unit content document.

Learning objectives

4.6 Delegate responsibility for the effective implementation of change including planning and implementation and delegating both responsibility and power to managers.

- What is meant by delegation and what are the requisite leadership behaviours that enable effective delegation
- Link to Hersey's model of situational leadership
- Support needed to be given in order to allow a delegated responsibility to work successfully: clear direction/sponsorship, recognised authority/mandate, appropriate resources, appropriate training and capabilities, reasonable timescales and communication support

- How to monitor and review delegated responsibilities and tasks
- Developing appropriate rewards and recognition associated with the successful delivery of delegated activities
- How a leader might take corrective action and redirect activities that have been delegated

4.7 Use force field analysis to identify forces and barriers to change and determine what needs to be done to develop and assist change.

- Bureaucracy: i.e. departmentalism, formality of management
- Resources
- Politics
- Insecurity
- Risk
- Blame culture
- Deference
- How individuals respond to change
- Link to Lewin's force field analysis
- Why some change programmes fail
- The principal barriers to effective change and the mitigating actions required to overcome resistance

Prior knowledge

Study sessions 14 to 17.

Resources

You will need internet access in order to complete this study session.

Timing

You should set aside about 6 hours to read and complete this session, including learning activities, self-assessment questions, the suggested further reading (if any) from the essential textbook for this unit and the revision question.

18.1 Effective delegation and leadership support

Mullins (2005) defines **delegation** as:

> 'the process of entrusting authority and responsibility to others through the various levels of the organisation, and the creation of a special manager–subordinate relationship'.

He argues that it is a critical management skill, particularly in larger organisations where work has to be largely done by the staff.

Learning activity 18.1

Critically evaluate the factors that need to be considered in 'delegation of tasks' from the perspective of the manager and the staff.

Feedback on page 262

Heathfield (2006) offers some useful guidelines to be an effective delegator, by arguing that leadership styles are situational. Situational requirements depend on the task, the team and people's capabilities and knowledge, the time and tools available and the results desired.

Managers and leaders make daily decisions about the appropriate leadership style to employ in each work situation. The purpose is to obtain employee involvement and employee empowerment to enable people to optimise their contribution at work.

Guidelines for effective delegation include:

- Whenever possible, when delegating, give the person a whole task to do. If the task is too extensive, people need to be aware of the overall goals, and how what they are doing contributes. People are most effective when they are aware of the big picture.
- Make sure people understand exactly what you want them to do. Question, observe and seek feedback to make sure that the goals are clear and the objectives are SMART.
- If you have a vision of what a successful outcome or output will look like, share that with people.
- Identify the key points of the project or dates when you want feedback about progress. Make sure progress is able to be tracked and related to clear deadlines and outcomes.
- Be absolutely clear how outcomes will be measured.
- Relate and link appropriate rewards to successful completion.

Poor delegation is characterised by:

- poor team and individual motivation and morale
- the team is confused, and this spills over into conflicts and tensions
- you get questions about delegated tasks too often.

Positive aspects of delegation include:

- higher efficiency
- increased motivation
- it develops the skills of your team
- better distribution of work through the group.

Responsibility for activities and tasks always lies ultimately with managers; delegation is not abrogation. Even though you have delegated a task to someone else, you are still responsible for making sure the task is done on time and correctly. If the task fails, you cannot point the finger. You delegated. It is your fault. You may have picked the wrong person for the job.

The amount of authority that is delegated is up to the manager and the situation. A good guide is that it should be enough for people to successfully complete the task.

There are several common problems with delegation which need to be considered and minimised:

- Managers can mistakenly assume that assigning a task is synonymous with delegating it. An assignment means telling someone what to do, when and how to do it, so it carries no real responsibility. It is just a way of getting someone else to do something for you. It is not necessarily wrong to assign something but it is not delegation.
- Some managers go too far in the other direction and assume that delegation means handing something over totally without any real direction or support. This can work if the person delegated is experienced and fully motivated to accomplish the goals, and has clear communication so that no misunderstandings are likely to occur.

Implicit in the above is that delegation is a developmental process. This will be considered further in the next section.

Self-assessment question 18.1

You are empowered to undertake a significant task. What help do you need from your leader?

Feedback on page 263

18.2 Situational leadership

Learning activity 18.2

Refer back to section 3.1 where leadership styles were considered in detail, and remind yourself about situational leadership.

Feedback on page 263

Hersey (1984) and Hersey et al (2000) developed the model of situational leadership as a particularly effective way of supporting staff in an appropriate way.

Their approach identifies the *situation or circumstance* as the key factor in determining which leadership style is most relevant and appropriate. It is a key skill of leadership to recognise what is going on, and then select the best behaviour or style to deal with that situation effectively (see figure 18.1).

Figure 18.1: Situational leadership model

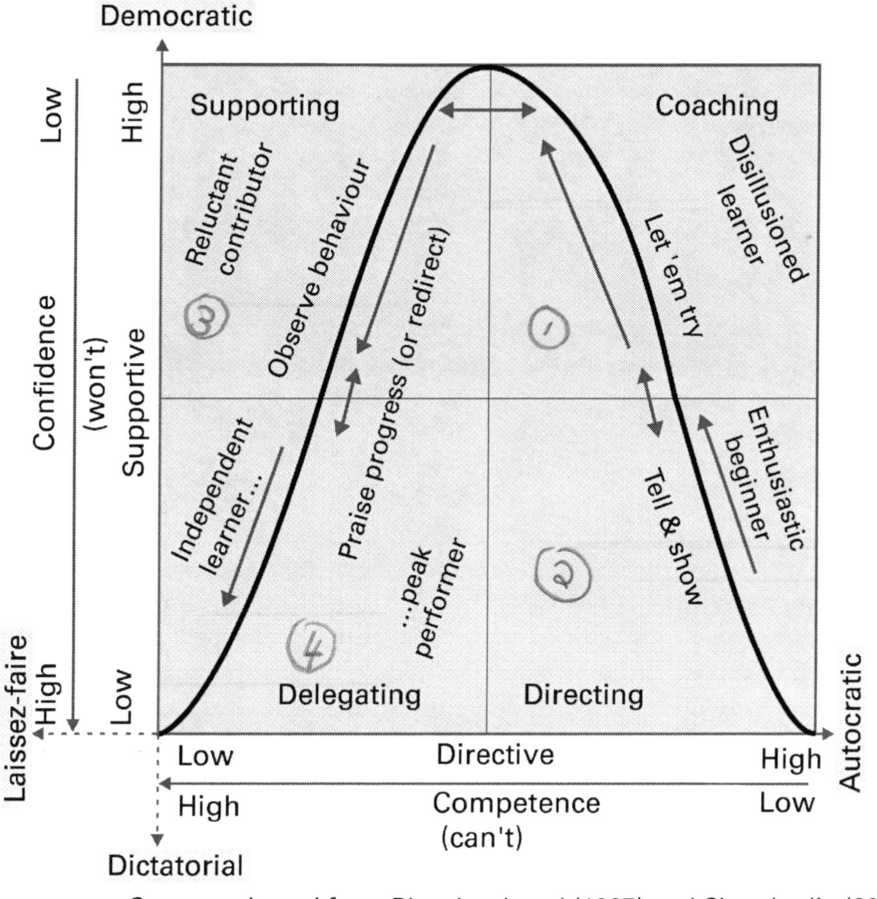

Source: adapted from Blanchard et al (1987) and Chamberlin (2002)

In order to assess the best behaviour or style that is appropriate the leader has to consider the 'state of readiness' of staff that the leading is attempting to influence. Readiness is a combination of ability, willingness and resources.

- Ability refers to skills, knowledge and so on.
- Willingness is attitudes – wanting to perform.
- Resources are those tangibles which actually provide assistance such as equipment, money, information and other people.

Managers and leaders therefore have to develop their people in all of the three dimensions in order to have effective staff. In essence, hard and soft skills are equally important.

Hersey et al identified four general states of readiness:

- R1 – low follower readiness; unable, unwilling, uncommitted and demotivated.
- R2 – low to moderate follower readiness; unable but willing and motivated.
- R3 – moderate to high follower readiness; able but unwilling and insecure.

- R4 – high follower readiness; able, willing and confident.

Depending on the state of readiness, four corresponding leadership styles are proposed:

- S1 – telling – requires a lot of guidance on the specific tasks to be completed.
- S2 – selling – high guidance on the task and two-way communication.
- S3 – participating – requires a lot of two-way communication, but less focus on task since the follower is capable.
- S4 – delegating – little direction or support needed because the follower is able and motivated.

In terms of effective delegation, S4 is appropriate and most effective when you have staff who are at R4, both competent and motivated to take full responsibility. Delegation style is most appropriate with a high follower readiness level.

The Hersey-Blanchard situational leadership theory is based on the amount of direction (task behaviour) and amount of socio-emotional support (relationship behaviour) a leader must provide given the situation and the 'level of maturity/state of readiness' of staff. Task behaviour is the extent to which the leader engages in spelling out the duties and responsibilities to an individual or group. This behaviour includes telling people what to do, how to do it, when to do it, where to do it, and who is to do it. In task behaviour the leader engages in one-way communication. Relationship behaviour is the extent to which the leader engages in two-way communications. This includes listening, facilitating and supportive behaviours. In relationship behaviour the leader engages in two-way communication by providing socio-emotional support. Maturity and readiness is the willingness and ability of a person to take responsibility for directing behaviour. People tend to have varying degrees of maturity, depending on the specific task, function or objective that a leader is attempting to accomplish through their efforts.

To determine the appropriate leadership style to use in a given situation, the leader must first determine the maturity level of the followers in relation to the specific task that the leader is attempting to accomplish through the effort of the followers. As the level of followers' maturity increases, the leader should begin to reduce his or her task behaviour and increase relationship behaviour until staff reach a moderate level of maturity. As the followers begin to move into an above-average level of maturity, the leader should decrease not only task behaviour but also relationship behaviour.

Self-assessment question 18.2

Try the following multiple-choice questions to test your knowledge of delegation and SL theory.

1 Empowerment of people is most effective by use of the following:
(a) Joint decision making
(b) Delegation

(continued on next page)

Self-assessment question 18.2 *(continued)*

(c) Proactive consultation
(d) Reactive consultation.

2 What is the most likely benefit from a participative style?
(a) The decision will be made more quickly
(b) The quality of the decision will be better
(c) People are more likely to accept decisions
(d) There will be greater agreement among the participants.

3 Which of the following was *not* recommended as a guideline for participative leadership?
(a) Present a proposal as tentative and encourage people to improve it
(b) Restate ideas and concerns expressed by someone to verify understanding
(c) Identify the best ideas and quickly dismiss any with obvious weaknesses
(d) Let people know how their ideas and suggestions were eventually used.

4 Which of the following is *not* likely to be a benefit from using delegation?
(a) Less responsibility for an overloaded manager
(b) More development of the subordinate's skills
(c) Increased commitment by the subordinate
(d) More efficient time management for the manager.

5 Delegation is most likely to occur when:
(a) The manager is confident and secure
(b) The task is important
(c) Subordinate jobs are highly interdependent
(d) Work procedures are highly standardised.

6 Which of the following was *not* a guideline for how to delegate effectively?
(a) Specify the subordinate's scope of authority and limits of discretion
(b) Explain the new responsibilities and the expected results
(c) Arrange for the subordinate to receive relevant information
(d) Tell the subordinate to report any problems immediately.

7 A manager should *not* delegate tasks that are:
(a) Unpleasant
(b) Symbolically important
(c) Complex and difficult
(d) Urgent but not important.

8 Decisions about what to delegate to staff are most likely to be influenced by:
(a) How much the subordinate wants the assignment
(b) How much the manager is overloaded with extra work
(c) How competent and trustworthy the subordinate is
(d) How long the subordinate has worked for the manager.

9 What is the *least* important reason for delegating to subordinates?
(a) Get rid of tedious tasks that are time wasters
(b) Develop subordinate skills and confidence
(c) Make the job of subordinates more interesting
(d) Increase subordinate commitment to a task.

Feedback on page 263

18.3 Monitoring, reviewing and rewarding of delegated tasks

Learning activity 18.3

Define 'monitor', 'review' and 'reward' in the context of achieving performance.

Feedback on page 263

Delegation is managers interacting with their people and as such is iterative and dynamic. It is a complex process that spans a variety of behaviours including preparatory activities, communication behaviours, monitoring, reviewing, feedback and reward.

Delegation is not abrogation and a manager still needs to provide support to the people to whom tasks and activities have been delegated:

- Clear direction is required in terms of specific goals and SMART objectives.
- The manager still provides sponsorship to people, in that the role of the manager is to be available to provide, help, support, guidance and resources throughout the tasks.
- Resources need to be supported by appropriate training to develop any additional skills and capabilities which may be needed by staff.
- The manager needs to underpin the authority of the people who have been delegated tasks by providing political support and status so that people will not be hindered by other stakeholders in achieving the tasks and objectives.

When managers have delegated tasks to their staff, they are still required to support, monitor and review the tasks that have been delegated. A number of factors and variables need to be monitored and reviewed such as:

- Planning/strategising about the methods that will be employed to achieve the tasks.
- Setting relevant and appropriate performance criteria.
- Scheduling deadlines and subtasks which are agreed with staff.
- Performance monitoring at appropriate intervals during the tasks.
- Performance evaluation and realisation of benefits on an ongoing basis, even after the tasks are completed.
- Making decisions about incentives and rewards for staff, which are agreed.
- Keeping running lists of the competencies and skills of staff and matching tasks to those skills and competencies.
- Being aware of new skills and competencies which may be needed in the future, and having development plans in place to obtain those over time.
- What communications need to be in place with people doing the task.
- What activities will build long-term trust with staff.
- Establishing an appropriate authority relationship with the staff being delegated.

Monitoring is a particular critical activity because it points to the basic conundrum of delegation. A manager may delegate authority and tasks, but there are times when the need to monitor performance takes so much time and effort that it detracts from other activities the manager must do. In these cases, the value of delegation can be nullified or even negative. Monitoring is an essential and time-consuming aspect of delegation.

Effective delegation

Delegation can work well when staff and their managers have the relevant experience and confidence in the task. Delegation involves both a loss of control over tasks and an increase in the ambiguity of a work situation because the delay in seeing results can be lengthy. Loss of control can be one of the key reasons for a manager failing to delegate. As a result of these factors, the ability of a manager to delegate well requires a great deal of personal confidence and knowledge about the task environment.

Delegation can work well when delegation rewards the participants appropriately. Incentives and rewards are a key element of successful delegation, and they have both direct, short-term influence as well as more indirect, longer-term influence on the process. Obviously, there are direct consequences of rewarding staff for good performance; evaluating and rewarding staff are among the important controls that managers have over staff. The reward structure for the manager and staff can directly determine whether delegation is pursued or not. When a manager is deciding to delegate, workload may interact with his/her incentive structure, that is, how performance evaluation and reward is done. When managers are rewarded for the total performance (of both managers and staff), the manager's most effective decision is often to delegate more. However, if individual performance can be measured and rewarded, it often is most rewarding to try to self-perform more of the tasks. In real-world organisations, total performance is often the easiest to measure and what matters most, so that delegation is common.

Delegation can also increase staff morale because staff are empowered to make their own decisions and this develops a greater sense of efficacy, control and self-worth. With delegation there is a significant element of autonomy for staff. In addition to building morale, delegation is also a means of developing the skills and leadership capabilities of the staff, to be even better in the future as a result of the delegated responsibilities.

The cost/benefit ratio for delegation to staff, then, includes not just the immediate benefits. Managers can treat the costs of delegating as an investment to be redeemed later. Staff who are delegated with more decision-making authority can tend to perform better in the future.

Self-assessment question 18.3

How does reward differ from recognition?

Feedback on page 264

18.4 Using force field analysis to enable successful change

In study session 15 you were introduced to the concept of force field analysis as developed by Lewin. Please refer back to this session to review what was explored at that time.

Learning activity 18.4

There are numerous models of change management. Spend some time doing an internet search to capture a flavour of the range of models which are available. Try and appreciate similarities and differences between them.

Feedback on page 264

In summary, Lewin (1951) argued that in any business situation there are both driving and restraining forces that influence the business dynamics:

- *Driving forces* are those forces affecting a situation that are pushing in a particular direction which tends to initiate a change and keep it going.
- *Restraining forces (resistance)* are forces acting to restrain or decrease the driving forces, and thus resist change.
- *Equilibrium* is reached when the sum of the driving forces equals the sum of the restraining forces.
- *Change* can only occur when the driving forces exceed the restraining forces. The challenge for organisations, as for individuals, is first to recognise the various forces, and second to ensure that there are sufficient driving forces in place to overcome the resistances.

There are many factors which have been identified as significant to change initiatives. Some of the most relevant ones are:

- *Bureaucracy* – the formal structure of the organisation in terms of positions, roles, responsibilities and cultural norms. Individualistic behaviours are usually discouraged by the rules. Departments are usually clearly identified and there are clear boundaries between various departments. The style of management is usually highly regulated and formalised. Change is not encouraged, and if required it is highly formalised and can take a long time to implement.
- *Resources* can inhibit or facilitate change depending on the appropriateness and amount of resources which are provided.
- *Politics* are the internal and external interactions with stakeholders, which depending on relative power and interest can be positive or negative influences on change.
- *Insecurity* can again work both ways depending upon whether insecurity is due to the current state of affairs or due to the uncertainties that change may bring in the future.
- *Risk* again has similar dimensions. Sometimes it is risky to stay as we are or it is riskier to change.

- *Blame culture* usually inhibits change. If people are likely to be blamed when change fails, then they are more likely to do nothing to avoid taking a risk, which may not work.
- *Deference* can also work both ways. Strong leadership, the sort of charismatic leadership that we encountered in study session 2, often means that staff follow the leader in driving or resisting change, depending on the leader's preference.

There are no hard and fast rules regarding driving forces and restraining forces when it comes to change. In every case the situation and the context of change will determine the likely responses.

In terms of individuals' reactions to change, Brewer (2003) suggests that 'resistance to change is a rational response as the change represents a threat, either real or perceived'.

Brewer (2003) identifies some of the causes of resistance to change in figure 18.2.

Figure 18.2: Some causes of resistance to change

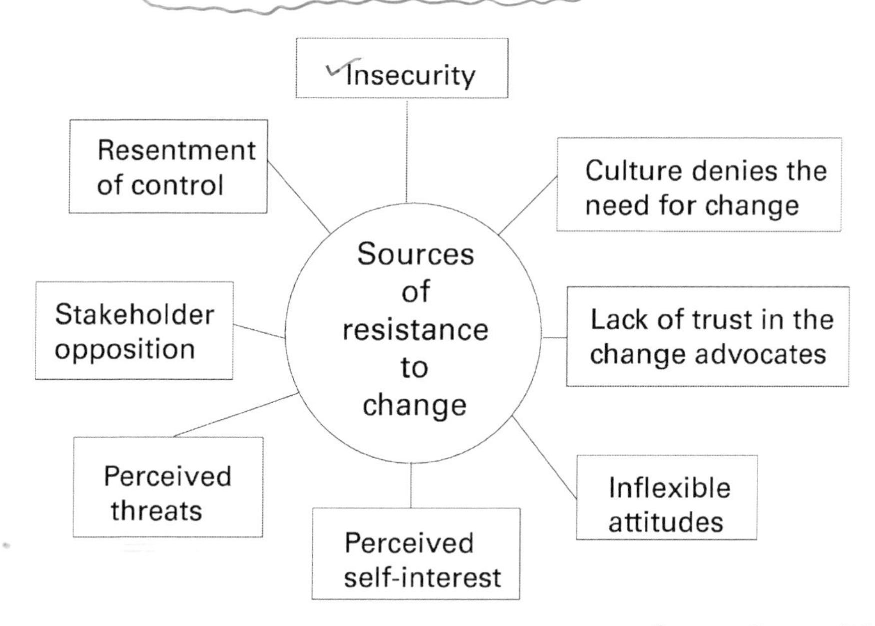

Source: Brewer (2003)

There are numerous models and practical guides from the academic and practitioner literature about how to successfully implement change initiatives, and why change fails. You will have already explored some of these in previous sessions. There are many others and just a couple are explored below.

Hammer and Stanton (1995) set out what they believe are the main reasons why dramatic change initiatives (BPR) actually fail. They base their views on extensive empirical research in a range of organisations which attempted BPR-type change programmes. Their top ten reasons were:

1 Make sure that you know what BPR is, then do it and not something else.

2 Before you 'do BPR', identify the process.
3 Understand existing processes as a first step, but do not spend too much time on this, as you will (probably) be doing something completely different.
4 Proper leadership is required to BPR. This requires a broad strategic perspective plus authority to allocate sufficient resources to support the required change.
5 Being timid about the SRD (service redesign) – be bold and imaginative.
6 Pilot your SRD before full implementation – de-bug and get rid of the gremlins.
7 BPR quickly – show some tangible results within a year, or you will lose momentum – get results fast.
8 Do not place anything 'off limits'. All processes are in the frame.
9 Be fast, improvise and be iterative 'quick and dirty'.
10 Consider the effects of the SRD on your people – what are the benefits for them? Ignore this and you will get DR of DREC (denial, resistance, exploration and commitment).

Kotter (1990) concluded that there are 'eight reasons why many change processes fail':

1 Allowing too much complexity – trying to achieve too much, and not breaking change down into a series of distinct phases.
2 Failing to build a substantial coalition of support from all the stakeholders who are affected by the change.
3 Failing to understand the need for a clear vision to create purpose and direction.
4 Failing to clearly communicate the vision.
5 Permitting roadblocks and resistance to be gathered against the vision.
6 Failing to plan carefully enough, not focusing on relatively simple short-term wins to create commitment and momentum.
7 Declaring victory too soon.
8 Not anchoring changes in corporate culture.

Kotter (1996) suggests an eight-step model to 'Transform your organisation' through what he suggests is a successful change approach:

1 *Establish a sense of urgency*. You need to examine market and competitive realities, and then identify and evaluate opportunities and threats.
2 *Form a powerful guiding coalition* by making sure that responsibility for change is entrusted to a group with enough power to lead the change effort. Power and ability is supported by teamwork.
3 *Create a vision*. The role of senior management, particularly the CEO, is to create a vision to help direct the change effort and to develop strategies for achieving that vision.
4 *Communicate the vision.* Kotter suggests that leaders 'use every vehicle possible to communicate the new vision and strategies' and also provide tangible support in an ongoing way.
5 *Empower others to act on the vision*. The leader also is a positive catalyst for change in a number of practical ways. Primarily the leader gets rid of obstacles to change. These obstacles can be cultural, technological or

structural. The leader has to be prepared to change systems or structures that seriously undermine the vision, and also to encourage risk taking and non-traditional ideas, activities and actions.

6. *Plan for and create short-term wins*. Along with urgency Kotter suggests that quick successes create a massive impetus and dramatically improve motivation. In the change programme there needs to be careful planning for visible performance improvements, systems in place to create improvements and recognition and reward for the staff who have been involved in delivering the improvements.
7. *Consolidate improvements and produce still more change*. Leaders should not rest on their laurels, but should use the quick wins to build on the impetus. Use success to change systems, structures and policies that do not fit the vision. Promote and develop staff who can implement the vision, and reinvigorate the process with new projects, themes and change agents.
8. *Institutionalise new approaches*. A final stage is to drive home the connections between the new behaviours and successful change. Success did not happen by chance, it was carefully planned and implemented and required staff to make significant alterations to behaviours.

Beckard and Harris (1977) suggest that successful change is about harnessing this momentum for change and creating a clear focus for change, but also making sure that the benefits for change are going to outweigh the costs of change.

$$f(V,D,S) > R$$

where V = vision of the future, D = dissatisfaction with the present, S = knowing what first steps to take, and R = cost of change.

Self-assessment question 18.4

http://www.change-management-toolbook.com/home/introduction.html presents a table which provides a broad overview of the different skills that change agents (the managers who are actually responsible for projects) need relating to change management in terms of self, team and system (table 18.1). It is by no means exhaustive, but gives a good starting point for analysis.

In terms of the situation and context of your organisation, what skills are more critical than others? Try and prioritise your choices in order of importance.

Table 18.1 Skills of change agents. X = strongly needed, (X) = partly needed

Skills the change agents need to acquire	Self	Team	System
Technical skills of the specific sector			
Quality management			
Listening and inquiry skills			
Defining objectives/visioning			
Understanding mental maps/shifting perspectives			
Resource orientation			

(continued on next page)

Self-assessment question 18.4 *(continued)*

Skills the change agents need to acquire	Self	Team	System
Dealing with complexity			
Learning from mistakes/feedback			
Coaching			
Leadership			
Training skills			
Facilitation skills			
Large system change tools			
Understanding and catalysing self-organisation			

Feedback on page 264

Revision question

Now try the revision question for this session on page 299.

Summary

Key learning points from this session:

- Delegation is a critical leadership skill. Staff, however, need appropriate support from their leaders if they are to respond and perform effectively.
- Hersey and Blanchard's model of situational leadership contrasts the state of readiness of staff with the appropriate style that is required of leaders. Leaders need a range of styles at their disposal to most effectively influence the performance of their staff.
- Delegation is not abrogation and delegated responsibilities need constant monitoring and reviewing. Appropriate reward and recognition is needed to underpin performance of staff.
- Force field analysis recognises the forces which drive and inhibit change. This model and other change management models have been explored to try and appreciate what needs to be done at an individual level and organisation-wide to enable successful change.

Suggested further reading

In addition to the further reading in study session 17, you should read in more depth authors such as Beckhard and Harris (1977), Hersey, Blanchard and Dewey (2000) and Kotter (1996 and 1990).

Feedback on learning activities and self-assessment questions

Feedback on learning activity 18.1

The manager has to consider:

- nature of the task
- circumstances of the task
- skills, attitudes and knowledge of the people

- resources available
- degree of delegation to be offered.

The staff have to consider in addition to the factors above:

- clarity of the task and objectives
- measurement of success
- rewards and recognition
- support, authority and resources that will be provided
- team issues.

Feedback on self-assessment question 18.1

- Clarity in terms of objectives (SMART goals).
- Tangible help in terms of all the various resources that will be required.
- Facilitation in terms of authority and responsibility, and the boundaries in terms of scope and autonomy.
- Clear communication and feedback routes.

Feedback on learning activity 18.2

Situational leadership starts with an understanding by the leader of the state of his/her staff's motivation and readiness. Depending on the staff situation then different leadership styles are required. Delegation is one of the four quadrants in the situational leadership model, which is appropriate style to adopt.

Feedback on self-assessment question 18.2

1 (b)
2 (c)
3 (c)
4 (a)
5 (a)
6 (d)
7 (b)
8 (c)
9 (a)

Feedback on learning activity 18.3

Monitor has a variety of nuances:

- to check the quality or content
- to keep track of systematically with a view to collecting information
- to test or sample, especially on a regular or ongoing basis
- to keep close watch over
- to direct.

Review has a variety of possible meanings:

- to look over, study, or examine again
- to consider retrospectively; look back on

- to examine with a degree of criticality, and to possibly correct
- to subject to a formal inspection, with a view to making improvements for the future.

Reward, too, has a number of components:

- something given or received in recompense for effective behaviour
- money offered or given for some special service
- a satisfying return or result; profit
- as a positive reinforcement for the performance of a desired task.

The key idea is to be aware that all are essential when delegating effectively. You have to measure to establish datum points, review to compare against what objectives were set, and reward appropriately for the achievement of objectives.

Feedback on self-assessment question 18.3

Refer to learning activity 18.3 for definitions of reward. Recognition is formal awareness that something has been perceived. Reward, however, has some connotation that something tangible such as money or a promotion is given to the people who have performed well and achieved tasks. Recognition may be more intangible, such as praise or even a simple 'thank you'. The key point is that either may be appropriate depending on the situation.

Feedback on learning activity 18.4

http://www.scu.edu.au/schools/gcm/ar/arp/argyris.html explores some of groundbreaking work of Argyris and Schon on the nature of individual and organisational learning, which has influenced many management theories.

http://www.onepine.info/mod1b.htm has an extensive discussion of change management models. http://www.leading-change.com/ suggests a range of practical change management tools and techniques.

Feedback on self-assessment question 18.4

Compare your answers with the generic skills suggested in the link (table 18.2).

Table 18.2 Skills of change agents. X = strongly needed, (X) = partly needed

Skills the change agents need to acquire	**Self**	**Team**	**System**
Technical skills of the specific sector			X
Quality management		X	X
Listening and inquiry skills		X	X
Defining objectives/visioning	X	X	X
Understanding mental maps/shifting perspectives	X	X	X
Resource Orientation	X	X	X
Dealing with complexity	(X)	(X)	X
Learning from mistakes/feedback	X	X	X

(continued on next page)

Table 18.2 *(continued)*

Coaching	X	X
Leadership	X	X
Training skills		X
Facilitation skills	X	X
Large system change tools	(X)	X
Understanding and catalysing self-organisation	(X)	X

Study session 19

Overcoming the barriers to change

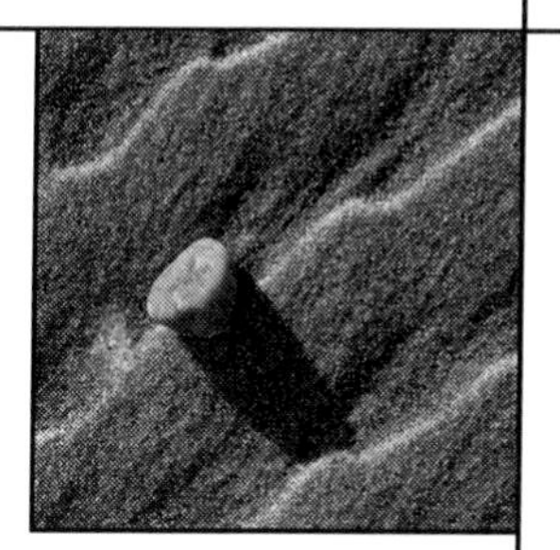

Introduction

This penultimate session considers a variety of aspects of 'negotiation' as a way of overcoming some of the barriers which hinder smooth relations within and between organisations. Negotiation is a mixture of systematic analysis and interpersonal skills, which is a key theme of how leaders provide leadership and influence others, which has been explored throughout this unit.

My father said: 'You must never try to make all the money that's in a deal. Let the other fellow make some money too, ... [else] you won't have many deals.'

Paul Getty

Session learning objectives

After completing this session you should be able to:

19.1 Describe the negotiation process, including the need for planning, stakeholder mapping and power/dependency mapping.
19.2 Explain structural power and its impact on negotiation.
19.3 Identify the areas for non-negotiation and potential concession.
19.4 Describe alignment within the negotiating team and the use of escalation for strategic issues.
19.5 Define 'industrial relations' and outline how this relates to the purchasing function.
19.6 Describe the differences between IR negotiation and commercial negotiation.

Unit content coverage

This study session covers the following topics from the official CIPS unit content document.

Learning objectives

4.8 Negotiate effectively in difficult leadership and management situations, including involvement in negotiating within industrial relations situations.

- The negotiation process and the need for planning a negotiation campaign (link to other units)
- How a complex negotiation needs careful stakeholder mapping and the importance of power/dependency mapping
- The concept of structural power (Cox) in a negotiation context and how this will impact the approach to negotiation
- The areas for non-negotiation and potential concession
- The need for alignment within the negotiating team and the way in which escalation can be used appropriately for strategic issues
- The term 'industrial relations' and the contexts in which such relations are appropriate

- When and how the purchasing function may become involved in IR situations
- How to approach an IR negotiation and the key differences from a commercial negotiation

Prior knowledge

Study sessions 14 to 18.

Resources

You will need internet access in order to complete this study session.

Timing

You should set aside about 6 hours to read and complete this session, including learning activities, self-assessment questions, the suggested further reading (if any) from the essential textbook for this unit and the revision question.

19.1 The negotiation process

Learning activity 19.1

Access the website http://news.bbc.co.uk/go/pr/fr/-/2/hi/europe/4538100.stm and read the case study, starting with the headline 'EU leaders hail new budget deal – European leaders say they are satisfied with the deal reached on the EU budget, after two days of tense talks' and ending at 'But Tony Blair has not achieved his grand project – to modernise the budget and focus it more on the challenges of globalisation rather than subsidising farmers, says our correspondent.' Reflect on the example of the negotiation process from the different perspectives of the various politicians involved.

You should consider in your reflection:

- Was the negotiation a clear process or an exercise in power politics?
- Who won and who lost?
- How many stakeholders were involved? Who were they and what were their motives?

Feedback on page 281

Kharbanda and Stallworthy (1991) suggest that negotiation is an ongoing activity for managers:

> 'We are negotiating all the time: with customers, suppliers, trade unions, our family – indeed, all with whom we come into contact. In business, in particular, negotiation needs management.'

http://www.wikipedia.org/wiki/negotiation gives this definition of negotiation:

> 'Negotiation is the process whereby interested parties resolve disputes, agree upon courses of action, bargain for individual or collective advantage, and/or attempt to craft outcomes which serve their mutual interests. It is usually regarded as a form of alternative dispute resolution.'

Put even more simply, negotiation can be regarded as the process of discussing an issue between two or more parties with competing interests with an aim of coming to an agreement. According to Bailey et al (2005):

> 'However defined, negotiation is seen as a process whereby agreement is sought.'

Processes do not just happen, they need to be carefully designed and planned, and negotiation is no exception. There are numerous models of negotiation from academic and business sources. Each of the negotiation models attempts to offer some unique insight into the negotiation process, yet at the same time similarities are also evident.

Kharbanda and Stallworthy (1991) suggest that negotiation is an eight-stage process:

- prepare
- argue
- signal
- propose
- present the package
- bargain
- close
- agree.

Farmer (1991) simplifies this to a three-stage process (pre-negotiation, negotiation and post-negotiation) with the negotiation stage having three substages (introduction, bargaining and agreement).

Farmer (1991) provides useful guidelines for each of the phases.

Pre-negotiation – this is the *planning phase*, which is essentially your preparation for the negotiation. This phase needs to be detailed and thorough, since inadequate preparation is often cited as the main reason why negotiations fail. Preparation is not just an internal focus on what you want to achieve, but is as much as trying to assess the actions and the reactions to the other parties to the negotiation. For yourself and the other party to the negotiation, you need to be clear about:

- objectives
- tactics
- individuals who will be doing the negotiation
- the venue – home, away or neutral territory
- timing
- assumptions
- strengths and weaknesses.

The introduction to the negotiation process is a complex interplay of factors, but is only the beginning of this active negotiation phase. Farmer suggests a range of sensible steps to take:

- Be on time.
- Understand the purpose of the negotiation.
- Establish and prioritise the issues which are relevant to you.
- Create a positive attitude which suggests that agreement is the main purpose.
- Test assumptions to ensure that they are accurate and mutual.
- Confirm the other parties' position, needs and objectives.
- Look for positive signals (verbal and non-verbal).
- Seek to build rapport at an individual level.
- Build from areas which are agreed.
- Understand that opening statements are often for effect and that you will both move.
- Early concessions should be relatively small and always seek something in return.
- Be precise and not vague.
- Information is potential power so seek to obtain information without giving too much away.
- Do not rush to make decisions.
- Agree timescales but be flexible.
- Pitch your opening bid at a level which can change the other parties' expectations.

The bargaining phase is the follow-on from the introduction phase. Factors to be aware of include:

- Stumbling blocks: If the other party comes up with objections at the introductory stage, try and find out why they object, and see if you can overcome this resistance at little impact to your position. This is a classic practical application of force field analysis.
- Pressure should be used in this bargaining phase to try and move to agreement. Time is often used to fix deadlines (which may or may not be fixed in reality!). There are other sorts of pressure such as the physical pressure of long sessions, which may mean that negotiators get tired and give in; financial pressure because of the potential cost/benefits involved in the outcomes as well as the cost of the process itself; psychological pressure because of the group and interpersonal dynamics involved. Refer back to study session 6 on tactics in terms of influencing people for some of the range of psychological approaches which are possible.
- Cooperation should also be emphasised as well as pressure. The whole underpinning to the negotiation is mutuality of interests, and therefore seeking a solution which will satisfy all parties. Cooperation is enforced by summarising areas of agreement and a focus on the positive rather than negative aspects. This can be reinforced by openness and sharing of information as a potential way of overcoming stumbling blocks and resistance. At the same time these should be considered reactions which underpin the serious and professional attitude that you are taking.
- If conflict or confrontation looks likely then keep calm and do not get over-emotional. Try and take an approach which defuses the situation, silence, recapitulation of the situation to date, delay by

seeking clarifications, and adjourn the meeting if need be to allow people time to collect their thoughts and reconsider.
- Underpinning this bargaining phase should be a balance between trust, questioning and listening skills.

Agreement follows on from the bargaining phase, where most of the issues should be resolved through skilled negotiation. Key points to note:

- Apparent deadlock can be overcome by careful attention to a variety of factors. You always need to understand the other parties' position and sometimes a degree of 'face-saving' is required – changing the tone or wording of certain clauses may not change the effect but may be more acceptable to the various stakeholders. Find reasons for you or the other party to make changes, which may make it more palatable. In extreme circumstances it may be that individual positions are so entrenched that a change of negotiators may be enough to break the deadlock.
- Agreement is often encouraged by getting into the detailed requirements. The who, what, where, when and how establishes the process which will ensure that whatever is agreed actually works effectively.
- General agreement may need to be developed into the detailed requirements of a contract, which should clarify potential ambiguities and specify details of quality, cost and time.
- These details then need to be communicated carefully within your organisation and to other relevant stakeholders.

Post-negotiation is when the agreement is followed up in all relevant details:

- Agreement needs to drafted, confirmed by both parties and treated as a de-facto contract.
- Obtain agreement from your internal stakeholders, that they understand what may be required of them, and that they are committed to deliver. Make sure the other party does the same.
- An official documentation which is required (such as purchase orders) fully reflects what was agreed.
- Check and review progress of the agreement at agreed intervals, to ensure that the agreement is followed but also to develop and underpin the relationship which the agreement has cemented. This review can also consider renewal and revision if the agreement is time bound.
- Review the whole negotiation process. Were objectives fully achieved? Did everything go according to plan? What could be done better in the future? What went well which we can learn from?

Table 19.1 presents a résumé of the negotiation process.

Table 19.1 The negotiation process in brief

Preparation and planning	Negotiation	Post-negotiation
Planning	The opening:	Summarise
Objective setting	• ritual • posture	Draft agreement

(continued on next page)

Table 19.1 *(continued)*

Preparation and planning	Negotiation	Post-negotiation
Develop: • postures • tactics • questions • outcomes • straw issues	The bargaining and agreement phases: • proposals • movement • signals • building • testing • questions • range of tactics • recess • closing • summarise	Review: • outcomes against plans • behaviour against results • trends and patterns of the negotiation

Source: CIPS (1990)

In the business environment negotiation rarely involves just two parties. Usually a number of stakeholders are involved with varying degrees of power and interest in the outcomes of negotiations. Stakeholders, stakeholder mapping and the importance of assessing power and interest have been covered in detail in study sessions 4, 5 and 17 and are clearly an important element of the negotiation process. Please revisit these sections and reflect how stakeholders are relevant to all the phases of a negotiation.

Self-assessment question 19.1

Define 'negotiation' and how it differs from other methods of influencing.

Feedback on page 281

19.2 Structural power: how this will impact on negotiation

Section 19.1 above concentrated on viewing negotiation as a method whereby agreement is reached on the basis of mutual interests. Andrew Cox and his colleagues at the Centre for Business Strategy and Procurement at the University of Birmingham have argued that relations between organisations are still fundamentally about power.

Cox et al (2000) argue that the debate over whether real partnership can exist is redundant. They say that despite popular belief, effective collaboration is about domination. They dispute the idea of cooperation between equal partners, or partnership, as best practice. By the same token, relationships based on power have been discouraged. Cox et al (2000) view this type of argument as a false dichotomy and say there is no reason why an inequality of power between purchasers and suppliers should be a barrier to a continuing close working relationship. They believe that purchasers should always seek to create a dominant position with suppliers, and that this should be used to enable a good relationship which aims to achieve better quality and lower costs.

Learning activity 19.2

Visit http://www.supplymanagement.com/edit/archiveresults.asp and access and read the full article by Cox et al, entitled 'Wielding influence', Supply Management, 6 April 2000. Briefly summarise the argument in the article. (You will need your CIPS membership number and password to access this page.)

Feedback on page 281

Cox et al (2000) suggest that careful study is required to analyse the structure of an industry, and its competitive dynamics, to determine the power relationships which are identifiable. They have studied the construction industry and the dairy industry to suggest that the structure will vary from industry to industry and at different times. In effect they take a situational approach to power, akin to Hersey's situational approach to leadership. It is this 'structural power' which determines the approach to sourcing strategies which are appropriate. These in turn relate to the negotiation stances that can be followed in the agreements which are the implementation of strategy in a daily operational context.

Cox et al (2000) have devised an analytical tool known as a power matrix (figure 19.1), built around the idea that all purchaser–supplier relationships depend on the relative usefulness and scarcity of the resources that are exchanged between the parties. Each party within a transaction can be located in one of four basic power positions: buyer dominance (>), interdependence (=), independence (0) and supplier dominance (<). It is important that buyers and suppliers should not only understand and 'manage the current power circumstance, but also use relationships to create new power circumstances that provide for a more congenial leverage position for them to maximise their often divergent economic objectives' (Cox et al 2000).

Figure 19.1: The power matrix

Buyer power attributes relative to supplier	Low (supplier power)	High (supplier power)
High	Buyer dominance	Interdependence
Low	Independence	Supplier dominance

Supplier power attributes relative to buyer

Source: adapted from Cox et al (2000)

Knowing the specific power circumstances between buyer and supplier is a first step. A second step is to decide whether they have the capability and resources to undertake first-tier relationship management, or work throughout the supply chain with suppliers from the first tier through all tiers down to raw-material suppliers. There are four sourcing options available for buyers to manage their suppliers and supply chains: supplier selection, supplier development, supply chain sourcing and supply chain management (see figure 19.2).

In their preparation for negotiations the buyer must think carefully about their internal capabilities and the external power circumstances they are involved in when they decide which sourcing option is the most appropriate one for a particular supplier and supply chain.

Key questions that need to be asked by buyers in assessing the situation:

- The balance between the number of buyers and suppliers.
- The salience of the buyer's expenditure to the supplier.
- The number of available alternative purchasers to the supplier.
- The extent of supplier switching costs.
- The extent of buyer switching costs.
- The extent to which the product or service is commoditised.
- The extent to which the product or service is standardised.
- The level of buyer search cost.
- The level of information asymmetry advantage that one party has over the other.

Figure 19.2: The four sourcing options for buyers

Focus of buyer relationship with supplier	First-tier	Supply chain
Proactive	Supplier development	Supply chain management
Reactive	Supplier selection	Supply chain sourcing

Scope of work with supplier and supplier chain

Source: adapted from Cox et al (2000)

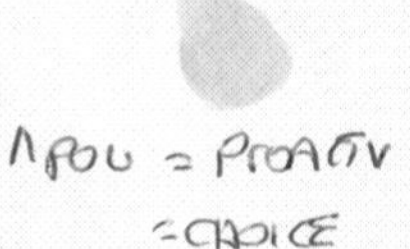

Self-assessment question 19.2

How can 'structural power' impact in a supply chain context with reference to the negotiation approach adopted?

Visit http://www.supplymanagement.com/edit/archiveitem.asp?id=6756 and read Cox's article 'Horses for courses' as background to the above question. (You will need your CIPS membership number and password to access this site.)

Feedback on page 282

19.3 The areas for non-negotiation and potential concession

Learning activity 19.3

In preparing for a negotiation how do we determine which are the areas for non-negotiation and concession?

Feedback on page 282

In preparing for a negotiation, Kennedy (1997) identifies three key considerations:

- What do we want? This requires careful analysis of the business environment within which the negotiation situation occurs and a clear identification of our needs in terms of SMART objectives. Generally the needs will be in terms of objectives such as quality, cost and time. SMART definition must quantify those needs very specifically, so that we know precisely the boundaries which are acceptable to us. Anything which is unacceptable therefore becomes non-negotiable. If we then do negotiate we are unlikely to achieve our objectives, or we did not define the objectives SMART-ly enough!
- How valuable is each of our wants? We may have a number of objectives which incorporate quality, cost and time. We should be absolutely clear which objectives have priority and are non-negotiable. Other objectives may be somewhat more flexible, and in these areas we may consider concessions.
- What are the entry and exit points? Entry points are opening bids, or starting points. These need to be carefully considered. Exit points are your 'walk away' position. The area in between is the area for 'bargaining'.

Bailey et al (2005) offer a simple diagram (figure 19.3) to explain the position very clearly. There is a range of possibilities. If the exit points are distinct then the gaps cannot be bridged. If there is an overlap then an agreement is possible by negotiation.

Figure 19.3

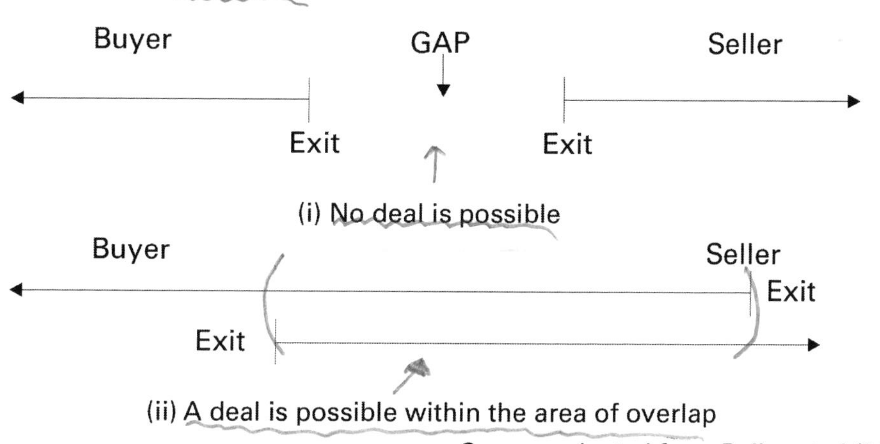

Source: adapted from Bailey et al (2005)

Making effective concessions

Malhotra (2004) suggests useful ways in which making concessions can build trust and lead to a successful outcome for all parties:

- A carefully planned unilateral concession can work wonders for trust, for it conveys to the other party that you consider the relationship to be a friendly one, with the potential for mutual gain and trust over time. A true unilateral concession requires no commitment or concession from the other side. Such concessions must come at little cost or risk to the provider, but be of high benefit to the recipient.
- Label your concessions. Concessions, unilateral or otherwise, are only influential in building trust or encouraging reciprocity if the receiver views them as concessions. Parties are often motivated to discount and devalue each other's concessions and contributions, because doing so relieves them of the obligation to reciprocate. As a result, many concessions go unnoticed or unacknowledged. When you have made a significant concession, communicate exactly how much you have given away and what the sacrifice means to you. By doing so, you will not only affect the other party's perceptions of your goodwill but trigger your partner's desire to reciprocate, and increase the level of mutual trust.
- Explain your demands. When you start a negotiation with someone new, you can expect they will assume the worst about your motives and intentions. In reality there may be constraints forcing you to stand firm. Psychologists have found that people tend to view themselves in the best possible light and others in a much less positive light – especially those with whom they are in conflict. For this reason, it is important that you make a clear explanation of your actions. An opening offer, if viewed by the other side as extreme, can diminish and even destroy trust. An offer that is explained and justified will preserve trust, and may enhance it.

http://www.getahead-direct.com/gwng09-bargaining-and-concession-trading.htm offers a much more transactional approach to concessions, which you may also wish to consider:

- Concession trading. Negotiation is the art of knowing how to exchange concessions. Concessions can become a way of life, eating away at an organisation's profit margin. This is why it is important to plan carefully the concessions that you are willing to make.
- Avoid making the first major concession. It is important to work hard at not being the first party to make a major concession. The psychological victory gained by the winner of the first major movement is so important that it may shape the overall outcome of the talks. If you do find yourself in this unenviable position then try to obtain an equally important concession in return.
- Offer concessions in reverse priority order. When the other side offers to make a concession they will usually expect you to make a concession in return.
- It is important to have your concessions listed in reverse priority so that you can offer a concession of your choice before they can ask for something specific. Alternatively you could opt to play 'hard-ball' and accept their offer without responding in kind.

- Make every concession contingent. Frame every concession you make in terms of 'If you agree to X, we will give in on Y'. If, however, the other side makes a contingent offer, you should aim to seek an advantage. For example you could counter with an offer like 'We will accept X and Y but only if you agree to Z'.
- Behave as if every concession that you make is important. The other side will not usually know how much importance you attach to the concessions that you make. If you give the impression that a concession that you have offered is of no consequence to you, then the other side may push for further concessions before making a significant movement in their position. When concessions are being offered, be wary of the negotiator who gives in too easily. They may be naive, they may know something that you do not or they may have misunderstood the consequences of agreeing to your demands. It is in both sides' interests to make sure that the implications are fully understood before entering into a formal agreement.
- Avoid goodwill concessions. Each concession made may be read either as a goodwill gesture, or as a sign of weakness. Even where a concession is taken as a sign of goodwill, there is no compelling reason for the other side to respond in kind. An experienced negotiator is more likely to accept the concession and feel confident that he can seek further movement from a party that is ready to make unilateral concessions.
- Concession management. The problem with making concessions is that making one from a position of weakness can lead to requests for you to make a series of follow-on concessions. Alternatively, if you are not in an obviously weak position, and are seen to be too ready to make concessions, then the other side may start to feel that the underlying deal must be biased to your advantage. Another important aim during the bargaining phase is to get the other side used to making concessions.

Self-assessment question 19.3

Assess the pros and cons of Malhotra and get-ahead.com approaches to concessions in negotiations.

Feedback on page 282

19.4 Negotiating teams – escalation and strategic issues

Learning activity 19.4

Define 'escalation' in the context of negotiations.

Feedback on page 283

Mannix (2005) offers some useful guidelines about the benefits of teams rather than individuals being involved in negotiations:

- Teams can create new opportunities for integrative solutions. Teams stimulate more discussion and more information sharing than do individuals.

- Team negotiators feel less competitive and pressured than do solo negotiators. With greater numbers comes a sense of security.
- Teams also bring a variety of technical and interpersonal skills, which is hard to emulate by solo negotiators.
- Familiarity with one another allows team members to share divergent information and engage in the constructive conflict necessary to find a solution.

Creating a true team environment requires a great deal of preparation, coordination and internal negotiation before you even meet the other side. The most adaptive teams are those that meet often and work intensely, developing effective methods to face and resolve their conflicts. The deep knowledge created through preparation is likely to result in greater flexibility and creativity at the bargaining table.

Self-assessment question 19.4

Mannix (2005) proposes benefits of teamworking for the negotiation process – what are the potential difficulties?

Feedback on page 283

19.5 Industrial relations and the purchasing function

Several definitions of industrial relations (IR) can be found from internet sources:

> 'A broad term that may refer to relations between unions and management, unions themselves, management and government, unions and government, or between employers and unorganised employees. Within this definition, specific attention may be directed toward industrial conflict or its regulation through the formulation of work rules or agreements.' Source: http://broadway.sfn.saskatoon.sk.ca/business/sdlc/gi.html.

> 'The field of labor relations looks at the relationship between management and workers, particularly groups of workers represented by a trade union.' Source: http://en.wikipedia.org/wiki/Industrial_relations.

Learning activity 19.5

Consider through your reading and research some of the various definitions of IR from academic and organisational sources.

Feedback on page 284

Mullins (2005) treats the term 'industrial relations' as the same as the term 'employment relations', defined as:

> 'concerned with the relationship between the policies and practices of the organisation and its staff, and the behaviour of work groups'.

Implicit in this definition is the suggestion of some interaction between the interests of the organisation via its leaders and managers, and the interests of the staff via trade unions and their officials. At the same time this interaction is increasingly affected by the legal framework which requires the exercise of rights and responsibilities, for both the organisation and staff.

It is widely accepted in developed, mature economies that there are definite benefits to be derived for the organisation by a positive approach to IR. Practices such as careful job design, supported by training, development and a cooperative/consultative culture, leads to increased commitment, motivation and satisfaction from staff, which in turn impacts positively on productivity, profitability and flexibility.

Self-assessment question 19.5

Outline when and how the purchasing function may become involved in IR situations.

Feedback on page 284

19.6 IR negotiation and commercial negotiation

Learning activity 19.6

Are there any distinctions between an IR negotiation and a commercial negotiation?

Feedback on page 284

http://changingminds.org/disciplines/negotiation/styles/industrial_relations.htm describes the IR negotiation in industrial situations as typified by trade union negotiations, where a team from the trade union seeks to gain better pay and working conditions from a reluctant management (or vice versa).

Confrontation and competition have traditionally been typical of IR negotiations between trade unions and managers. By their very nature these can be very confrontational and competitive. Characteristic of traditional IR negotiations is robustness of style from both sides, backed often by powerful brinkmanship. It was often necessary to employ third parties (via arbitration, mediation or some alternative dispute resolution method) to eventually resolve matters.

Ashcroft (2004) suggests that commercial negotiations require high levels of personal qualities and skills on the part of negotiators. Ashcroft defines commercial negotiation as:

> 'the process for resolving differences of opinion which arise in contract dealings between a buyer and seller'.

Ashcroft concludes that commercial negotiations should be founded on mutual trust and respect. They should be conducted within a problem-solving atmosphere, with sufficient time to tackle all issues. Great care should be given to providing communication channels to each side's senior management and advisers. Commercial negotiation done correctly always pays dividends. Theory, planning and practice indicate that logical persuasion and genuine business objectives are essential requirements of professional commercial negotiation behaviour.

Self-assessment question 19.6

How would you approach an IR negotiation as part of the purchasing role?

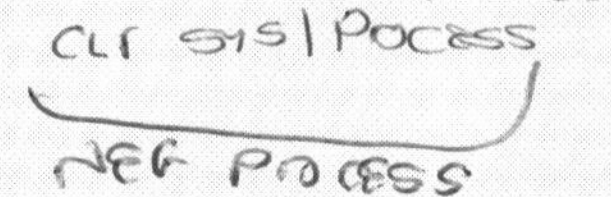

Feedback on page 284

Revision question

Now try the revision question for this session on page 299.

Summary

Key learning points in this session are:

- Evaluation of the stages required for a negotiation process and particularly the importance of preparation and planning.
- That negotiation is not only about compromise and seeking accommodation. Cox et al (2000) suggest that power is still a significant factor in a negotiation context and describe how this will impact the approach to negotiation.
- Clear definition of objectives and purpose assist negotiators to identify the areas for non-negotiation and potential concession.
- If teams are involved in a complex negotiation then there is a need for alignment within the team.
- IR and commercial negotiations can be regarded as different or similar, depending on which perspective is taken. Regardless of the distinctions, the purchasing function may become involved in both situations.

Suggested further reading

Of particular reference to the supply context are Bailey, Farmer, Jessop and Jones (2005) and a range of publications by Cox, Sanderson and Watson

(2000) and Cox (1997, 2001, 2002 and 2003). There are any number of guides to successful negotiation.

Feedback on learning activities and self-assessment questions

Feedback on learning activity 19.1

You should consider in your reflection:

- Was the negotiation a clear process or an exercise in power politics? A clear process is in place (the budgeting process) but it was overtaken by power politics and competing interests and the tight timescales involved.
- Who won and who lost? In financial terms Germany, the UK and France will have to raise their contributions, so they 'lost financially'. However, the French conceded little re the Common Agricultural Policy, and the Germans gained political capital from their conciliatory approach. The UK gained credibility within the EU by reaching an agreement which had seemed unlikely at times. At the same time Mr Blair faced considerable criticism from within the UK. The initial winners seem to be Poland and the other smaller states who are new to the EU and as yet are less easy to predict.
- How many stakeholders were involved? Who were they and what were their motives? Main stakeholders are the larger countries, the smaller states, the EU Commission, and the various local interests within each of the member states. Motives vary significantly depending on what they wish to achieve.

Feedback on self-assessment question 19.1

A number of valid definitions can be considered from the literature (see earlier in this session).

Bailey et al (2005) suggest alternatives to negotiation:

- Persuasion – encourage the other party to accept your views with no concessions required from you.
- Give in – accept totally what the other side offers.
- Coerce – insist the other side accedes to your wishes or you will apply some sanction or penalty (which you presumably have the power to deliver).
- Problem solve – remove the issue by solving the problem so that negotiation is not needed.

Feedback on learning activity 19.2

Key points made are:

- Power can still support beneficial arrangements between purchaser and seller.

- The Japanese context and philosophy is different from Western norms.
- Power is key to managing supply.
- There are four different generic relationship types, none of which is superior. The manager should choose the one that fits the circumstances best.
- The power situation with any given supplier can change over time.
- The balance of power between a buyer and supplier is determined by the power resources each party has at its disposal.
- The analysis must be extended to the wider context of the supply chain.

Feedback on self-assessment question 19.2

The boxes in figure 19.2 impact on negotiation stances depending on the power dynamics which are in evidence. More relative power means you can be proactive as opposed to reactive. More relative power means you can take a much wider strategic approach which encompasses the whole supply chain (a tendency towards the upper right-hand quadrant). However, they can also be 'reactive' – the dominant party has a choice. Furthermore, the selection of different sourcing strategies is included in the discussion rather than how relative power affects negotiation. At a simple level the relative power structure determines the ability of a party to achieve a good deal. More critically, a negotiator should consider the strategic factors (power resources) that affect dominance in order to protect or improve their negotiating position (salience, switching costs, number of suppliers, and so on).

Feedback on learning activity 19.3

The answer is in careful preparation. Note the guidance at the beginning of section 19.1:

For yourself and the other party to the negotiation, you need to be clear about:

- objectives
- tactics
- individuals who will be doing the negotiation
- the venue – home, away or neutral territory
- timing
- assumptions
- strengths and weaknesses.

This careful analysis determines entry and exit points with some certainty for your own situation. It may not always be possible for you to be so sure about the other party, but careful preparation may at least establish parameters, and a well-planned introduction phase should answer many of the unknown factors.

Feedback on self-assessment question 19.3

Both approaches could be argued to be excessively extreme, but can be usefully contrasted as in table 19.2.

Table 19.2

Malhotra	Get-ahead.com
Risk that concessions are automatically expected	Risk that concessions are automatically expected
Unilateral concessions are a sign of weakness	'Do not make the first concession' may result in a deadlock
Small concessions perhaps suggest you are not serious	Small concessions indicate that bigger ones will follow
Seeking a trusting relationship may imply naivety on your part	Contingency suggests you will always be pushy and maybe excessive in your demands
Naivety can be taken advantage of	Excessive suspicion of the other side's motives may fuel mutual mistrust
Careful communication and explanation takes time and requires a variety of media to be used, which may add to cost and complexity	This mistrust may spill over into hostility and conflict which could destroy the negotiation

Feedback on learning activity 19.4

There are a variety of definitions, most of which broadly encompass the definition suggested here:

> An escalator clause is a provision in a contract stipulating an increase or a decrease, as in wages, benefits or prices, under certain conditions, such as changes in the cost of living.

In terms of negotiation there may well be situations in a negotiation which cannot be predicted with certainty over the lifetime of an agreement. To try and set clear parameters may be to the disadvantage of one of the parties to the negotiation. Yet it is crucial to the strategic success of the relationship that uncertainty is managed. Rather than allowing this uncertainty to potentially hinder agreement, the parties agree a method whereby this uncertainty is mitigated. A good example is by relating prices to the Retail Price Index or to the rate of inflation, so that they can be increased or decreased accordingly. This saves detailed and costly renegotiation or disputes.

Feedback on self-assessment question 19.4

Almost every positive benefit suggested by Mannix could have potentially negative aspects!

- Integration can be difficult if you have a wide variety of views to consider. Teams can inhibit discussion and more information sharing due to lack of familiarity or through dynamics which create repressive norms of behaviour.
- Team negotiators could feel more competitive and pressured than do solo negotiators. With greater numbers comes a sense of competition between team members.
- Good solo negotiators can call on technical expertise to help them to prepare for negotiation, but then carry out the negotiation phase solo, which allows them the personal opportunity to be effective.

- Familiarity with one another could inhibit team members to engage in the constructive conflict necessary to find a solution. Concern for team maintenance could overshadow achievement of the objectives.

Feedback on learning activity 19.5

Compare your definitions with ideas suggested in the text.

Feedback on self-assessment question 19.5

The purchasing function can be involved in IR just like any other individual member of staff. Purchasing staff can be affected positively or negatively by management policies regarding job design, training, development and cooperative/consultative approaches regarding strategy development.

In specific purchasing terms the purchasing function may well be involved in implementing policies which impact on staff within other parts of the organisation. Outsourcing, delayering, downsizing, supplier rationalisation and development often require the active involvement of the purchasing function, which may well create conflicts with other internal staff and stakeholders.

Feedback on learning activity 19.6

There have been suggestions that IR negotiations are more confrontational because of the traditional nature of IR in the UK context, which required win–lose strategies to be the norm. Commercial negotiations in contrast suggest that transactional approaches for mutual benefit and win–win are the norm.

It has been demonstrated that there is no consensus to the commercial negotiation view – refer to Cox et al (2000) in section 19.2. It is also suggested that the confrontational view of IR has been replaced by the view that partnership between staff and the management is the way forward in the current competitive business environment.

Those of you from other business environments and cultures may wish to reflect and consider the nature of IR and commercial negotiations in your own countries, which may well be significantly different from that described in this session.

Feedback on self-assessment question 19.6

It is very difficult to offer clear guidelines to a question such as this. Context and circumstance are everything, but a clear system such as that proposed in section 19.1 will be helpful. The negotiation process is a balance between systematic analysis and interpersonal skills, and these both need to be acknowledged in your response.

Study session 20

Change and performance: change for the better...

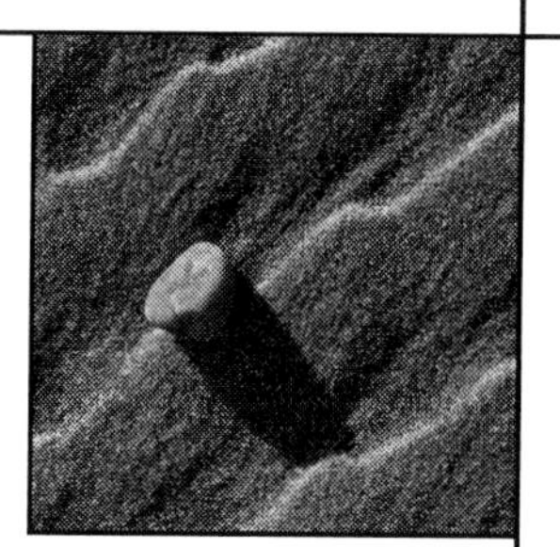

'It is not the strongest of the species that survive, nor the most intelligent, but the one most responsive to change.'

Charles Darwin

Introduction

This session considers the final aspects of the syllabus and the section on 'Leading change through people'. The session concentrates on how change impacts on performance, in terms of tangible, measurable achievements which can be monitored and quantified.

Session learning objectives

After completing this session you should be able to:

20.1 Monitor and control the impact of change processes on supply chain performance – quantitative measures.
20.2 Monitor and control the impact of change processes on the supply chain performance – qualitative measures.
20.3 Understand the practical considerations in change processes.
20.4 Describe how a supplier implementation programme is organised, including trial/pilot period and ramp-up/ramp-down phases.
20.5 Describe how existing suppliers can be managed and incentivised.

Unit content coverage

This study session covers the following topics from the official CIPS unit content document.

Learning objectives

4.9 Monitor and control the impact of the change process on the supply chain performance including:

- Budgets
- Projects measurement
- Benchmarking
- Auditing
- Employee and stakeholder reactions
- Appropriate communication programmes involving third parties regarding internal changes

4.10 Manage continuity of performance while implementing change.

- The importance of maintaining a 'business as usual' approach for managing supply
- The process of internal handover from one individual or team to another
- How a supplier implementation programme is organised, including the potential benefits of a trial/pilot period and the ramp-up/ramp-down phases

- How existing suppliers can be managed and incentivised to see out the full terms of their contracts without disruption to supply or service levels

Prior knowledge

Study sessions 14 to 19.

Resources

In order to complete this study session you will need internet access.

Timing

You should set aside about 6 hours to read and complete this session, including learning activities, self-assessment questions, the suggested further reading (if any) from the essential textbook for this unit and the revision question.

20.1 Change processes and impact on supply chain performance – quantitative measures

Van Weele (2005) suggests that:

> 'the question of how to measure and evaluate purchasing performance is not easily answered … to date no single, practical approach that produces consistent results in different types of companies has been found'.

How results are measured depends upon how managers view the role and importance of the purchasing function (see table 20.1).

Table 20.1 The management view of the purchasing function

Management view	Position of purchasing	Performance measure
Administrative activity	Low status	Orders Order backlog Lead time Adherence to procedures etc.
Commercial activity	Reporting to management	Savings, price reductions Financial measures
Part of integrated logistics	Integrated within logistics	Savings, cost reductions Supplier delivery Reliability Gradual improvement metrics Target costing
Strategic business area (supply chain perspective)	Represented at senior management levels	Supplier development and involvement Make-or-buy decisions Supplier rationalisation Dramatic improvement metrics

Source: Van Wheele (2005)

When purchasing is seen as an operational and administrative function, then measures are largely quantitative in character. Purchasing and performance is largely evaluated in terms of costs allocations, and the control of purchasing as a non-value-added activity. Typical measures are expressed largely in terms of budgets, adhered to measurement against specific project areas, benchmarking and auditing metrics. Purchasing is measured mostly in terms of efficiency.

Learning activity 20.1

Define the following terms:

- budget
- benchmarking
- purchasing audit.

Feedback on page 293

When purchasing is considered to be a strategic business area, then measures are more qualitative and judgemental. A variety of complex measures of procedures and guidelines are employed to focus much more on effectiveness, and the potential to add value to the business. Significant improvements in performance can be delivered by making radical changes to the way purchasing and the supply chain are organised and managed.

Self-assessment question 20.1

What performance measures are used to evaluate change in the supply chain in an organisation with which you are familiar? Consider your response in terms of the factors identified by Van Weele in table 20.1.

Feedback on page 294

20.2 Change processes and impact on supply chain performance – qualitative measures

Learning activity 20.2

Define the following terms and consider why they are regarded as more qualitative measures of performance:

- target costing
- supplier development and involvement

(continued on next page)

Learning activity 20.2 *(continued)*

- make or buy decisions
- supplier rationalisation.

Feedback on page 294

We have considered within several sessions the importance of perception and reactions of both employees and other stakeholders to change initiatives and programmes. Revisit relevant sessions to remind yourself about the range of factors to be considered.

This section will not revisit these areas in any detail, suffice to emphasise the importance of communication regarding change.

It is suggested that staff are resistant to change for a number of reasons, principally:

- lack of awareness about the change
- comfort with the ways things are
- fear of the unknown.

Fenson (2000) suggests that change is inevitable, but exactly what and how it is communicated can make a major impact on how change is perceived in your company.

While organisational change requires more than ten tips, here are ten key factors to keep in mind when planning, announcing, implementing and communicating a change initiative.

1. There's no one perfect way to communicate change. Change is uncomfortable, and adapting to change can be complex. Tasks and activities are easy to list, but behaviour and habits are not easy to change. Be prepared to adapt the approaches for your organisation.
2. What exactly is changing and why. Too many change programmes are heavy on jargon and light on substance of what the changes actually mean for staff.
3. Know what results you want, from both the change initiative and the communication programme.
4. Include communication specialists from the start so that the message is properly communicated.
5. Share information with staff as soon as possible.
6. Accuracy of the message quality and consistency are crucial.
7. Change effort starts with the announcement or a merger or change initiative. Many leaders and managers underestimate the length of time required to implement change successfully.
8. Use a variety of communication pathways and vehicles.
9. Do not confuse process with communication. While those meetings and processes can be communication vehicles if designed mindfully and handled in the context of a broader programme, they are not adequate to meet change communication needs.
10. Provide staff with opportunities to share concerns, ask questions and offer ideas, and make following up with answers and updates a top priority. The more people are involved in the process, the more likely they are to provide support to the change initiative.

Self-assessment question 20.2

Assess the effectiveness of different ways of 'communicating successfully' to external stakeholders and staff.

Feedback on page 295

20.3 Practical considerations in change processes

Change management programmes by their very nature are risky and uncertain. There is a complex interplay to be considered which is dynamic and subject to external influences. At the same time leaders wish to plan and control change in such a way that objectives are achieved. In essence there is a need to preserve some elements of continuity or 'business as usual' at the same time as change occurs.

Learning activity 20.3

Consider where poor current performance can affect the future success of change initiatives.

Feedback on page 295

If it were easy to achieve continuity and change, then change initiatives would be much more successful than they appear to be in reality. The challenge for leadership, particularly in terms of managing supply, is to consider what strategies can be adopted which can steer a course between these apparently contradictory forces.

Among the forces for change and continuity are the following:

- Technological developments in e-commerce.
- A focus on savings in costs.
- A balance between centralising and decentralising decision making.
- The cultural habits and norms which resist change.
- The training and development which needs to underpin the requirements of change.
- Internal and external stakeholder reactions.
- The need to maintain continuity of performance while change initiatives come to fruition.

Handover of change projects and initiatives needs careful planning, and sufficient time and support must be allowed in order to effect a smooth transition from the project team to the operational team. Support includes sufficient initial training to ensure that sufficient skills and knowledge are in place. After suitable initial training, mentoring and ongoing contact to reinforce behaviours should also be planned into the process of transition and handover.

Self-assessment question 20.3

Access http://www.supplymanagement.com/edit/archiveitem.asp?id=1311 and read the article from *Supply Management* (March 2000), starting at 'Procurement central. The Office of Government Commerce starts work on 1 April with a huge task ahead of it' and ending 'From a global perspective, UK government procurement is pretty advanced and could become even more of an example for the rest of the world.' (You will need your CIPS membership number and password in order to access this page.)

Consider the article in terms of the continuity and change issues which are identified.

Feedback on page 295

20.4 Organising new suppliers

Visit the website Office of Government Commerce: http://www.ogc.gov.uk/sdtoolkit/reference/ogc_library/contractmanagement.html which has a whole range of advice and guidance on contract management and advice on transitions and how to manage them, published by the OGC. The following text is a summary.

Overview

OCG outlines the tasks needed to carry out successful implementation and transition to a new contract. The contract must fully reflect the commercial deal. It must clearly document the work and/or services to be provided, quality plan, implementation plans and milestones, the performance regime that will apply, payment approaches and charges, the responsibilities of the parties and mechanisms for dealing with change. The project team will also need to establish a framework for managing the relationship with the provider and/or partners; the expectations of both parties should be set out in the contract.

Readiness checklist

Readiness for a new service means that a number of key elements are brought together – successful implementation requires that:

- the organisation is ready
- staff are ready
- the public are ready
- providers are ready
- contract management is in place
- service management is in place

- benefits management is in place
- performance measurement is in place
- changes ahead have been thought about.

Managing the transition

There are organisational, people-related and technical issues that have to be managed when an organisation changes the way it works. The management task is to ensure that the transition is as smooth as possible between the old and the new ways of working. A major change should always be managed formally as a project, perhaps as part of a wider programme of change.

The preparatory work should already have been undertaken during the full proposal and draft contract stages, so that staff know exactly what will happen. A detailed transition plan will have been included in the draft contract, drawn up after detailed discussions in which both customer and provider demonstrate their shared understanding of what is involved, the risks and the responsibilities of both parties.

Acceptance

The purpose of acceptance testing is to confirm that the service is ready for operational use. This is a condition of most model contracts. The provider's service should meet the requirements outlined in some form of requirements specification (and finalised during negotiations, where negotiations are part of the procurement strategy). Acceptance is closely tied to ongoing contract management; the timing of acceptance will vary depending on the type of service that has been provided.

Outsourcing

The provider has to demonstrate their readiness before the contract starts. However, with outsourced services there is often limited scope for testing readiness. The service may have been implemented in a 'big bang' over a weekend, replacing whatever was there before. There is therefore a need for regular contract reviews, conducted by the contract management team.

Acceptance will be most relevant to a new service that has not previously been available, the transfer of an on-site service to a remote location or a phased (incremental) implementation where a sub-set of the total service is provided in each phase. In these cases it should be possible to pilot test or simulate the quality and responsiveness of the service before formally accepting it and allowing it to 'go live'.

Learning activity 20.4

Give examples of practical experience that you have had bringing on board new suppliers and new contracts – what worked well and what did not work so well?

Feedback on page 295

Now attempt the following question.

Self-assessment question 20.4

Give an example of successful working from learning activity 20.4 above in a supply chain context – what were the learning points and actions that ensued as a result of your experiences?

Feedback on page 296

20.5 Managing and incentivising existing suppliers

Contracts do come to an end, and it may well be that for a variety of commercial reasons you decide to change suppliers.

It could be that the existing supplier has failed to perform according to the contract terms and your expectations. Or new suppliers have emerged who offer quality, cost or time performance improvements which are commercially attractive.

What needs to be done to ensure a smooth transition from one supplier to another?

There are no hard-and-fast rules, but among the factors to be considered are:

- A contract may have a finite timescale, and the contract terms should contain clear reference to transitional arrangements. The current supplier is still bound by the terms of the existing contract and the benefits and obligations that are enshrined in the contract.
- The contract may not necessarily be the end of the relationship between you and your existing supplier. They may still be able to bid for new contracts which may come along in the future, and it may well be to their benefit to end the contract on good terms.
- Poor handover may well damage the reputation of the existing supplier and also leave them open to redress if they fail to honour all their contract obligations.
- Maybe a balance of carrot (through a loyalty or performance-related incentive) and stick (through insistence that the contract clauses are honoured) is the best way to manage the transition.

Learning activity 20.5

How do you select the appropriate balance between reward and compliance? Legal considerations may also have an impact.

Feedback on page 296

Now attempt the following question.

Self-assessment question 20.5

Read up on examples of transitional arrangements when new contracts or legislation is enacted which make significant changes that affect stakeholders.

Feedback on page 296

Revision question

Now try the revision question for this session on page 299.

Summary

Key learning points in this session:

- Monitoring and control of the impact of the change process on supply chain performance involves both qualitative and quantitative measures.
- Continuity and change both need to be managed carefully to ensure successful change.
- Introduction of new suppliers needs to be carefully organised. Particularly where it is difficult to test performance fully, then trial or pilot periods provide some indication of likely issues.
- Suppliers who come to the end of a contract should be managed and incentivised to see out the full terms of their contract without disruption to supply or service levels.

Suggested further reading

Mullins (2005) provides a good generic treatment in this area, and Van Wheele (2005) relates change and performance management to the supply context.

Feedback on learning activities and self-assessment questions

Feedback on learning activity 20.1

A variety of definitions are possible. Suggestions which capture the essence of each term include the following.

Budget: A plan of financial operations embodying an estimate of proposed expenditures for a given period and the proposed means of financing them.

Benchmarking for the logistics and supply chain professional is a key method for determining the competitive position of your firm from both logistics cost and service perspectives.

Benchmarking is a performance comparison of organisational business processes against an internal or external standard of recognised leaders. Most often the comparison is made against a similar process in another organisation considered to be 'world class'.

Audit: the application of a comprehensive knowledge of generally accepted accounting principles and auditing standards to the auditing of the accounts and financial records of individuals, businesses, non-profit organisations or public services governments to determine their accuracy and reasonableness, to establish or verify costs, or to confirm the compliance of transactions with the provisions of statutes, regulations, agreements or contracts.

Purchasing audit is to analyse all elements of an audit as defined above, and related specifically to purchasing activities within organisations in order to confirm their current position.

Feedback on self-assessment question 20.1

Management view	**Position of purchasing**	***Performance measures in your organisation?***
Administrative activity	Low status	
Commercial activity	Reporting to management	
Part of integrated logistics	Integrated within logistics	
Strategic business area (supply chain perspective)	Represented on the senior management levels	

Feedback on learning activity 20.2

- Target costing: A cost control technique that lays down the maximum amount that a particular product should cost. The cost determined by deducting a required profit margin from the price that the product is expected to sell at in a competitive market. Qualitative because selling price is a matter of judgement without any absolute degree of certainty.
- Supplier development and involvement: Supplier involvement is the process whereby suppliers are actively included in an organisation's change management initiatives, ideally at an early stage in the process. This enables the organisation to benefit from skills, knowledge and attitudes that the supplier can bring to the change management considerations. Supplier development is the development of a long-term relationship with the supplier for mutual benefits for both parties. Both are qualitative assessments, backed by a degree of quantitative measures, but with no certainty that these measures will continue into the future.
- Make-or-buy decisions are decisions about whether an organisation should make the products or services that it sells in-house, or purchase in whole or part from other external sources. The decision is partly a financial one, but also considers wider areas of core competence, resource allocation and value-added activities.
- Supplier rationalisation is a process designed to reduce the overall number of suppliers, in favour of fewer, but strategically more critical suppliers. A qualitative assessment is required as to what constitutes an ideal number of suppliers.

Feedback on self-assessment question 20.2

Consider among a variety of factors:

- use of appropriate communication media
- range of communication media available
- frequency of communication
- availability and use of feedback mechanisms
- measures that will be used to judge effectiveness of communication.

Feedback on learning activity 20.3

You need to reflect particularly on situations where a one-size-fits-all solution is contemplated, without a holistic appreciation of all the factors that are involved.

An example could be where an organisation relies completely on technology and assumes that the culture will change to accommodate new ways of working. If the technology fails to perform then the situation can be made far worse than before.

Another example could be when an organisation drives through a restructuring of the various departments without doing anything about culture or allowing enough time to embed the changes.

Feedback on self-assessment question 20.3

The following table summarises some of the issues that you could have identified.

Continuity	**Change**
Best-practice philosophy	E-commerce developments
Business as usual	Significant savings
Decentralisation in departments will continue at national and local government levels	Economies of scale
Certain departments (MOD) excluded	Best practice in contract management
Credibility needs to be maintained during the change transition	Performance management at the heart of the new strategy
	Development of purchasing cards and internet tendering
	From procurement as an administrative to a strategic function

Feedback on learning activity 20.4

Reflect on some of the issues raised in the OCG guidelines. Was it possible to verify in advance that a supplier could actually perform to the standard required? Could it have been possible to pilot test before a complete roll-out? Did the nature of the contract, the nature of the supplier and the specific situation make a significant difference to the outcomes that you experienced?

Feedback on self-assessment question 20.4

It is difficult to provide specific feedback to your own situations so you need to reflect more yourselves. Questions that you could consider are:

- Are there any particular circumstances which are specific to supply chains?
- The general trend to outsourcing and off-shoring seems to pose new issues and problems.
- Particular concern seems to be in overcoming the challenges faced by off-shoring critical items which were previously delivered in-house or by a local supplier.
- There appear to be compelling commercial reasons for off-shoring, but what are the less tangible 'costs' of the off-shoring decision?

Feedback on learning activity 20.5

Situational and contingent factors need to be considered, such as size and importance of the contract, track record and impact on customers.

Feedback on self-assessment question 20.5

There are a range of possible scenarios to this question and no real hard-and-fast rules. You should by now be adept at internet searches to provide relevant examples of public and private sector transitional arrangements and initiatives.

Revision questions

Revision question for study session 1

'Management implies leadership, and in fact the success or failure of managers can be judged on their leadership qualities' (Hannagan, 2005). Critically assess the validity of this statement.

Feedback on page 301

Revision question for study session 2

Tannenbaum and Schmidt (1973) defined leadership style as 'the behaviour of leaders towards subordinates, the manner in which tasks and functions of leadership are conducted'. Develop this definition to explain how this relates to the range of leadership styles that they proposed.

Feedback on page 301

Revision question for study session 3

Propose a range of styles which can de adopted by leaders, and suggest circumstances where each style is most appropriate.

Feedback on page 302

Revision question for study session 4

Assess French and Raven's five sources of power and apply them to the purchasing context of an organisation with which you are familiar.

Feedback on page 302

Revision question for study session 5

Critically assess the concept of 'managing in four directions' and explain why it is beneficial for managers to do so.

Feedback on page 303

Revision question for study session 6

Explain *four* different methods of influencing in the supply chain and assess the 'effectiveness' of each of the alternative tactics that you have identified.

Feedback on page 304

Revision question for study session 7

Explain how you can assess the success of influencing tactics.

Feedback on page 305

Revision question for study session 8

Compare and contrast the 'team leader' and the 'solo leader' as discussed by Belbin (1981).

Feedback on page 306

Revision question for study session 9

Give reasons for what differentiates a successful team from less successful teams. State what makes the difference in performance.

Feedback on page 306

Revision question for study session 10

Critically evaluate how effective teams deal with conflict.

Feedback on page 307

Revision question for study session 11

Critically assess the benefits of diversity in the workplace and evaluate the advantages and disadvantages. Relate the benefits specifically to the context of an organisation with which you are familiar.

Feedback on page 307

Revision question for study session 12

Give reasons why it is important to develop people in the workplace, and state the approaches that could be adopted.

Feedback on page 308

Revision question for study session 13

Write a management report to your senior management, with a critical evaluation of how effective project leadership can improve performance and bring benefits in the purchasing department.

Feedback on page 309

Revision question for study session 14

(a) Outline the approaches an organisation may adopt to strategy development.

(b) Demonstrate how an organisation's strategic purpose can be disseminated throughout the business.

Feedback on page 310

Revision question for study session 15

Appraise two different models of change management. What factors would you consider in the implementation of a change management programme? Relate the factors specifically to the context of the purchasing department of an organisation with which you are familiar.

Feedback on page 310

Revision question for study session 16

Describe the seven key skills, according to Crainer (1998), that managers should possess in order to effectively manage change.

Feedback on page 311

Revision question for study session 17

Compare and contrast Kaizen and re-engineering as approaches to business improvement. State which approach you prefer and why.

Feedback on page 312

Revision question for study session 18

Assess what is meant by delegation and identify the requisite leadership behaviours that enable effective delegation.

Feedback on page 313

Revision question for study session 19

Define the term 'negotiation' and critically assess *two models* which consider the negotiation process.

Feedback on page 313

Revision question for study session 20

State the performance measures that you would consider to be important with regard to the purchasing function in an organisation with which you are familiar.

Feedback on page 314

Feedback on revision questions

Feedback on revision question for study session 1

This question is an opportunity for students to clarify their understanding of the similarities and distinctions between leadership and management.

You have a lot of leeway in answering this sort of question, since there are a number of viewpoints that can be cited. The debate about leadership and management has ebbed and flowed over recent decades and is unlikely to reach any firm consensus in the future. The quote from Hannagan is there to provoke and enable critical assessment – so better answers will use it to illustrate whichever view they are proposing. Better marks will be awarded to those who reflect a range of theories which support their views but still acknowledge some balance about difference between leadership and management. Clearly Hannagan is suggesting that leadership qualities such as setting and articulating a clear vision, setting a good example, being innovative and creative, and motivating and inspiring others are in his view an essential part of good management.

Relevant management theory should as a minimum consider styles, behaviours, actions and traits.

Feedback on revision question for study session 2

Figure 21.1

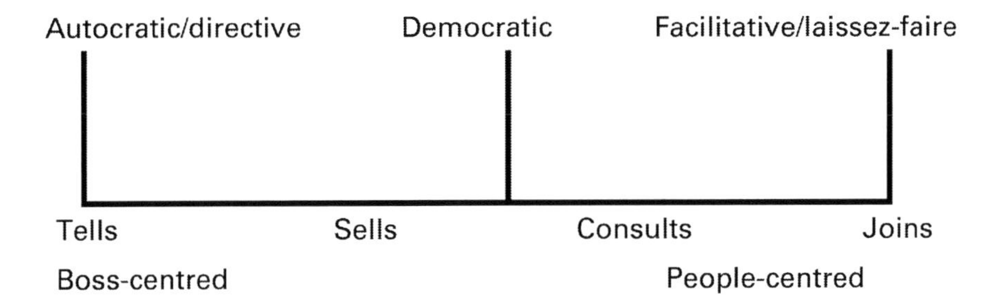

Tannenbaum and Schmidt used the definition above and identified a continuum of leadership styles from autocratic to laissez-faire, based on the behaviour of leaders towards their subordinates (figure 21.1). The behaviour links also to the way they communicate and interact with their people:

- Tells – the leader identifies a problem, chooses a solution and announces this to staff. Staff are then expected to implement this solution, as directed by the leader. This is often referred to as a top-down approach.

- Sells – the leader identifies the problem, chooses a solution, but recognises that a bold announcement may encounter resistance from staff. He/she therefore attempts to persuade staff to accept the decision by spending some time in explaining the rationale behind the decision-making process that has been followed.
- Consults – the leader identifies the problem, but consults staff before making a decision. The consultation involves listening to the advice and options proposed by staff, and taking those views into consideration when making the decision.
- Joins – the leader defines the problem and most likely sets some constraints within which the solution is bound (quality, cost and time). The group is then given the responsibility and authority to make decisions. The leader may or may not be available in an advisory role as needed.

Feedback on revision question for study session 3

Your discussion requires some brief description of leadership styles and a range of the common approaches which you should be referring to from the bullets below.

- The three main classifications of leadership styles: authoritarian, democratic and laissez-faire, and how they relate to McGregor's Theory X and Theory Y view of people. Authoritarian styles based on a Theory X perspective, and democratic and laissez-faire based on Theory Y.
- A continuum of different leadership styles from facilitative through to directive, and how they reflect in the contrasting methods of tell and sell and the other two broad categories of leadership style: consult and join.
- The merits of a situational approach to leadership, based on the state of readiness of staff.
- Transactional leadership and transformational leadership.

The relevant circumstances will depend on the situation, the staff and the objectives to be achieved, and the leader should be aware that different leadership styles may be required in different circumstances.

Feedback on revision question for study session 4

French and Raven (1959) identified five broad sources of power:

- Legitimate power. The target of influence perceives the legitimacy of power due to position or status of the holder of the power. For example, middle managers and first-line managers have authority because of their position within the formal structure of the organisation. This is often referred to as position power. In purchasing this could relate to the power of senior managers relative to their subordinates and staff.
- Reward power. Authority to use organisational resources for rewards or recognition as perceived by the follower. For example, senior managers in the purchasing department having control over staff pay, promotions, increased responsibility, career progression and perks in general.
- Coercive power. Threat of sanctions or punishment and the ability to carry them through. For example, senior managers in the purchasing

department withholding or delaying pay, promotion, increased responsibility, perks.
- Referent power. Ability to identify with and be influenced by the manager. Based on the perception of attractive personal traits in the manager – charisma. The manager in the purchasing department is popular and a good communicator and shows sincere concern for his staff. You are attracted to their personality and thus are happy to follow their lead. In these cases they may not be senior managers, or even managers at all, but have power because they attract willing followers.
- Expertise power. Authority based on the perception of skill, competence, expertise and/or experience of the person, who again need not be a manager. Based on credibility and clear evidence of expertise in previous situations, by the person.

More critical answers may also mention that the French and Raven definitions of power are also relevant and considered in a number of other practical ways in the purchasing function such as by the use of:

- power/interest matrix
- competence/care matrix
- Kraljic matrix.

Feedback on revision question for study session 5

Figure 21.2

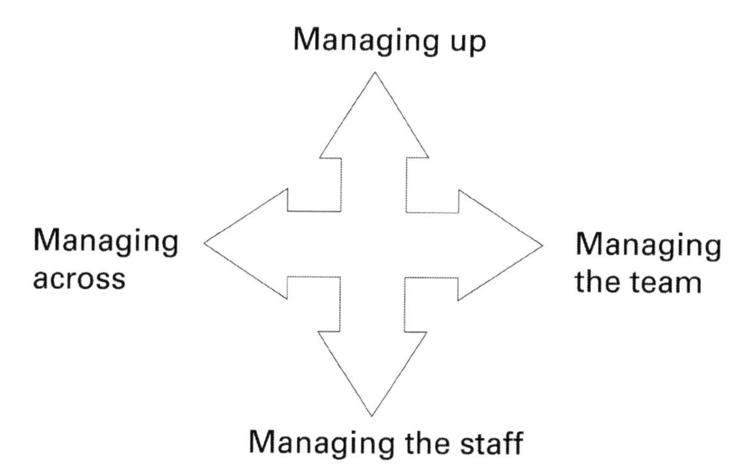

Managing upwards: Middle and first-line managers often claim that a lack of top-management support is one of the most common reasons why they cannot work effectively and run into difficulties. It is useful to be able to get senior management support to help solve problems, to provide resources or to show a sense of ownership towards project or normal day-to-day activities.

Managing the team: Managing your team is how you as a manager respond to the state of readiness of your staff, but also how you can influence your team members to make improvements in attitudes, behaviours and performance, to achieve improvements in readiness.

Managing the staff: A sense of involvement has to be created among those who will be working or using new systems and procedures. The most visible group are the people whose work is directly altered by the new ideas and who will be living with the results in their daily work. They have to set up the system, and run it thereafter. It is essential to involve those who will be the users of your changes, so that they contribute to solutions and gain commitment from being involved. A good rule of thumb is that a change imposed from above will not be accepted as readily as one to which staff have contributed.

Managing stakeholders: A key management skill is to create a sense of ownership in your stakeholders (inside or outside your organisation). Stakeholders need to 'own' the issues that you are addressing before they will be willing to invest time and effort into making a change work. The manager must build a sense of ownership among other departments and external stakeholders towards the new ideas, so that it is not seen as someone else's problem. The manager also expects and needs support from other departments to meet deadlines set, come up with ideas to overcome difficulties and generally to support the new work publicly. This will only happen if the staff in the respective functions and stakeholders feel a sense of ownership and responsibility towards the new ideas.

It is beneficial for managers to be aware of the concept of 'managing in four directions' because projects are formed and delivered in a dynamic environment, where different groups (the four directions) are involved in the project to a greater or lesser degree.

The manager needs to be:

- aware of the various groups
- aware of the different levels of power and interest that the various groups can exert
- able to consider and then develop a range of strategies to ensure that the various groups can be managed to support and assist the manager in achieving the project goals.

Feedback on revision question for study session 6

Yukl identified a range of influencing tactics available to managers; you should select any four of these.

- Rational persuasion involves use of explanations, logical arguments and factual evidence to demonstrate that a request or suggestion is feasible and relevant to the task at hand. This tends to work best when objectives are shared, but that the way the objective is to be achieved is unclear to the staff involved.
- Apprising involves the leader explaining the benefits to staff as to why they should support the leader. It appeals to the 'what's in this for me?' attitude which some staff may have. This tends to work best if the leader actually has the credibility to deliver the benefits which are being proffered.
- Inspirational appeal involves an emotional and value-laden appeal, intended to focus on the emotions of staff, rather than the logic of rational persuasion. This works well when the issue directly influences the situation of staff and can result in some significant change for them.

- Consultation occurs when staff are invited to participate in planning how to implement a proposed action or proposal. Their input can be useful at a technical level, but also it is likely that consultation achieves commitment and support from staff, and a drive to ensure that the idea achieves its intended outcome.
- Collaboration involves an offer to provide resources if staff agree to carry out the request of the leader. This works best when there is some mutual benefit involved. The leader helps and supports staff by providing resources that help them to do the task successfully.
- Ingratiation attempts to influence staff's attitude, and get them to be more positive about the leader. The leader gives compliments, does favours, praises and shows respect, such that staff respond appropriately. Sincerity is the key to effective use of this tactic. You have to mean it, or staff will see through falseness.
- Personal appeal is influence based on friendship or loyalty to the leader. If friendship and loyalty are genuine and strong, then there is a high likelihood that this tactic will be successful.
- Exchange involves an explicit or implicit offer of some reward for staff in return for their compliance and support. Exchange is about increasing benefits, such that it is worthwhile for staff to agree. It is very much about finding the appropriate 'carrot', and showing that you are able to deliver the promised reward.
- Coalition involves bringing in other people to help influence staff. This may be peers, superiors, subordinates or stakeholders whose views staff respect.
- Legitimating tactics involve attempts to establish authority of the leader. For routine issues this is unlikely to be important, but if requests are unusual and appear to be outside your remit, you may have to establish authority through 'proving' that you have it.
- Pressure tactics include threats, warnings, assertive behaviour and frequent requests to see if requests have been complied with. A careful balance has to be taken with this approach. Pressure may succeed in achieving compliance, but can engender resentment and a lack of commitment on behalf of staff because willingness is ignored.

Feedback on revision question for study session 7

Responses to influencing tactics broadly fall into three categories:

- Commitment. Subordinates agree with request from the leader, and make every effort to do what has been asked of them, in an enthusiastic way. Commitment is usually regarded as the most desirable outcome from influence tactics.
- Compliance. Subordinates are willing to do what is asked of them, but are not always enthusiastic and positive. Behaviour has been influenced, but attitudes have not. Compliance may be enough to achieve relatively simple tasks, but if the task is complex and difficult then it may not be sufficient.
- Resistance. Subordinates are opposed to the request, and actively try and avoid doing it. Resistance can be more or less significant depending upon the strength of feeling involved.

In a simplistic sense the tactic can be regarded as effective if the desired outcome (goal) is achieved. At a deeper level you also want positive support from staff, so that learning can take place.

Feedback on revision question for study session 8

The solo leader rules in an autocratic manner, is directive, expects compliance from staff and often leads from the front. Belbin suggests solo leaders can be effective in times of crisis because they act swiftly and decisively, but if they fail this can have serious consequences. Solo leaders clearly have a Theory X view of their people.

In contrast, team leaders act in a much more participative and structured manner. They have a Theory Y view of people and therefore consult, delegate and trust their people to perform well. Belbin suggests that this approach is more likely to be successful in most situations (see table 21.1).

Table 21.1

	Solo leader	Team leader
1.	He knows everything best (interferes)	Chooses to limit his roles and delegates other roles to those who can do better
2.	Conformity – tries to make everybody be the same	Builds on diversity – values the differences in different people
3.	Collects admirers and 'yes men'	Seeks talented people and does not feel threatened by them
4.	Tells subordinates what to do	Encourages colleagues to use their particular strengths in their own way
5.	Management by objectives – makes it clear exactly what everyone is supposed to do	Creates mission – helps to clarify the vision which others act on as they think best

Feedback on revision question for study session 9

A range of reasons and how these impact on performance can all be suggested with equal validity:

- Common goals and vision form the glue that binds a team together.
- Cross-functional teamworking – to harness the diverse skills of people in a cooperative and participative manner, by getting people from different technical functions to work together to achieve common goals.
- Sheard and Kakabadse (2002) expanded and combined previous thinking by Tuckman, Kubler-Ross and Adair into a multi-factor model of effective team development – see (table 21.2).

Table 21.2

Key factor	Effective team	Focus
Clearly defined goals	Common and understood	Task
Priorities	Team alignment	Task
Roles and responsibilities	Agreed and understood	Individual
Self-awareness	Appropriate to team needs	Individual
Leadership	Catalytic and facilitative	Group
Group dynamics	Established and agreed	Group

(continued on next page)

Table 21.2 *(continued)*

Key factor	Effective team	Focus
Communications	Open	Group
Content	Influenced but not controlled by the organisation	Environment
Infrastructure	Stable support by organisational infrastructure	Environment

Feedback on revision question for study session 10

You should possibly start by considering different perspectives on conflict:

- Unitary perspective seeks to develop an organisation that is integrated and harmonious throughout, and regards conflict as dysfunctional and harmful.
- Pluralist perspective sees conflict between competing groups within an organisation as inevitable, and inherent in the functional and hierarchical structure of most organisations.
- Radical perspective sees organisations in terms of a conflict of power and control. Conflict reflects the inequalities within an organisation and is the natural means whereby change is effected.

Mullins (2005) suggests that managers can focus on a number of strategies for managing conflict within teams, in order that creative conflict can work positively without degenerating into destructive and divisive conflict:

- Clarification of goals and objectives avoids misunderstandings and provides a clear common focus for all.
- Resource distribution to be clearly justified so that people understand why and how resources have been allocated throughout the organisation.
- HRM policies and procedures which are fair and equitable. Clear job analysis, recruitment, selection, rewards and punishments help to create a level playing field for all staff.
- Non-monetary rewards can be emphasised through challenges, delegation and empowerment and so on.
- Development and training in group process skills, such as communication, problem solving and so on.
- Group activities and careful team selection reduces role/style conflicts.
- Leadership and management to be more participative and supportive. Demonstration of respect, trust, developing people and so on.
- Creating appropriate infrastructure processes to reduce unnecessary bureaucracy.
- A systems approach which encompasses the social and psychological aspects of work as well as the structural aspects.

Feedback on revision question for study session 11

Answers will depend on the specific context of your own organisation, but should include some reference to the following issues.

Benefits:

- improves employee retention
- increases customer confidence

- that in a global and diverse marketplace, a company whose make-up mirrors the make-up of the marketplace it serves is better equipped to thrive
- provides organisations with a more global and international perspective
- broader range of skills and backgrounds improves creativity and innovation
- better business results and performance.

Advantages:

- broad base of culture, attitudes and behaviours
- different talents and experiences
- opportunity for synergy, creativity and innovation
- inclusive and wide spread of skills.

Disadvantages:

- needs a broader range of management skills
- cultures, attitudes and behaviour can clash, leading to overt conflict, or isolation and polarisation
- loss of focus on organisational goals in favour of specialist interests
- divisive and energy sapping with disagreements and misunderstandings.

Feedback on revision question for study session 12

You could usefully start by contrasting the people as 'cost' with the people as 'asset' approach (table 21.3).

Table 21.3

Cost	Asset
Training is expensive and adds to costs	People interact with other resources and with customers
Increased costs decrease profits	The more they are trained the better they do the work
Managers know what is needed, people provide the labour	More training means more creativity and innovation
Managers can better control a compliant workforce	More learning leads to better performance, motivation and satisfaction

Then there are the benefits of 'learning' for the individuals concerned, for their organisations and for society in general (table 21.4).

Table 21.4

Individuals	Organisations	Society
Developing potential	Developing capacity	Survival and growth
Learning *how* to learn	Achieving goals effectively	Cohesion and consensus
Ability to change	Clear purpose, vision, etc.	Underpinning of democratic choices
Learning for life	Learning produces solutions	Creation of a fulfilled society
Learning is formal and informal	Balances short- and long-term perspectives	

Approaches to be adopted: you should briefly consider aspects of all of these.

- Training – 'an instructor-led and content-based intervention leading to desired changes in behaviour' Sloman (2005).
- Learning – 'a self-directed, work-based process'.
- Development – 'leading to increased adaptive capacity'.

Feedback on revision question for study session 13

Candidates need to consider critically the challenges that good project leadership needs to address:

- balance of technical and interpersonal skills
- balance of project objectives and broad strategy
- creation of vision, mission, objectives, SMART goals and so on
- managing and motivating the project team –

in short, *all* aspects of managing in four directions.

Specific skills and capabilities include:

- Shaping goals: setting or receiving overall objectives and directions, interpreting them, reacting to changes in them, clarifying the problem and setting boundaries to it.
- Obtaining resources: identifying them, negotiating for their release, retaining them, managing their effective use.
- Building roles and structures: clarifying and modifying their own, and those of other functions.
- Establishing good communications: linking the diverse groups or individuals contributing to the project, to obtain their support and commitment.
- Seeing the whole picture: taking a helicopter view, managing time and other resources, anticipating reactions from stakeholders, spotting links and unexpected events.
- Moving things forward: taking action and risks to keep the project going, especially through difficult phases.

Additional interpersonal skills include:

- Communicating – sensitivity; structures; links; written, oral, and face-to-face presentations and listening.
- Negotiating – resolving conflicts; informal and formal.
- Team-building – energy and enthusiasm; role clarity; selection of the team and group development.
- Involving users and staff – ownership and commitment; education and training; reassurance (support and back-up); consultation, listening and awareness.

Candidates need to focus on performance – in relation to quality, cost, time, or other appropriate performance measures. So tangible specific measures need to be highlighted.

Candidates need to produce an answer that relates specifically to the purchasing department rather than to be generic to the whole organisation.

Feedback on revision question for study session 14

This question was set in the CIPS Strategy paper in May 2005, so you can usefully refer to the Examiner's Report. Some of the key points made in that Report are reproduced below.

(a) You should give an overview of the rational and emergent approaches to strategy development. The discussion of the rational approach should mention its top-down, formal, long-term, predictive nature and the problems of inflexibility, unresponsiveness and implementation difficulties. The discussion of the emergent approach should include its bottom-up, informal and responsive nature, but also allude to its lack of direction and focus. The compromise solution of logical incrementalism could also be mentioned.
Better answers will provide an overview of the rational and emergent approaches to strategy development and its hybrid solution of logical incrementalism.
However, other approaches can be considered and proposed, such as soft systems methodology, scenario planning, brainstorming, the adaptive approach and so on.

(b) An organisation's strategic purpose can be disseminated throughout the organisation by means of vision and mission statements, specific objectives, policies and plans. You should demonstrate a clear understanding of these methods and how they link together through the strategy hierarchy of corporate, business and functional levels of the organisation.
Good answers should demonstrate a clear understanding of vision and mission statements, objectives, policies and plans combined with an awareness of how they link together through the corporate, business and functional levels of the enterprise and how they can be facilitated by good communication channels and media. Try and achieve a balanced discussion and avoid too much of a focus solely on the generic communication issues or on change management issues. Try and balance the two because they are equally important. The purpose of an organisation is relatively unchanging, therefore its effective dissemination is more concerned with getting the message right through processes and structures rather than the soft change management issues.

Feedback on revision question for study session 15

'Appraise' means you need to assess the pros and cons of two from a range of different models of change management. Better marks come from *breadth and depth* of discussion – your choice of two models can come from any of these considered in this unit, plus other relevant models:

- Lewin's force field analysis
- Organisational development movement
- The action research model
- Kaizen and BPR as philosophies of change
- Forced and evolutionary change
- Any other change management model which you feel is appropriate.

Practical implementation is affected by factors such as:

- time
- cost
- difficulty
- culture and politics
- market dynamics.

When you relate this to your organisation and the purchasing department, you should explore the role of the purchasing function and its potential to take a leading role within the organisation.

What can a leader do to assist effective change? The role is a balance between facilitator and visionary. The leader is provider of appropriate resources and also acts as a broker to gain support from other stakeholders. The leader can, for instance, set an example.

Feedback on revision question for study session 16

- Managing conflict – the ability to manage conflict in a constructive way so that positive outcomes can emerge. Conflict of itself is not seen as negative. Indeed constructive conflict and openness can unearth disagreements, which can stimulate innovative and creative solutions. Conversely managers also need the skills to diffuse and divert conflict that is potentially destructive and counter-productive.
- Interpersonal skills. The effective change manager will have a range of soft interpersonal skills, such as communication, empathy, listening and motivation, such that people are likely to respond positively to him/her.
- Project management skills – a blend of the systematic skills of being able to deliver to the required level of quality, cost and time in a complex environment, with the team-building skills to get the best out of the people involved in the project.
- Leadership and flexibility – the ability to set clear objectives and to motivate people to achieve them. At the same time understanding that the business environment is capable of rapid change, to which flexible, innovative and creative responses may be required.
- Managing processes. Processes are 'how things get done'. Change managers need the ability to manage these carefully so that processes are properly designed, planned and controlled, and improved as necessary.
- Managing strategy – staying mindful of the contribution of the proposed changes to the overall strategic aims and objectives of the organisation, so that the changes align smoothly and make a positive contribution.
- Managing their own development – the ability to take responsibility for one's own learning in the context of the organisation and how it is evolving. Particularly important is the acknowledgement that self-development is a lifelong process which never ends.

Crainer argues that managers who possess these seven skills are much less likely to be reactive when it comes to change situations. They will be capable of actively promoting and initiating change in a positive and constructive way.

Feedback on revision question for study session 17

Kaizen is seeking to achieve small improvements in any element of the organisation's activities, but to do so continuously and consistently over time. Step-change, often referred to as business process re-engineering (BPR) or transformational change, is altogether more radical, seeking to achieve significant improvement in activities in a relatively restricted timescale.

Mullins (2005) identifies the following main components of a kaizen approach to change:

- Detailed analysis of all the steps in a process, via process mapping.
- The process mapping demonstrates where changes can be made, by looking at eliminating any non-value-added activities.
- Improvements can be in equipment (better machinery), materials (the items that are used) or in behaviours of employees.
- Kaizen looks at eliminating non-value-added activities and expressing the savings in terms of time or money.

BPR has been defined by Hammer and Champy (1993) as 'the fundamental rethinking and radical redesign of business processes to achieve dramatic improvements in critical, contemporary measures of performance, such as cost, quality, service and speed'.

Distinctive features of BPR are, among others:

- A zero-based approach which means starting from scratch, and largely ignoring past trends in performance. This approach is often referred to as *greenfield thinking.*
- A focus on process, how we deliver goods and services to the customer across the organisation.
- A focus on radical thinking to achieve significant improvements.

Comparison may actually incorporate both approaches.

- BPR if properly implemented can lead to dramatic, quantifiable improvements in a short time frame. Hammer and Champy (1993) suggest that BPR initiatives, even if they are extensive, should be capable of producing measurable benefits within a year.
- At the same time BPR is often complex, difficult and risky. This means that clear leadership and management is an absolutely essential component for success.
- Kaizen is often easier than BPR because only small improvements are needed, which may require far less complexity and can often be driven and initiated by staff themselves since often relatively small amounts of resources are required.
- At the same time, kaizen may not deliver sufficient improvements to catch up or keep pace with competitors who are working and improving at a faster rate than your organisation. There is a risk that you may be falling behind by proceeding too slowly. But if you are ahead of the competition, then kaizen helps you to keep ahead by not getting complacent and over-confident.

Feedback on revision question for study session 18

Mullins (2005) defines delegation as 'the process of entrusting authority and responsibility to others through the various levels of the organisation, and the creation of a special manager–subordinate relationship'.

Guidelines for effective delegation include:

- Whenever possible, when delegating, give the person a whole task to do. If the task is too extensive, people need to be aware of the overall goals, and how what they are doing contributes. People are most effective when they are aware of the big picture.
- Make sure people understand exactly what you want them to do. Question, observe and seek feedback to make sure that the goals are clear and the objectives are SMART.
- If you have a vision of what a successful outcome or output will look like, share that with people.
- Identify the key points of the project or dates when you want feedback about progress. Make sure progress is able to be tracked and related to clear deadlines and outcomes.
- Be absolutely clear how outcomes will be measured.
- Relate and link appropriate rewards to successful completion.

Poor delegation is characterised by:

- poor team and individual motivation and morale
- the team is confused, and this spills over into conflicts and tensions
- you get questions about delegated tasks too often.

Delegation and leadership styles are also linked to Hersey and Blanchard's situational leadership model.

Feedback on revision question for study session 19

Among many possible definitions are just two suggestions:

> 'Negotiation is the process whereby interested parties resolve disputes, agree upon courses of action, bargain for individual or collective advantage, and/or attempt to craft outcomes which serve their mutual interests. It is usually regarded as a form of alternative dispute resolution.'

Negotiation can be regarded as the process of discussing an issue between two or more parties with competing interests with an aim of coming to an agreement.

Kharbanda and Stallworthy (1991) suggest that negotiation is an eight-stage process:

- prepare
- argue
- signal
- propose

- present the package
- bargain
- close
- agree.

The above approach can suggest that negotiation is a linear process, which could be regarded as simplistic.

Table 21.5 A Model for Negotiation

Pre-negotiation	The negotiation			Post-negotiation
Pre-negotiation	Introduction	Bargaining	Agreement	Post-negotiation

Source: Farmer (1991)

Farmer's approach (table 21.5) breaks the linearity of Kharbanda and Stallworthy into three distinct phases, which will vary significantly in terms of effort and content required, and perhaps more realistically reflects the iterative nature of the negotiation process.

Feedback on revision question for study session 20

Van Weele (2005) suggests that 'the question of how to measure and evaluate purchasing performance is not easily answered'. How results are measured depends upon how managers view the role and importance of the purchasing function (table 21.6).

Table 21.6

Management view	**Position of purchasing**	**Performance measure**
Administrative activity	Low status	• Orders • Order backlog • Lead time • Adherence to procedures etc.
Commercial activity	Reporting to management	• Savings, price reductions • Financial measures
Part of integrated logistics	Integrated within logistics	• Savings, cost reductions • Supplier delivery • Reliability • Gradual improvement metrics
Strategic business area (supply chain perspective)	Represented at senior management levels	• Target costing • Supplier development and involvement • Make-or-buy decisions • Supplier rationalisation • Dramatic improvement metrics

When purchasing is seen as an operational and administrative function, then measures are largely quantitative in character. Purchasing and performance is largely evaluated in terms of costs allocations, and the control of purchasing as a non-value-added activity. Typical measures are expressed largely in terms of budgets, adhered to measurement against specific project areas, benchmarking and auditing metrics. Purchasing is measured mostly in terms of efficiency.

When purchasing is considered to be a strategic business area, then measures are more qualitative and judgemental. A variety of complex measures of procedures and guidelines are employed to focus much more on effectiveness and the potential to add value to the business. Significant improvements in performance can be delivered by making radical changes to the way purchasing and the supply chain is organised and managed.

References and bibliography

This section contains a complete A–Z listing of all publications, materials or websites referred to in this course book. Books, articles and research are listed under the first author's (or in some cases the editor's) surname. Where no author name has been given, the publication is listed under the name of the organisation that published it. Websites are listed under the name of the organisation providing the website.

Adair, J (1979) *Action-Centred Leadership.* London: Gower Publishing.

Adair, J (1986) *Effective Teambuilding.* London: Gower Publishing.

Anderson, LA and D Anderson (2006) *Identifying your Drivers of Change,* at http://www.beingfirst.com/products/books/bcm/.

Arminas, D (2000) 'Procurement Central', *Supply Management,* March.

Ashcroft, S (2004) 'Commercial negotiation skills', *Industrial and Commercial Training,* 36(6) pp229–33.

Association for Project Management: http://www.apm.org.uk.

Atherton, JS (2005) Learning and Teaching: *Experiential Learning* [On-line] UK: Learning and Teaching: http://www.learningandteaching.info/learning/experience.htm.

Baily, P, D Farmer, D Jessop and D Jones (2005) *Purchasing Principles and Management,* 9th edition. London: FT Prentice-Hall.

Bass, BM (1985) *Leadership and Performance Beyond Expectations.* New York: Free Press.

Beckhard, R (1969) *Organisational Development: Strategies and Models.* Reading, MA: Addison-Wesley.

Beckhard, R and RT Harris (1977) *Managing Complex Change.* Reading, MA: Addison-Wesley.

Belbin, RM (1993) *Team Roles at Work.* Oxford: Butterworth-Heinemann.

Belbin, RM (2000) *Beyond the Team.* Oxford: Butterworth-Heinemann.

Blake, RR and JS Mouton (1964) *The Managerial Grid.* Houston, TX: Gulf Publishing.

Boddy, D (2002) *Management: an Introduction,* 2nd edition. Harlow: Prentice-Hall.

Brewer, R (2003) *Managing Human Resources In Purchasing and Supply.* CIPS Study Guide. Stamford: CIPS.

Brown, JAC (1986) *The Social Psychology of Industry: Human Relations in the Factory.* Harmondsworth, Middlesex: Penguin.

Buchanan, D and D Boddy (1992) *The Expertise of the Change Agent: Public Performance and Backstage Activity.* London: Prentice Hall.

Burgoyne, J, I Cunningham, B Garratt, P Honey, A Mayo, A Mumford, M Pearn and M Pedler (1999) 'The debate starts here', in *People Management in Perspective.* London: Institute of Personnel & Development.

Burke, R (2003) *Project Management: Planning and Control Techniques*, 4th edition. Chichester: Wiley.

Burns, JW (1978) *Leadership.* New York: Harper & Row.

Charbonneau, D (2004) 'Influence tactics and perceptions of transformational leadership', *Leadership & Organization Development Journal,* 25(7) pp565–76.

The Chartered Institute of Purchasing and Supply: http://www.cips.org

Chartered Institute of Purchasing and Supply (1990) *Successful Negotiation: Preparation, Planning and Process*, IPS Briefing Publication. Stamford: CIPS.

Collins, J (1996) *Aligning Action and Values: Leader to Leader.* Drucker Foundation and Jossey-Bass Publishers, Summer.

Cousins, P (1992) 'Purchasing Partnerships: a professional approach', *Purchasing and Supply Management,* December, pp33–5.

Couzins, M and S Beagrie (2003) 'How to... manage upwards', *Personnel Today,* 11 November.

Cox, A (1997) 'On power, appropriateness and procurement competence', *Supply Management*, 2 October, 24–7.

Cox, A, J Sanderson and G Watson (2000) *Power Regimes: Mapping the DNA of Business and Supply Chain Relationships.* Stratford-upon-Avon: Earlsgate Press.

Cox, A, J Sanderson and G Watson (2000) 'Wielding influence', *Supply Management,* 6 April.

Cox, A (2001) 'The power perspective in procurement and supply management', *Journal of Supply Chain Management,* 32, Special Edition, pp4–7.

Cox, A (2003) 'Horses for courses', *Supply Management,* 30 January.

Cox, A, P Ireland, C Lonsdale, J Sanderson and G Watson (2002) Supply Chains, Market and Power: Strategies for Appropriating Value. London: Routledge.

Crainer, S (1998) *Key Management Ideas: Thinkers that Changed the Management World*, 3rd edition. London: FT-Prentice Hall.

Creating a Compelling Vision: http://leadinginsight.com/compelling_vision.htm.

Drucker, PD (1954) *The Practice of Management.* Oxford: Butterworth-Heinemann.

Drucker, PF (1999) *Management Challenges for the 21st Century.* New York: Harper Collins.

Dunphy, D and D Stace (1993) 'The strategic management of corporate change', *Human Relations*, 46(8), pp905–20.

Effecting Change in Higher Education: http://www.effectingchange.luton.ac.uk/approaches_to_change/index.php?content=actionresearch.

EU campaign, For Diversity, Against Discrimination: http://www.stop-discrimination.info.

Farmer, D (1991) *The Successful Negotiator's Handbook.* Swansea: Malcolm Press.

Farrell, M and W Schroeder (1999) 'Power and influence in the buying centre', *European Journal of Marketing*, 33(11/12), pp1161–70.

Fenson, S (2000) *10 Tips for Communicating Change.* Inc.com – small business resources for the entrepreneur: http://www.inc.com/articles/2000/06/19312.html.

Floyd, S and W Wooldridge (1996) *The Strategic Middle Manager.* San Francisco: Jossey-Bass.

Follett, MP (1924) *Creative Experience.* New York: Longman Green and Co.

Gadiesh, O and JL Gilbert (2001) 'Transforming Corner-Office Strategy into Frontline Action', *Harvard Business Review*, May.

Gardiner, PD (2005) *Project Management: A Strategic Planning Approach.* Basingstoke: Palgrave Macmillan.

Goldberg, B (1997) 'Corporate vision', *Executive Excellence*, March.

Goleman, D (1995) *Emotional Intelligence.* New York: Bantam Books.

Hammer, M and J Champy (1993) *Re-engineering the Corporation: A Manifesto for Business Revolution.* London: Nicholas Brearley.

Hammer, M and SA Stanton (1995) *The Re-engineering Revolution.* New York: Harper Collins.

Hannagan, T (2005) *Management Concepts and Practices.* Harlow: FT Prentice-Hall.

Heathfield, SM About Human Resources: http://humanresources.about.com/cs/manageperformance/a/delegation.htm.

Hersey, P (1984) *The Situational Leader.* New York: Centre for Leadership Studies.

Hersey, P, KH Blanchard and K Dewey (2000) *Management of Organisational Behaviour: Utilising Human Resources,* 8th edition. New York: Prentice-Hall.

Herzberg, F, B Mausner and BB Snyderman (1959) *The Motivation to Work,* 2nd edition. London: Chapman & Hall.

Hofstede, G (1981) *Culture's Consequences: International Differences in Work-Related Values.* London: Sage Publications.

Huczynski, A and D Buchanan (2001) *Organizational Behaviour: An Introductory Text,* 4th edition. London: FT Prentice-Hall.

Johnson, G and K Scholes (2004) *Exploring Corporate Strategy: Texts and Cases,* 7th edition. London: FT Prentice-Hall.

Johnson, G, K Scholes and R Whittington (2004) *Exploring Corporate Strategy: Texts and Cases,* 7th edition. London: FT Prentice-Hall.

Jungalwalla, R (2000) 'Transforming groups into teams', *Executive Education*, 17(2).

Kelman, HC (1958) 'Compliance, identification and internalization: three processes of attitude change', *Journal of Conflict Resolution,* 2, pp51–6.

Kennedy, G (1997) *Kennedy on Negotiation*. London: Gower Publishing.

Kharbanda, OP and EA Stallworthy (1991) 'Negotiation: an essential management skill', *Journal of Managerial Psychology*, 6(4).

Kotter, JP (1990) *A Force for Change: How Leadership Differs from Management.* New York: Free Press.

Kotter, JP (1996) *Leading Change.* Boston, MA: Harvard Business School Press.

Kreitner, R (2001) *Management,* 8th edition. Boston, MA: Houghton Mifflin.

Lengel, RH and RL Daft (1988) 'The selection of communication media as an executive skill', *Academy of Management Executive*, 2(3), 225–32.

Lewin, K (1951) *Field Theory in Social Science.* New York: Harper & Row.

Lock, D (2003) *Project Management*, 8th edition. Aldershot: Gower Publishing.

Lysons, K and R Brewer (2003) *Managing Human Resources in Purchasing and Supply,* revised edition. Stamford: CIPS.

Malhotra, D (2004) 'Six ways to build trust in negotiations', *Negotiation,* 5 April. Harvard Business School Press.

Mannix, EA (2005) 'Strength in numbers: working in teams', *Negotiation,* 8(5), May. Harvard Business School Press.

Maslen, R and KW Platts (1994) 'Force field analysis: a technique to help SMEs realise their intended manufacturing strategy', in *Operations Strategy and Performance,* 1st European Operations Management Association Conference, University of Cambridge, June, pp587–88.

Maylor, H (2003) *Project Management,* 3rd edition. London: Pearson.

McGregor, D (1960) *The Human Side of Enterprise.* London: Penguin.

Meredith, JR and SW Mantel (2000) *Project Management: A Managerial Approach.* New York: Prentice Hall.

Meredith, JR and SW Mantel (2003) *Project Management: A Managerial Approach,* international edition, 5th edition. New York; Chichester: Wiley.

Mullins, LJ (2005) *Management and Organisational Behaviour,* 7th edition. London: FT Prentice-Hall.

Nanus, B (1992) *Visionary Leadership.* San Francisco: Jossey Bass.

Nonanka, I and H Tageuchi (1995) *The Knowledge Creating Company.* Oxford: Oxford University Press.

Noypayak, W and M Speece (1998) 'Tactics to influence subordinates among Thai managers', *Journal of Managerial Psychology,* 13(5/6) pp343–58.

Office of Government Commerce: http://www.ogc.gov.uk/sdtoolkit/deliveryteam/briefings/businesschange/manag_transit.

One Workplace Equal Rights: http://www.oneworkplace.co.uk.

Ouchi, WG (1981) Theory Z: How American Business Can Meet the Japanese Challenge. New York: Addison-Wesley.

Peters, T and RS Waterman (1982) *In Search of Excellence.* New York: Random House.

projectmanagement.com: http://www.projectmanagement.com.

PMI (2001) A Guide to the Project Management Body of Knowledge. London, Project Management Institute.

Rajkhowa, G (2003) *Business Organisation and Processes,* revised edition. Stamford: CIPS.

Reynolds, J (2004) *Helping People Learn: Strategies for Moving from Training to Learning*. London: CIPD.

Saunders, M (1997) *Strategic Purchasing and Supply Chain Management*, 2nd edition. London: Prentice-Hall.

Saunders, M (1988) 'Strategic and policy considerations', *Purchasing and Supply Management*, April, pp34–5.

Schein, EH (1998) *Organisational Psychology*, 3rd edition. Englewood Cliffs, NJ: Prentice-Hall.

Scholtes, PR (1998) *The Leader's Handbook: making things happen, getting things done*. New York; London: McGraw Hill.

Sheard, AG and AP Kakabadse (2002) 'From loose groups to effective teams', *Journal of Management Development*, 27(2), pp131–53.

Slack, N, S Chamber and R Johnston (2004) *Operations Management*, 4th edition. London: FT Prentice-Hall.

Sloman, M (2005) Training to Learning. London: CIPD.

Smith, A (1998) *Training and Development in Australia*. Sydney: Butterworths.

socionics.com: http://www.socionics.com/main/types.htm.

Stannack, P (2003) *Commercial Relationships*. Stamford: CIPS.

Suh, KS (1999) 'Impact of communication medium on task performance and satisfaction: an examination of media-richness theory', *Information & Management*, 35, pp 295–312.

Tannenbaum, R and WH Schmidt (1973) 'How to choose a leadership pattern', *Harvard Business Review*, May–June.

Thomas, J (1985) 'Force field analysis: a new way to evaluate your strategy', *Long Range Planning*, 18(6), pp54–9.

Thomas-Kilmann Conflict Mode Instrument. Palo Alto, CA: Consulting Psychologists Press.

Townsend, R (1985) *Further up the Organisation*. London: Coronet.

Tuckman, BW (1965) 'Development sequence in small groups', *Psychological Bulletin*, 63, pp384–99.

UK Government website: http://www.direct.gov.uk.

Van Weele, A (2005) *Purchasing and Supply Chain Management: Analysis, Strategy, Planning and Practice*, 4th edition. London: Thomson Learning.

Wickens, PD (1995) 'Getting the most out of your people', *People Management*, 9 March.

Wickens, PD (1998) *The Ascendant Organisation*. London: Macmillan Business Press.

Wikipedia: http://en.wikipedia.org.

Yukl, GA (2006) *Leadership in Organizations*, 6th edition. Englewood Cliffs, NJ; London: Prentice-Hall.

Index